Peter Pfister (ed.)

Eugenio Pacelli – Pius XII (1876–1958)
In the View of Scholarship

SCHNELL + STEINER

Bibliographic information published by the Deutsche Nationalbibliothek
The Deutsche Nationalbibliothek lists this publication in the Deutsche Nationalbibliografie;
detailed bibliographic data are available in the Internet at http://dnb.d-nb.de.

1st edition 2012
© 2012 Verlag Schnell & Steiner GmbH, Leibnizstraße 13, 93055 Regensburg
Layout: Vollnhals Fotosatz, Neustadt a. d. Donau
Cover design: Anna Braungart, Tübingen
Print: Erhardi Druck GmbH, Regensburg
Translation: Christof Morrissey

ISBN 978-3-7954-2566-1

Further information about our publications can be found under:
www.schnell-und-steiner.de

Contents

Contents

Preface

9 October 2008 marked the 50th anniversary of Pope Pius XII's death. Taking up a suggestion by Pope Benedict XVI, the Papal Committee for Historical Scholarship honored the life and works of Pius XII in an exhibition. Following stations in Rome and Berlin, the exhibition was presented in Munich from 17 March to 3 May 2009, in the city where Eugenio Pacelli served as nuncio from 1917 to 1925 and which became his second hometown.

The exhibition portrayed Eugenio Pacelli's life's journey in chronological sequence. Using photos, documents, and works of art, it traced – in the words of the exhibition catalogue – the "steep career of the young and highly promising Roman priest Don Eugenio Pacelli in the realm of papal diplomacy and the Congregation for Extraordinary Ecclesiastical Affairs, as papal nuncio in the diplomatic posts of Munich and Berlin, then at the head of the Secretariat of State, and finally on the See of St. Peter".

In order to complement this chronological portrayal of Pius XII's life's journey through additional thematic information, the Most Reverend Reinhard Cardinal Marx, archbishop of Munich and Freising, invited four renowned scholars to hold presentations that addressed the topics of "Pius XII and Modernity", "Pius XII and the Jews", "Pius XII and Michael Cardinal Faulhaber", and "Pius XII in the Judgment of Posterity". The resonance of these accompanying presentations, which were held in the auditorium of the Bavarian Main State Archive, was extraordinarily gratifying. The present publication now makes these papers – supplemented by the moderators' statements, the presentations from the exhibition's opening in Munich, and an article about sources on Eugenio Pacelli/Pope Pius XII in church archives in Munich – accessible to a wider public.

I cordially thank all the presenters and moderators who contributed to the success of this accompanying event. The outstanding cooperation between the Bavarian State Archives, the Munich City Archive, and the Archive of the Archdiocese of Munich and Freising, which first occurred during the Faulhaber exhibition in the year 2002, was continued with the accompanying program for the exhibition on Pius XII. I thank General Director Dr. Margit Ksoll-Marcon and Executive Archive Director Dr. Michael Stephan for their willingness to support and help organize these events.

I hope that the articles published in this volume will contribute to the scholarly debate on the life and works of Pope Pius XII.

Munich, 15 August 2011,   Deacon Dr. Peter Pfister
the Feast of the Assumption   Archive and Library Director

Greeting at the Opening of the exhibition "Opus Iustitiae Pax"

Archbishop Reinhard Cardinal Marx

Ladies and Gentlemen,

I was glad to comply with the wish of our Holy Father to present the exhibition on Pope Pius XII in Munich, following its previous stints in Rome and Berlin. Eugenio Pacelli had a special relationship with Munich and with Bavaria. Munich was his first station as apostolic nuncio. With one of my predecessors in the office of Archbishop of Munich and Freising, Michael Cardinal von Faulhaber, he saw eye to eye on a wide range of political and church matters. These good ties are vividly symbolized by the replica of the Marian column situated in the display case at the entrance. This exhibition piece was given as a farewell gift by the members of the Freising Bishops Conference, headed by their chairman Cardinal Faulhaber, to Nuncio Pacelli upon his departure from Munich. The good relations between Munich and Rome remained in place during Pacelli's tenure as Cardinal Secretary of State and his pontificate as Pius XII.

The close ties between the Church in Munich and Freising and Pope Pius XII are further documented by the commemorative stone that was set down in my cathedral in 1942. The city of Munich too, and not only the Church, demonstrated its close relationship to Pope Pius XII. On the occasion of his 75th birthday, the city council decided to rename the Pfandhausstraße as Pacellistraße. In 1956, the city fathers sent the pope a chalice as a birthday present. Pius XII expressed his thanks in a personal letter, elaborating: "Your wishes and your gift are a new reminder to Us of the happy years of joyful work in your humane city, shaped by its own, authentic culture, which We regarded as a second father city and whose sons and daughters always gave us special pleasure with their custom".

It therefore goes without saying that an exhibition on the life and work of Eugenio Pacelli is in the right place here in Munich. This exhibition represents a way station for scholarly research into the personality of this great pope; Pope Benedict has announced that the files from the entire period of Pius XII's pontificate will be opened in 2014. We in Munich have already done our share of the groundwork by making the files of Michael Cardinal Faulhaber accessible. By

2014, the records of Joseph Cardinal Wendel will be opened as well. The historical record of my predecessors during the time of Pius XII will thereby be accessible in its entirety for scholarly research. The Church does not need to fear the truth. Only on the basis of sources will it be possible to bring to light the historical truth and thereby enable a just verdict on the life and work of Pius XII during very eventful times.

Following the words of the esteemed prelate and the extensive introduction by Dr. Hummel, there remain but three things for me to do.

First, I would like to express my appreciation of this exhibition, which so impressively enables us to visualize the life of Pope Pius XII.

Second, I would like to point out that, attendant to this exhibition, four presentations covering individual aspects of Pacelli's biography will be held in the Bavarian Main State Archive in March and April. These presentations will be arranged, with the customary good cooperation, by the General Directorate of the (Bavarian) State Archives, the Munich City Archive, and the Archive of the Archdiocese. To that end, I would especially like to thank General Director Dr. Ksoll-Marcon, Dr. Stephan, and Dr. Pfister.

Finally, I hereby declare the exhibition "Opus Iustitiae Pax. Eugenio Pacelli – Pius XII" opened. I hope it attracts many visitors and will help them acquire a more balanced view of this important pope.

Translated by Christof Morrissey

Remarks on the Opening of the Exhibition "Opus Iustitiae Pax. Eugenio Pacelli – Pius XII (1876–1958)" in Munich

Walter Cardinal Brandmüller

"As in a dream, a dream of greatness, I absorbed all of this" – "and like a strong dream that penetrates the mind, it lives on and continues to work within me. The non-believer and heir to Protestant culture bent his knee, without the slightest reservation, in front of Pius XII and kissed the fisherman's ring; for it was neither a man nor a politician in front of whom I kneeled but rather a white idol, which – enveloped by the most measured clerical-courtly ceremonial – gently, and suffering a little, emblematized two thousand years of Western Civilization". So wrote Thomas Mann on 3 May 1953.

In 1949, when Pius XII celebrated the 50th anniversary of his ordination to the priesthood, Ernst Reuter, following a resolution by the West Berlin Senate, sent the pope a congratulatory message that revealed great admiration and also informed him that the city's Caecilien-Allee was to be renamed Pacelli-Allee. When the pope died on 9 October 1958, it was Mayor Willy Brandt who ordered that Berlin's flags be flown at half-mast, both on that day and on the day of the funeral.

In 1963, Rolf Hochhuth's play *The Deputy* premiered in Berlin. Its communist director Erwin Piscator enjoyed – for whatever reason – resounding success with the piece, a success that shaped a certain image of this pope, which the work of numerous top-tier historians has been unable to shake to this day. For many, Pius XII remains "Hitler's Pope". As late as 2007, Hochhuth was still able to call Pacelli a satanic coward and the most contemptuous of all people with impunity. What, one asks, happened in that decade between Thomas Mann and *The Deputy*? What led to this monumental reversal in the public opinion of a nation for whom Pacelli, following the catastrophe of 1945 – which had brought not only the end of the Nazi regime but also the collapse of Germany – had opened wide the door to return to the international community? In 1946, Pius XII had rejected the notion of the German people's collective guilt for the Second World War and stunningly appointed three German cardinals – Frings of Cologne, Preysing of Berlin, and Count Galen. Was it not also Pius XII who, in concert with de Gasperi, Adenauer, and Robert Schuman, had worked for a united Europe?

There may be various reasons for this swing in opinion. Ultimately, however, I believe that the wider public's evaluation of popes is largely determined by the way in which the erratic phenomenon of the Roman papacy, indeed of the whole Catholic Church, is contemporarily perceived. This perception, in turn, determines the standards by which a pope is measured. In most cases, these are the standards of one's own times – and the tripwires of anachronism are rarely avoided. And naturally enough, how "the pope" or "the Church" is conceived in the first place also plays a decisive role.

In the case of Pius XII, it is clear that he is generally seen as a political figure and that it is almost exclusively his conduct toward the warring powers in World War II, and toward the totalitarian regimes and ideologies, that is examined. This reductionism, which considers reality only selectively and entirely ignores certain decisive points, must be corrected through an all-encompassing consideration of the papacy and its primarily religious dimension if we wish to gain a historical picture that accurately reflects reality. Only if that happens – and it will require a certain intellectual discipline – can the writing of history, as well as its reflection and interpretation, do justice to the complex reality of the Roman papacy. The *grandeur et misère* of the popes can only be appropriately measured by the standards of their own mission and their self-image as successors to the Apostle Peter.

That mission is primarily, indeed exclusively, religious in nature. It is to preserve intact through the centuries and make known anew to every generation the message proclaimed by Jesus Christ. That this message has consequences for the material life of the individual as well as for the community goes without saying. Only in this sense does a political context become recognizable at all. It is through this lens, then, that we should examine the work of Eugenio Pacelli, Pope Pius XII.

It must be kept in mind that the distortions his image has undergone in the last 40 years are not supported by historical research but have obviously been fueled by political motivations and have themselves served as means to political ends. In the meantime, we have learned that the signal for a systematic campaign against Pius XII radiated from Moscow, and just at that moment, in 1948, when the pope stymied the Communists' attempt to seize power in Italy with his well-known communist decrees. This was followed by the spectacular success of a publicity-hungry playwright who, whatever his motivations, had jumped on the bandwagon launched by Moscow.

To the image of Pius XII shaped by these developments, even the most thoroughly researched scholarship produced under the aegis of the Kommission für

Zeitgeschichte – the results currently fill 152 published volumes – has been able to effect only slight changes. For a long time, these findings were simply ignored. Some circles refuse to allow their prefabricated, clichéd view of history to be demolished by historical facts. On the subject of society's perception of a pope, an axiom from scholastic philosophy comes to mind: *Quidquid percipitur ad modum percipientis percipitur* (Whatever is perceived is perceived in the manner of the perceiver). In other words, the product generated by this perception will tell us not only something about what is being perceived but just as much about the one doing the perceiving.

When the Scotsman Thomas B. Macaulay, a historian and leading political figure, reviewed the English translation of Ranke's *History of the Popes* in the *Edinburgh Review* in 1840, one could read there (I cite in shortened form): "There is not, and never there was on this earth, a work of human policy so well deserving of examination as the Roman Catholic Church [...] The proudest royal houses are but of yesterday, when compared with the line of the supreme pontiffs [...] The Republic of Venice came next in antiquity [...] the Republic of Venice has gone and the Papacy remains [...] full of life and youthful vigour" and, he continues, "she may still exist in undiminished vigour when some traveller from New Zealand shall, in the midst of a vast solitude, take his stand on a broken arch of London Bridge to sketch the ruins of St. Paul's".

Neither Thomas Mann nor Thomas Macaulay were Catholics, yet their perceptions of the papacy, of a pope, stand in sharp contrast to those of many of our contemporaries. This tells us not a little about the perceivers. It is the declared intention of this exhibition to help revise the reductionist consideration and appreciation of Pius XII discussed above, through a more comprehensive presentation of this pope, who in his person and in his actions embodied the very essence of the papacy for many contemporaries. Now the question may justifiably be posed as to why the exhibition leaves out the subject of Pius XII's magisterium work, which so distinguished his pontificate. The answer is that a conference dedicated to just that theme and titled "Eredità del magistero di Pio XII" already took place in connection with this exhibition, held at our request by the papal Gregorian and Lateran Universities.

The results of that conference revealed Pius XII as a teacher of the Church who was so forward-looking that he was cited more frequently in the texts of the Second Vatican Council than any other pope. This fact, along with all the other evidence in the sources, also shows that the last council is just as clearly in the mainstream of the Church's unbroken tradition as the ones that preceded it. For this reason, Pope Benedict XVI always emphasizes the necessity of interpreting Vatican II within the hermeneutical horizon of the entire tradition. It represents a "point of no return" in the sense that no council can contradict the preceding one.

My thanks to all of you, ladies and gentlemen, for accepting our invitation.

Translated by Christof Morrissey

Eugenio Pacelli – Pope Pius XII: From Pre-Judgment to Historical Justice. Notes on a changing historical Image

Karl-Joseph Hummel

The exhibition "Opus Iustitiae Pax: Eugenio Pacelli – Pius XII (1876–1958)", which, after running in Rome and Berlin, was also presented in Munich, is an impertinence. It impertinently demands that we take leave of a historical image that many had held to be immutable – some out of concurring conviction, others out of pessimistic apprehension. For nearly five decades, the attempt was made to present the theatrical reality of *The Deputy* (Der Stellvertreter) that Rolf Hochhuth staged in 1963 at the Freie Volksbühne in Berlin as an accurate and enduring interpretation of historic reality. But the hope that the image of the pope portrayed on stage would be able to withstand the corrective pressure from historical research has not been met. Even today – after the opening of the Vatican archives up to 1939[1] – the kind of situation that occurred more than once in the past, wherein scholarly findings were questioned because they conflicted with the interpretation of Hochhuth's "Christian tragedy", can no longer be repeated as such. Anyone who wants to know "how it really was" will no longer seek the answer in the theater.

When we look back on the five decades that have passed since Pius XII's death on 9 October 1958 and remember Eugenio Pacelli (1876–1958), we can see that the unanimously positive evaluations – among believers and non-believers, Christians and Jews – voiced on the occasion of his death have in the meantime, amid fierce controversy, largely been pushed to the margins. About no other pope do the judgments of posterity diverge so greatly, nor is the discrepancy between a popular black-and-white image, on the one hand, and the differentiated findings of historical research, on the other, as pronounced as in the case of Pacelli[2].

---

[1] The archives, which at the moment have been opened to 10 February 1939, the day Pope Pius XI died, will likely be opened in five to six years' time for the entire papacy of Pius XII, from 1939 to 1958. Cf. an announcement by the Prefect of the Vatican Secret Archive, Bishop Sergio Pagano, Katholische Nachrichten-Agentur (KNA), Vatikan/Ausland/EU, 3 July 2009, 2.

[2] See Karl-Joseph Hummel, "Der Nuntius, die Deutschen und der Papst: Zum Stand der Debatte um Eugenio Pacelli nach Öffnung der Archive bis 1939", in: Pontifical Committee of Historical Sciences, ed., *Opus Iustitiae Pax: Eugenio Pacelli – Pius XII. (1876–1958)*, (Regensburg, 2009), 55–66.

I will therefore, in the first half of my presentation, offer some reflections on the extraordinary bandwidth of this historical image to clarify why the judgment of posterity changed so fundamentally within such a short time – from 1958 to 1963 – and why we are now witnessing the pendulum swinging back again. In the second part, I will use a portrait of Eugenio Pacelli's nunciature in Munich from 1917 to 1925 to demonstrate what new insights historical scholarship has already gained since the opening of the Vatican archives up to 1939.

I. Contemporary History as Contested History

The Deputy, the first play by a then largely unknown 30 year-old Protestant publishing firm employee from Gütersloh – it premiered on 20 February 1963 – reflected the mood of the times and became a worldwide success[3]. "A deputy of Christ", Hochhuth has the "Jesuit Father" Riccardo Fontana say to his own father, a legal counsel with the Holy See, in Act II, a deputy of Christ who visualizes internally scenes of deportations of Jews to extermination camps and "nonetheless remains silent, for reasons of state, who reflects just *one* day, hesitates only one *hour*, before raising the voice of his pain to a curse that will cause even the last person on this earth to tremble – such a pope is [...] a criminal"[4]. Compared with some of Hochhuth's later pronouncements, this characterization, bound as it is to particular presuppositions, sounds almost rational. Later, Hochhuth described Pope Pius XII as the "most contemptible of all popes"[5], as the "ethically most abysmal failure on the see of St. Peter"[6] or as a "satanic coward"[7].

---

[3]   Erwin Piscator, director of the Freie Volksbühne, telegraphed the publisher Ledig-Rowohlt after a brief initial review of the manuscript: "Who is hiding behind the pseudonym Hochhuth?" Reported by Rolf Hochhuth in an interview with Johannes Honsell and Oliver Das Gupta, "Rolf Hochhuth wird 75: 'Ich hatte ein sagenhaftes Glück'", ‹http://www.sueddeutsche. de/kultur/554/406331/text› of 31 March 2006 (12 December 2008). In connection with the accusations that he had been part of a cooperation between the Soviet and Romanian secret services, Hochhuth himself said about his level of recognition in 1963 that it would be absurd to assume the East Bloc intelligence agencies would "slip [their papers] to a young man in Gütersloh who had never before published a word". See Rolf Hochhuth, "Papst Pius XII. war ein satanischer Feigling", ‹http://www.welt.de/kultur/article899192/Papst_Pius_XII_war_ein_ satanischer_Feigling.html› (26 May 2007).

[4]   "Jesuit pater" Riccardo Fontana to his father, in: Rolf Hochhuth, *Der Stellvertreter*, Act II (Reinbek, ³⁹2006), 137.

[5]   Hochhuth spoke out in connection with Pope Pius XII's speech before the College of Cardinals on Christmas Eve 1942 and has repeated his vituperation on numerous occasions, almost word for word, for example in: "Eine ungeheure Lüge", in: *Die Zeit*, Nr. 13, 1998, then in: "Hitlers

The "stage pope" was presented as a portrait of historical-documentary precision. Director Erwin Piscator reported about "persistent historical research conducted over years"; the piece aimed "for an objectifying history writing, not story writing, that examined the totality of human behavior"[8]. According to his own claims, however, Hochhuth never set foot in a Vatican archive[9] and he neglected to speak with the most important contemporary witnesses, such as Pius XII's personal secretary Robert Leiber SJ, even once. Instead, he relied on "murky

Papst", in: *Der Spiegel*, 15 November 1999, 246, or in: "Alles über Pius XII: Zur Schließung des Vatikan-Archivs für Historiker", in: *Die Welt*, 22 August 2001. Cf. Thomas Brechenmacher, "Angesichts einer entchristlichten, sich in einem hoffnungslosen Krieg befindlichen Welt, forderte der Papst die Kardinäle auf, nicht in kleinmütiger Klage zu versinken, sondern als wahre Diener der Kirche 'die Wahrheit und die Tugend' zu verteidigen. Diese Haltung schließe eine besondere Art der Klage und Trauer nicht aus, nämlich jene, 'die auf dem Herz des Erlösers lastete [...] beim Anblick Jerusalems, das seiner Einladung und seiner Gnade mit starrer Verblendung und hartnäckiger Verleugnung entgegentrat, die es auf dem Wege der Schuld, bis hin zum Gottesmord geführt hat'. Pius XII. griff hier ein Zentralverdikt des religiösen Antijudaismus auf – dasjenige des Gottesmordes. Die Wahl dieser Bildlichkeit war vor dem Hintergrund der aktuellen Ereignisse sicherlich nicht besonders glücklich. Freilich sollte nicht vergessen werden, dass Pacelli nicht über die Situation der Juden in dem von NS-Deutschland beherrschten Europa sprach, sondern unter Zuhilfenahme eines althergebrachten Bildes einen Appell an die Kardinäle formulierte. Die theologische Aussage war keine politische"; Thomas Brechenmacher, "Katholische Kirche und Judenverfolgung", in: bistum-erfurt.de, Dokumentationen, 10. ("Regarding a de-Christianized world mired in a hopeless war, the Pope challenged the cardinals not to descend into faint-hearted plaintiveness but to defend 'the truth and virtue' as true servants of the Church. Such a stance still left open the possibility of a particular kind of lamentation and mourning, the kind 'that weighed on the heart of the Redeemer [...] upon seeing Jerusalem, which opposed His invitation and His mercy with unbending blindness and dogged denial, which led it onto the path of guilt, and ultimately to deicide'. Here, Pius took up a core judgment of religious anti-Semitism, that of the deicide. Against the background of events taking place in 1942, the choice of this particular representation was undoubtedly ill-considered. We should keep in mind, however, that Pacelli was not talking about the situation of the Jews in a Europe dominated by Nazi Germany; rather, using a time-honored image, he was issuing an appeal to theologically trained cardinals – and only to them. The Pope's theological pronouncement was intended to be not political but metaphorical").

[6] Hochhuth, "Hitlers Papst".

[7] Matthias Matussek and Alexander Smoltczyk, "'Ein satanischer Feigling': Dramatiker Rolf Hochhuth über die neuen Kontroversen zu seinem Papst-Stück *Der Stellvertreter* und Pius XII.", in: *Der Spiegel*, 26 May 2007, 158f.

[8] Hochhuth, *Der Stellvertreter*: Piscator, Preface, 12.

[9] Hochhuth: "Um zu wissen, wie sich ein Kardinal oder ein Bischof bewegt, wie ein Prälat spricht, musste ich die Atmosphäre im Vatikan kennenlernen." ("To know how a cardinal or bishop moved, how a prelate speaks, I had to get to know the atmosphere of the Vatican.") In: "'Mein Pius ist keine Karikatur': Spiegel-Gespräch mit Dramatiker Rolf Hochhuth", in: *Der Spiegel*, 24 April 1963, 90–96, here 90.

sources", as the Vatican-based journalist Hansjakob Stehle described them[10], and on the personal disloyalty of a German Curia prelate, Bruno Wüstenberg[11], who provided him with information from the Vatican Secretariat of State[12]. Right up to today, Hochhuth has had to contest with legal means claims made by members of intelligence services that they conducted parts of the research[13].

A dramatist, according to Hochhuth, cannot employ a single element of reality as he finds it. In his attempt to expand "scientifically compiled material in an

[10] According to a report by the journalist Hansjakob Stehle, who was active for many years in Rome, Hochhuth traveled "to Rome for six weeks in 1959, for preliminary studies for his play, but spent – as he revealed to me in a conversation 'at the scene of the crime' in 1987 – most of his time in Grottaferrata, twenty kilometers away. Here, banished and embittered in his little house, lived [...] Alois Hudal." "He conceals his murky source, Bishop Alois Hudal, although he could know better today", in: Hansjakob Stehle, "Streitfall Papst Pius XII.: Rolf Hochhuths weltbekanntes Stück *Der Stellvertreter* stützt sich auf Angaben eines trüben Gewährsmanns", in: *Focus*, Nr. 26, 1998. The rumor that Monsignor Hudal supplied Hochhuth with documents is also propagated in Pascalina Lehnert, *Ich durfte ihm dienen* (Würzburg, 1982), 127. Hochhuth responded to this: "I was in Grottaferrata one late afternoon – and never on any other occasion – and spent an hour with the fascist Bishop Hudal, embittered because he had been neutralized by the Vatican." See Rolf Hochhuth, "Der 'Stellvertreter' und seine Kronzeugen", in: *Focus*, Nr. 31, 1998. Cf. also Michael F. Feldkamp, "Hochhuths Quellen sind ziemlich trübe", in: *Vatican magazin*, Nr. 3, 2007, 26–28.

[11] Bruno Wüstenberg (1912–1984), Dr. iur.can.; from 1945 to 1949, head of the German-language section of the relief agency for prisoners of war in the Vatican; from 1945 to 1966, head of the department for German-speaking countries in the Secretariat of State; from 1966 pro nuncio in Japan.

[12] In 1963, *Der Spiegel* asked Hochhuth: "So you weren't in the archives. But otherwise you obviously found good contacts within the Vatican, thanks to the help of a prelate, whom you mention multiple times. Is that how it was?" Answer: "I have to say bluntly that I don't want to talk about that at all." Question: "You mentioned several times that that you were granted an hour-long audience at the Vatican Secretariat of State. [...] Were you with the cardinal secretary of state or in the Secretariat of State?" Answer: "I was at the secretariat of state. I'll say no more about it." See *Der Spiegel*, 24 April 1963, 90–92. In 2000, Hochhuth answered in an interview: "Today I can say the name but to protect him I would of course never have named him before he was dead. It was Monsignore Bruno Wüstenberg." In: "Rolf Hochhuth Dramatiker im Gespräch mit Wolfgang Küpper", ⟨http://www.br-online.de/alpha/forum/vor0002/20000228. shtml⟩ of 28 February 2000 (21 July 2009). In 2007, Hochhuth answered the question "Where did you get your inside information about the Vatican?" with "I didn't have a single one, and didn't need any?" See *Der Spiegel*, 26 May 2007, 90–92.

[13] Cf. Thomas Brechenmacher, "Hochhuths Quellen: War der 'Stellvertreter' vom KGB inspiriert?", in: *Frankfurter Allgemeine Zeitung*, 26 April 2007, 36. In a rebuttal of 8 May 2007, Rolf Hochhuth wrote: "At no point in my publications did I use materials that intelligence services provided me [...] the KGB was never a source of my criticism of pope Pius XII." *Frankfurter Allgemeine Zeitung*, 11 May 2007.

artistically formulated" way[14], he was forced to "purge" reality[15] and adapt Pope Pius XII to the demands of the moralistic theater. In the process, Hochhuth, with creative imagination, placed an artificial figure on the stage[16] that has as much in common with the historical Pope Pius XII as Eugenio Pacelli does with Rolf Hochhuth.

At first, this weakness did not hinder the play's success; it may even have been a prerequisite for it, because it enabled Hochhuth's pope to be fitted with the classic function of the scapegoat who can be made responsible – as a "deputy" – for things with which he has nothing to do, but which one can attribute to him, or at least consider him capable of doing. This weakness, however, contributes greatly to the fact that Hochhuth's play, after a mere four decades, no longer attracts much interest among theater audiences.

A differentiated approach based on a critical source analysis derived from scholarly investigation would only have diluted the drama's moral message. The change of roles from scholarly historian to moralizing author, on the other hand, granted the dramatist the freedom of the character sketch. The playwright Hochhuth could, for example, take note of the positive memories of Pope Pius XII in the Jewish community in Rome, which he well perceived during his 1959 stay in that city, but decide to leave them out of his play, and instead content himself with an interview comment: "It is odd that particularly the Jews in Rome are of the opinion that the pope did a lot for them"[17].

Scholarly progress toward the historical truth was not exactly facilitated by the pre-judgment from the stage; at the same time, Hochhuth's play did have an uncommonly motivational effect on research into church history. Pius XII became the best-researched pope of recent church history and Rolf Hochhuth found himself increasingly forced to dodge a debate with scholarly critics by invoking the comment: "I am not a historian"[18].

Why was this "tragedy" taken so uncommonly seriously in the early 1960s, in intellectual discussions of the day, in academia and politics, even in the form of parliamentary inquiries and diplomatic activity? Why was it staged all over the world (if not everywhere – some theaters rejected the piece on grounds of lacking

---

[14] *Der Stellvertreter*: Hochhuth, "Historische Streiflichter", 381; Piscator, Preface, 12.
[15] *Der Stellvertreter*: Hochhuth, "Historische Streiflichter", 381.
[16] Hochhuth invokes Friedrich Schiller, saying a literary work must be ideal in all its parts if it is to have reality as a whole; *Der Stellvertreter*: Hochhuth, "Historische Streiflichter", 381.
[17] Hochhuth, "Mein Pius", 90.
[18] Ibid.

quality)[19]? And why has the moral drawing power of this theater piece already elapsed after only 45 years?

I have taken the liberty of summarizing the answers to these questions in part using five thesis-style points. First: Hochhuth's script featured compelling content and found its way into the right hands at the right time. The timing of *The Deputy* may not have been thoroughly planned, step by step, but it still proved to be nearly perfect. Five years after the death of a pope who was highly admired around the world and across denominations, the public frontal attack against Pius XII satisfied, for widely differing reasons, the most varied contemporary moods and expectations. Following a radio discussion on 25 October 1963, Karl Jaspers wrote to Hannah Arendt: "I was thrilled to see a thirty year-old German, an autodidact (e.g. with no university education and no *Abitur*), passionate about the question of the murder of the Jews, superior to the attending Catholic professor (modern and contemporary history) in his concrete knowledge, so that he silenced him through facts and questions"[20].

Second: Jaspers, Hannah Arendt, and other Hochhuth supporters recognized with a sure sense the explosive power of an attack on the representative of the last remaining global institution that made a claim to morality. "The Jews are not that interesting. But an attack on the pope has drawing power"[21]. But that alone did not guarantee the play success. The manuscript had already been in existence for two and a half years, lying for eighteen months at the publisher Ledig-Rowohlt, before Piscator recognized the piece's potential and decided, within an hour: "I'm putting on this play"[22]. Helped by his rich experience as a theater director, Piscator turned Hochhuth's meandering text into a piece of condensed political agitation and did not shy from the expected scandal. Piscator's experience told him that it was impossible to stir up dust without making some people cough.

Third: at the beginning of the 1960s, institutions such as the Catholic Church or the universities fell under the general suspicion of mustiness of 1000 years, of culpable failure, and of covering up or making apologetic excuses for their conduct.

---

[19] See an overview of the public response in the first months in Fritz J. Raddatz, ed., *Summa iniuria oder Durfte der Papst schweigen?* (Reinbek, 1963), as well as Walter Adolph, *Verfälschte Geschichte: Antwort an Rolf Hochhuth* (Berlin, 1963). Cf. also Hochhuth in a discussion with Küpper: *The Deputy* "didn't actually become a bestseller in the German language sphere anyway. For example, it was not performed south of the Main and in the Rhineland, except in Basle and Vienna."

[20] In Lotte Köhler and Hans Saner, eds. *Hannah Arendt Karl Jaspers Briefwechsel 1926–1969* (Munich, 1985), 563f.

[21] *Der Stellvertreter*: Karl Jaspers, "Nicht Schweigen!", 502.

[22] Cited from an interview with Hochhuth on his 75th birthday in sueddeutsche.de (see n. 3).

Concurrent with the first scholarly investigations of the Third Reich, in general as well as in church history[23], the first critical questions were raised as to the moral responsibility of the "Pacelli generation" for the murder of the European Jews. In the immediate post-war period, an extensive discussion about guilt and responsibility took place, which even to this date has experienced only scant reception[24]. Its leading exponents – for example, Stefan Andres (1906–1970), Werner Bergengruen (1892–1964), Gertrud von Le Fort (1876–1971) and Reinhold Schneider (1903–1958) – could no longer, after years of silence, take up their previous roles. In their stead, the jurist Ernst Wolfgang Böckenförde (born 1930) and the authors Carl Amery (1922–2005) and Heinrich Böll (1917–1985) took center stage in the Catholic discourse of the time.

With his path-breaking study of the demise of the Center Party, the historian Rudolf Morsey had in 1960 already unleashed a lively discussion among experts on the Third Reich's early years. When Böckenförde published his essay "Der deutsche Katholizismus im Jahre 1933: Eine kritische Betrachtung" (German Catholicism in the year 1933: a critical view) in *Hochland* in 1960–1961[25], a clamorous public debate ensued. Böckenförde's analysis of long-term trends in German Catholicism was held up as a welcome historical corrective to the memories of the generation that had lived through those events.

Böckenförde placed the German bishops' momentous reversal of opinion of 28 March 1933, the Reich Concordat, and the demise of political Catholicism at the center of his interest. He initially determined that German Catholics, "led and encouraged by their bishops and the clergy", had "on the whole, courageously resisted". However, Böckenförde then continued: this self-assessment "was understandably not well suited for asking and debating the question whether and to what extent the Catholics and their spiritual leaders may have helped to consolidate Nazi rule in its beginnings and offered it their own collaboration. [...] German Catholics received advice and directives from their bishops, bestowed with episcopal authority, regarding their political conduct, which they would have

---

[23] Cf. Rudolf Morsey, "Gründung und Gründer der Kommission für Zeitgeschichte 1960–1962", in: *Historisches Jahrbuch* 115 (1995) 119–151; Christoph Kösters, "NS-Vergangenheit und Katholizismusforschung: Ein Beitrag zur Erinnerungskultur und Zeitgeschichtsschreibung nach 1945", in: *Zeitschrift für Kirchengeschichte* 120 (2009) 27–57.

[24] Cf. Karl-Joseph Hummel, "Gedeutete Fakten: Geschichtsbilder im deutschen Katholizismus", in: Karl-Joseph Hummel and Christoph Kösters, eds., *Kirchen im Krieg. Europa 1939–1945* (Paderborn et al., 2007), 508–567, here 508–523.

[25] Ernst Wolfgang Böckenförde, "Der deutsche Katholizismus im Jahre 1933: Eine kritische Betrachtung", in: *Hochland* 53 (1960/61) 215–239.

been better off not following. That would have been correct from the standpoint of national policy"[26].

Searching for an explanation, Böckenförde particularly criticized the reduction of the bishops' understanding of politics to the cultural realm and diagnosed a fundamental inner distance of the Catholic Church to modern state and society. He also identified, as a consequence of a deeply rooted anti-liberalism, a worrying susceptibility to authoritarian conceptions. "Open Catholic voices of opposition had even less of a chance in that they would have not only have confronted the authorities but would also have had to turn against authoritative declarations of the bishops and the overwhelming majority of Catholic public opinion. [...] How could it come to pass that the clerics and spiritual leaders of German Catholicism in the year 1933 saw in Hitler and the Nazi state trailblazers for a comprehensive renewal and expressly called for positive cooperation with, and support of, the Nazi regime?"[27]

Böckenförde's theses – his view of the Catholicism's religious-ideological unity under the political leadership of the bishops and clergy, on the one hand, and of its inner distance from state and society in the modern era, on the other; his assessment of a deeply rooted anti-liberalism and a corresponding susceptibility to authoritarian approaches; and his diagnosis of a political understanding among bishops and other clergy that was restricted to the cultural realm – took up an interpretation that the publicist Walter Dirks had already undertaken in 1931 and then republished in the *Frankfurter Hefte* in 1963[28].

Fourth: in the epoch of the Cold War, the common anti-totalitarian consensus of the past had broken into anti-fascism and anti-communism. Anti-fascism, claimed by those who represented the superior morality of a humanistic future, was imbued with a morally positive meaning, whereas in the era of "rapprochement through dialogue", anti-communism was reserved for those who were still living in the past.

---

[26] Ibid., 239.

[27] Ibid., 230, 232.

[28] In "Katholizismus und Nationalsozialismus" (1931), Dirks did not question that Catholicism found itself in a "declared defensive war against National Socialism" in the spheres of ideology and church politics: "The ideology of National Socialism is alien to the Church." However, "the social situation in which they grew powerful is close enough to the Catholics." Dirks saw the actual danger in the "conditions and processes within very specific social layers", in the middle classes, the lower middle class, and among the peasants, and feared that social tensions there would erupt into action. "The social objectives represented by political Catholicism – democracy, the rule of law, the corporate state – are too feeble to withstand competition with the more powerful folkloristic ideals of the fascists." In: *Die Arbeit* (Berlin) 8 (1931) 201–209 and *Frankfurter Hefte* 18 (1963) 515–522, cited in: *Gesammelte Schriften*, vol. 6: *Politik aus dem Glauben: Aufsätze zu Theologie und Kirche*, (Zürich, 1989), 21–36.

Fifth: On the eve of the Second Vatican Council, the Catholic Church itself was in a state of upheaval. In the papacy, a succession had taken place in 1958, after 19 years, which brought with it numerous changes. Pius XII's and John XXIII's differing auras were already unmistakable. The disciplined ideal figure of Eugenio Pacelli, which always appeared somehow fragile, was followed by the life-affirming, energetic pope Roncalli. The legally trained, gaunt diplomat and Holy Father was succeeded by a genial, pastoral, and baroque pontiff. None other than Angelo Giuseppe Roncalli, who as nuncio in Turkey had saved the lives of countless Jews, directly succeed that pope who, supposedly, had culpably "kept silent" on the destruction of the European Jews. Within the Church, Pius XII had stood for clear principles, authority, tradition, and obedience. Externally, he was perceived as the personal embodiment of anti-communism. Both views made him the symbolic figure of "yesterday's Church". Anyone who defended him and his conception of the Catholic Church during those forward-looking years of the *Aggiornamento* automatically assumed the unappealing mantle of a pre-conciliar apologist.

Why, despite the worldwide success of Hochhuth's play, was it only a question of time before his fictional character relinquished its power to persuade?

The play itself did not possess the literary quality that would have enabled it to break through as a classic. Over the course of time, *The Deputy* grew ever more self-referential. The strength of evidence from findings backed up by scholarship became overpowering because the stage pope had almost no connection to reality. The unintended consequence cited above, whereby the challenge posed by *The Deputy* led to Pius XII becoming perhaps the best-researched person in recent church history, further increased the pressure. In the meantime, Pope Pius XII is perceived in the full breadth of his personality and his actions; for this reason, too, he is no longer cut out for a one-dimensional caricature. Anyone who wants to know better can now do so as a result of many long-running debates. At the same time, the supporting function of non-literary props – the favorable circumstances of the time, which were substantial for *The Deputy*'s initial success and enabled its rise to global success – grew weaker. Politically, the end of the Cold War has greatly reduced the relevance of ideological conflicts over communism and anti-communism. From 1963 to 2009, an evermore rapidly secularizing society has steadily lost interest in the moral questions raised by *The Deputy*.

In the discussions of the last few weeks, stereotypes from the Hochhuth debate that were presumed obsolete have once more been reflexively revived – at least among members of a certain generation. On the 70th anniversary of Pius XII's election as pope, Hans Küng, in an interview that would be worth reading for its consistent one-sidedness alone[29], added up myriad accusations from the last 50 years to paint a negative portrait and then connected "his" Pius XII to positions from current Church politics. Küng's attributions bespeak an impressive reading effort, but of course one worth only half as much because he considers only those "politically correct" arguments about history and church policies from the Hochhuth controversy. This discussion copies the pattern that is familiar from the 1960s. The arguments wear the mantle of the past but take aim at the present. The war over *The Deputy* thereby becomes a "war of deputies". What was once an attack, however, has since mutated into a rearguard action. Hans Küng misses the current state of the debate because he clings to a black-and-white view and unwaveringly relies mainly on arguments that have long been discounted. Just one example from the theologian Küng's Tübingen history workshop: Pope Pius XII, claims Küng without any reference to his sources, "considered the Nazi system less offensive than the communist one. He was aware of the affinity between his own, authoritarian conception of the Church – he was anti-Protestant, anti-modern, anti-liberal, and anti-socialist – and the fascist view of the state. With an eye toward the notions of 'unity', 'order', 'discipline', 'the leadership principle', he presumed to recognize commonalities in the ideology of Nazism. The Nazis had similar aims at the state level as the Catholic Church in the religious and supernatural sphere"[30]. With such estimations, Küng's declared goal, that "Pope Pius XII deserves fair judgment", is difficult to achieve. Can that which is provably wrong in a historical sense be correct in a theological one? Or, put differently: how much historical justice can morality tolerate?

II. Eugenio Pacelli, Nuncio in Munich, 1917–1925

The opening of the Vatican archives up to 1939 changed the historiographical landscape more than many had anticipated. These archival materials enable us, for the first time, to view internal church processes and developments. With the aid of these new sources, the Vatican's deliberations and decision-making processes can now be traced. Perhaps even more fascinating, historians are uncovering traces of those actions that did not get carried out, of decisions that were prepared but never made, or of measures and reactions that were undertaken without the public

---

[29] Küng on the *Deputy* pope Pius XII, "Hitler war das kleinere Übel", Oliver Das Gupta im Gespräch mit Hans Küng, ‹http://www.sueddeutsche.de/politik/372/460009/text/print.html› 2 March 2009 (14 March 2009).

[30] Ibid.

finding out about them to this day. The inspection and analysis of the voluminous sources, and in part the publication of edited collections, has only begun[31]. Already, an intense debate has arisen over the evaluation and interpretation of the preliminary findings[32].

The late Protestant historian Klaus Scholder considered the appointment of Eugenio Pacelli as nuncio in the Kingdom of Bavaria "among the most important dates of German Catholicism in the 20th century"[33]. Following his studies, ordination to the priesthood, and – since 1903 – a diplomatic preparatory phase in the Vatican Secretariat of State, the native Roman Pacelli represented the Holy See for more than twelve years as apostolic nuncio in Bavaria and the German Reich, from 1917 to 1925 in Munich and, holding down two posts at once, from 1920 to 1929 in Berlin.

Pacelli was considered an extremely promising young diplomat with bright career prospects, "a man of the future" who "could even be found worthy someday, if the conditions are right, to be elected pope"[34]. Baron Ritter zu Groenesteyn, Bavarian chargé d'affaires at the Holy See, fittingly ascribed to his friend Pacelli[35]

[31] The over 6,000 reports of Nuncio Pacelli from Germany in the years 1917–1929 are being edited, annotated, and evaluated in a mutual online project of the Vatican Secret Archive, the German Historical Institute in Rome, and working group headed by Prof. Hubert Wolf of the University of Münster. A critical online edition of the reports of Pacelli's successor, Nuncio Cesare Orsenigo, initially for the years 1930–1939, as well as a select edition in German translation, are being prepared in cooperation between the Vatican Secret Archive, the German Historical Institute, and the Kommission für Zeitgeschichte in Bonn.

[32] Hubert Wolf, *Papst & Teufel: Die Archive des Vatikan und das Dritte Reich* (Munich, 2008) (Engl.: Hubert Wolf, Pope and Devil. The Vatican's Archives and the Third Reich (Cambridge and London, 2010)); Hubert Wolf, "Eine deutsche Mission und zwei Traumata", in: *Frankfurter Allgemeine Zeitung*, 9 October 2008; Karl-Joseph Hummel, "Der Teufel steckt meistens im Detail", in: *Frankfurter Allgemeine Zeitung*, 19 January 2009.

[33] Klaus Scholder, "Eugenio Pacelli und Karl Barth", in: Klaus Scholder, *Die Kirchen zwischen Republik und Gewaltherrschaft* (Berlin, 1988), 99; Klaus Scholder, *Die Kirchen und das Dritte Reich*, vol. 1: *Vorgeschichte und Zeit der Illusionen 1918–1934* (Frankfurt/Main, Berlin, and Vienna, 1977), 67. Other seminal articles include: Winfried Becker, "Neue Freiheit vom Staat – Bewährung im Nationalsozialismus: 1918–1945", in: Walter Brandmüller, ed., *Handbuch der Bayerischen Kirchengeschichte*, vol. 3 (St. Ottilien, 1991), 337–392; Heinz Hürten, "Bayern im deutschen Katholizismus der Weimarer Zeit", in: *Zeitschrift für bayerische Landesgeschichte* 55 (1992) 375–388, and Rudolf Morsey, "Eugenio Pacelli als Nuntius in Deutschland", in: Herbert Schambeck, ed., *Pius XII. zum Gedächtnis*, (Berlin, 1977), 103–139.

[34] Correspondence from the Royal Bavarian Legation at the Holy See to the Königliche Staatsministerium des Königlichen Hauses und des Aeußern (Royal State Ministry of the Royal House and External Affairs), 15 May 1917; BayHStA MA 92013.

[35] Cf. Georg Franz-Willing, *Die Bayerische Vatikangesandtschaft 1803–1934* (Munich, 1965), 135–151; Personal letter of condolence from Pope Pius XII to Michael Cardinal von Faulhaber, 27 January 1940, on the death of Baron Ritter zu Groenesteyn; EAM NL Faulhaber 1152; also see the obituary of Msgr. Weissthanner; ASMA K 31,20.

"tireless activity, quick intelligence, and purest devotion to the Holy See", and characterized him as a man who had earned high esteem "through his noble character and his tactful bearing." "There are today only a few clerics in the Vatican who know how to combine spiritual dignity with pleasant social manners. [...] Monsignor Pacelli, despite his somewhat ascetic reserve, constituted a noteworthy exception"[36].

Immediately on taking up his office, the 40 year-old Pacelli was given the most difficult mission that papal diplomacy of the First World War could assign: the international peace initiative to end the hostilities. Through the mediation of Georg von Hertling, Pacelli had already conducted talks in Switzerland even before his arrival in Munich, scheduled appointments in Berlin, and then immediately visited Kaiser Wilhelm II in his headquarters in Bad Kreuznach, in order to give him Pope Benedict XV's peace proposal. In doing so, he had, according to general consensus, presented a *bella figura*[37]. It was not Pacelli's doing that the peace initiative failed after months of negotiations. But this experience stayed with him until the Second World War and inspired him to maintain strict political neutrality in future.

Officially, the papal chargé d'affaires in Munich was accredited with the Kingdom of Bavaria; in practice, however, the Munich nunciature had, since the formation of the German Empire, taken on a de facto responsibility for the country as a whole[38]. The question of establishing a nunciature in Prussia or for the entire German Reich preoccupied the new nuncio from the start. In Munich, there was concern that if the nuncio left there, he would not be replaced. In that event, Baron Ritter zu Groenesteyn had as early as 1920 far-sightedly envisioned a consolation: "For a man of the future such as Monsignor Pacelli, however, following

---

[36] Ibid.

[37] Letter from the just appointed Nuncio Pacelli to the State Minister of the Royal House and for External Affairs (Staatsminister des Königlichen Hauses und des Aeußern) Georg Graf von Hertling, 21 April 1917; BayHStA MA 92013; Letter of 19 June 1917, letter of 1 October 1917; BayHStA MA 976. There are different accounts of the nuncio's half-hour audience with the German Kaiser in: Kaiser Wilhelm II., *Ereignisse und Gestalten aus den Jahren 1878–1918* (Leipzig, 1922), 225–230; Theobald von Bethmann Hollweg, *Betrachtungen zum Weltkriege. Zweiter Teil: Während des Krieges* (Essen, 1989), 253–255, 379–399; Wolfgang Steglich, *Der Friedensappell Papst Benedikts XV. vom 1. August 1917 und die Mittelmächte* (Wiesbaden, 1970), 90–328; Morsey, 107–112. On Nuncio Pacelli's denials of Kaiser Wilhelm II's memoirs, see Steglich, 655–661. The *Osservatore Romano* published the declaration on 18 October 1922; the same day, the nunciature publication appeared in German, in the *Bayerischer Kurier*, Nr. 382, 18 October 1922.

[38] Cf. Hubert Wolf, "München als Reichsnuntiatur", in: *Zeitschrift für Kirchengeschichte* 103 (1992) 231–242.

the establishment of a nunciature in Berlin, the nunciature in Munich no longer offers an adequate field of operations in order to retain his previous high standing in the eyes of the Vatican, where he already has jealous rivals"[39]. It could "now already be an advantage for Bavaria if the Holy See is represented in Berlin by such an honest friend of Bavaria"[40]. "Therefore, we can do without now, in order to be compensated later, when Monsignor Pacelli returns to Rome for a higher calling"[41].

In 1921, Pacelli had already looked for a secretary for Berlin and decided on the Cologne parish priest Joseph Frings. But the establishment of the Berlin nunciature was then delayed until the conclusion of the Bavarian Concordat in 1925, so that Frings was no longer available[42]. Some elements of the Center Party did not regret the delay; they feared being "leashed in by Rome" and argued that the nuncio would be less troublesome in Munich than in the Reich capital[43]. The Center Party Reichstag deputy Matthias Erzberger (1875–1921), who had a fixed view on this question, issued a telling warning against a quick relocation: "In this area, His Majesty the King of Bavaria is especially sensitive"[44].

Pacelli owed his reputation as a well-informed diplomat – in Munich as well as later in Berlin – to his tightly woven, very diverse personal network, which still has by no means been comprehensively researched. I name first and foremost Michael von Faulhaber, appointed archbishop through His Majesty the King of Bavaria on 26 May 1917, cardinal from 7 March 1921; Konrad von Preysing, cathedral preacher in Munich in the 1920s, later bishop in Eichstätt and Berlin, appointed cardinal in 1945; as well as Father Rupert Mayer, Pacelli's confessor in Munich[45], and Johannes Neuhäusler. Pacelli maintained close contacts not only to the Wittelsbach royal

---

[39] Baron Ritter zu Groenesteyn to Archbishop von Faulhaber, 14 May 1920; EAM NL Faulhaber 1352.

[40] Ibid.

[41] Ibid.; Ritter zu Groenesteyn continued to use the old stationery. "Königlich Bayerische Gesandtschaft" was crossed through and replaced by "Bayerische Gesandtschaft".

[42] On 7 March 1921, Nuncio Pacelli wrote to the Deputy General Vicar of Cologne, Otto Paschen, that it was not foreseeable at the moment when he would call on the services of Dr. Josef Frings, who had been designated secretary for the Berlin nunciature, though he did express thanks that Frings had been made available. In his memoirs, Frings wrote: "I had declared myself prepared but the matter was protracted. There must have been difficulties related to the Bavarian Concordat." Josef Frings, *Für die Menschen bestellt* (Cologne, 1973), 14; cf. also Norbert Trippen, *Josef Kardinal Frings (1887–1978)*, vol. I (Veröffentlichungen der Kommission für Zeitgeschichte, Reihe B: Forschungen 94) (Paderborn et al., 2003), 30f.

[43] Cited in: Wolf, 235.

[44] Erzberger on 2 March 1917 in a letter to Nuncio Aversa; replicated in: Wolf, 239f.

[45] Wilhelm Sandfuchs, *Pater Rupert Mayer* (Würzburg, 1981), 107.

family[46] but also to Hans Lang, who portrayed Christ at Oberammergau. Pacelli's contacts included politicians of different parties: Matthias Erzberger and Georg von Hertling, Gustav Stresemann, whom he valued highly, and Reichstag president Paul Löbe. His conversation partners included the Protestant theologian Adolf von Harnack, the educator Friedrich Wilhelm Foerster, and, later in Berlin, Albert Einstein and other leading members of the Kaiser Wilhelm Society, as well as Clemens August Count von Galen, who was the priest assigned to the nunciature. A connection to Colonel General Ludwig Beck, which has often been claimed[47], probably existed only indirectly, through Pacelli's contact to Josef Müller[48].

Not least in this rapidly established network were the personal assistants who were employed, in some cases for decades, to the limits of their abilities. These included Pater Robert Leiber, Pacelli's personal secretary, and the Trier canon and Center Party politician Ludwig Kaas. As a 23 year-old in 1918, Sister Pascalina Lehnert was delegated from her convent at Altötting to assist for just a two-month period. With her dispensation renewed twice, she headed Pacelli's household for over 40 years[49].

The "hurried Father" (eiliger Vater) was nearly omnipresent: at liturgical festivals, where he represented the frequently ill Munich archbishop; at Catholic congresses; at tours of factories; as honorary member of the student association "Trifels"; at the funeral of the Görres Society's deceased president[50]; on an excursion to the Wendelstein; on a test flight for VIPs on the new all-metal Junkers aircraft in 1924[51]. In the realm of charity, Pacelli worked to the limits of his powers

[46] Nuncio Pacelli – representing Archbishop Faulhaber, who had taken ill – celebrated the wedding mass for Crown Prince Rupprecht of Bavaria and Antonia of Luxembourg on 7 April 1921 in Lenggries, with the assistance of Konrad von Preysing. Later, he baptized two of the couple's children. See also Jean Louis Schlim, *Antonia von Luxemburg, Bayerns letzte Kronprinzessin* (Munich, 2006) und Dieter J. Weiss, *Kronprinz Rupprecht von Bayern* (Regensburg, 2007).

[47] Cf. Klaus-Jürgen Müller, *Generaloberst Ludwig Beck* (Paderborn et al., 2008), 411–416.

[48] Johannes Neuhäusler was, among other things, General Secretary of the Ludwig-Missionsverein in the 1920s and in 1925 founded the Bavarian Pilgrim's Office (Bayerisches Pilgerbüro); General Secretary of the Archdiocese from 1933 on, he worked closely with Josef Müller, a lawyer, who reliably brought Neuhäusler's secret reports to Pope Pius XI to the Vatican. See also Josef Müller, *Bis zur letzten Konsequenz* (Munich, 1975).

[49] See Martha Schad, *Gottes mächtige Dienerin: Schwester Pascalina und Papst Pius XII.* (Munich, 2007).

[50] Hermann Grauert was buried on 13 March 1924 in the presence of Cardinal Faulhaber und Nuncio Pacelli. See Rudolf Morsey, "Die Görres-Gesellschaft unter ihrem Präsidenten Hermann von Grauert (1919/20–1924)", in: *Jahres- und Tagungsbericht der Görres-Gesellschaft 2005*, 73–114, here 111.

[51] Cf. the account of a flight from Munich to Oberammergau in: Hans Baur, *Mit Mächtigen zwischen Himmel und Erde* (Pr. Oldendorf, 1982), 33f. (with photo). On 14 October 1924, the press reported on a 30-minute air journey that took place on 11 October 1924.

for the Papal Information Office for the Missing, as well as for the physical and spiritual well-being of prisoners of war. By order of the Holy Father, he inspected German prison camps and distributed food, clothing, and medication. In 1921, he arranged for 3 million Reichsmarks of charitable support from the Vatican, supplied the inter-confessional Munich student support organization with oil and tropical fruit, and secured donations from American Catholics as well as a 200,000 Lira benefaction for sick German students[52].

Nuncio Pacelli did much good behind the scenes; on the other hand, he also devoted much attention to the media and to public relations work. Baron Ritter zu Groenesteyn was correct in his observations: "The current holy Father considers it important that his nuncios are talked about in the public sphere"[53]. The general instructions (Generalinstruktion) for Pacelli from November 1916 declared: "Since the enormous influence of the press on public opinion, its immense advantages but also its tremendous disadvantages for the Holy See, for the Church, and for religion are well known to the most reverend Nuncio, he will undertake every effort to support and distribute the good press"[54]. In his press and publicity work, Pacelli left nothing to chance. When the departure of the nuncio from Munich to Berlin seemed imminent in 1920, a suggestion coming from Rome by way of the Bavarian legation inquired whether it "could not perhaps appear as an announcement, to prove to the departing nuncio Bavaria's gratitude for his self-sacrificing activity in difficult circumstances in the form of a farewell celebration put on for him by the Catholic associations. [...] At the very least, it would be desirable for Bavaria's Catholic press to dedicate words of farewell and gratitude to the nuncio in a non-mundane fashion"[55]. When the *völkisch* German press directed "the most exorbitant and most unjust attacks against the Holy See" in 1924, the nuncio informed Cardinal Bertram that the Holy See would actively welcome it "if the German episcopate would (issue) a common public protest in a form that it deemed appropriate." "I would be especially grateful if I could learn what Your Eminence, in union with the other Most Reverend bishops in Germany,

---

52 Cf. the letter of thanks from Archbishop Faulhaber to Pope Benedict XV, 25 March 1921, in: Ludwig Volk, ed., *Akten Kardinal Michael von Faulhabers 1917–1945*, vol. 1 (Veröffentlichungen der Kommission für Zeitgeschichte, Reihe A: Quellen 17) (Mainz, 1975), 179f., Doc. 88, the letter of thanks, 4 April 1924, as well as Faulhaber's 1921 Christmas letter to Pope Pius XI; EAM NL Faulhaber 1151. See also Stadtarchiv München, Bürgermeister und Rat 312/1.
53 Letter from Baron Ritter zu Groenesteyn to Archbishop Faulhaber, 14 May 1920; EAM NL Faulhaber 1352.
54 Cited in: Wolf, 27f.
55 Letter from Baron Ritter zu Groenesteyn, 14 May 1920; see n. 53.

thinks to do in this matter"[56]. In such situations, Pacelli not only expected that something be done but also that it be done quickly. Cardinal Secretary of State Pacelli's request to Cardinal Faulhaber in 1935 had, in its essence, already been expressed by Nuncio Pacelli only a few weeks after assuming that office and on various occasions thereafter: "I would be especially grateful for a prompt resolution, since I would not like to see the method of some German state agencies to let matters of this type, which by their nature are urgent, stagnate for months being emulated within the Secretariat of State"[57].

Nuncio Pacelli experienced the communist Bavarian Soviet Republic in Munich in 1918–1919 as a culture shock and personal threat, which became the foundations for his lasting emotional reservations about bolshevism. After the deposition of King Ludwig III, to whom Pacelli had given his credentials on 29 May 1917, an active group of littérateurs, pacifists, anarchists, and young communist revolutionaries from the Soviet Union attempted to install a soviet republic until May 1919. In violation of all diplomatic conventions and assurances, the nunciature in Brienner Straße was attacked by a soviet revolutionary unit in April and later shot at by government troops[58]. Both incidents impelled the nuncio to leave Munich for the time being and seek safety in Switzerland[59].

The Secretariat of State permitted a nuncio to leave his post only in the event of physical or life-threatening danger. Such a situation had not directly obtained in Munich. A difference of opinion between Munich and Rome arose over this matter, in which Archbishop Faulhaber sided with the nuncio. He believed "that the reaction of our highly esteemed Apostolic Nuncio Monsignor Pacelli was guided only by the highest church considerations"[60].

---

[56] Letter from the Apostolic Nunciature in Bavaria to Adolf Cardinal Bertram, 14 May 1924; copy in: EAM NL Faulhaber 1320.

[57] Letter from Cardinal Secretary of State Pacelli to Michael Cardinal Faulhaber, 17 November 1935, in: Ludwig Volk, ed., *Akten Kardinal Michael von Faulhabers 1917–1945*, vol. 2 (Veröffentlichungen der Kommission für Zeitgeschichte, Reihe A: Quellen 26) (Mainz, 1978), 79f., Doc. 508. Cf. Pacelli's letter to Baron Ritter zu Groenesteyn. 21 June 1917, in: Franz-Willing, 127f., 146f.

[58] See Heinz Hürten, "Legenden um Pacelli: Die Münchener Vatikangesandtschaft 1918/19", in: Konrad Ackermann et al., ed., *Bayern. Vom Stamm zum Staat. Festschrift für Andreas Kraus zum 80. Geburtstag*, (Munich, 2002), 503–511.

[59] Presumably, this was for the time between 22 November 1918 and 31 January 1919 and from 29 April 1919 until 8 August 1919. In his farewell speech in 1925, Cardinal Faulhaber mentioned only the attack by the soviet republicans on the nunciature on 29 April 1919. At his request, and on his own responsibility, Pacelli went to Switzerland for a short time. Cf. Faulhaber's statement on the nunciature's files of 7 July 1921 in: EAM NL Faulhaber 1320.

[60] Ibid., statement of 7 July 1921.

In Munich, Pacelli followed Archbishop Faulhaber's advice to avoid personal contact with the Bavarian Soviet regime at all costs, to exclude any appearance of recognition and legitimation. At the same time, he inquired in Rome whether a papal nunciature was even permissible in the case of a communist government[61]. The anticipated fundamental decision by the Vatican Secretariat of State has so far not been found, if one ever existed in the first place.

Pacelli's report of 18 April 1919 on the situation at the soviet communists' revolutionary headquarters has been stylized by John Cornwell, through translation errors, as purported evidence of Pacelli's anti-Semitism. In Cornwell's translation, "a throng of young women" becomes a "gang", "at the head of this group of women" is rendered as "the chief of this female scum", while "with expressionless eyes" is transposed as "with eyes marked by drug abuse"[62]. In fact, this was not even an eyewitness account by the nuncio himself; rather, the report was by his assistant Monsignore Schioppa, the *uditore* at the nunciature, who had been charged with approaching the government. Through his signature, Pacelli then bestowed this version with the status of an official report.

Politically, Pacelli also experienced the rise of the second totalitarian ideology of the 20th century, National Socialism. In his report on the Hitler putsch, he had already demonstrated concern over the movement's anti-Catholic tendencies[63]. After reading *Mein Kampf*, at the latest, he had no doubts that Adolf Hitler, for personal as well as ideological reasons, could not be considered as a political partner. Nuncio Pacelli and Hitler never encountered one another in Munich. In connection with the Hitler putsch, however, Pacelli earned himself a rebuke because Cardinal Gasparri wanted to have been informed earlier and more comprehensively. But Cardinal Faulhaber cleared up any ill feeling during his *ad limina* visit to the Vatican shortly thereafter. "I explained why Pacelli hadn't telegraphed during the Hitler Putsch, that he had been working through the night on the concordat"[64].

---

[61] See John Cornwell, *Pius XII.: Der Papst, der geschwiegen hat* (Munich, 1999), 98ff.

[62] Goldhagen nonetheless considers this letter the "authentic expression of the later pope's beliefs about the Jews", for a "barrage of anti-Semitic stereotypes and accusations [...] in which the demonizing views of Jews resonate". There may possibly have been more such pronouncements, which, however, were either taken to the grave by his conversation partners or kept under lock and key by the Vatican. Daniel Jonah Goldhagen, *Die katholische Kirche und der Holocaust: Eine Untersuchung über Schuld und Sühne* (Berlin, 2002), 63f.

[63] Gerhard Besier, *Der Heilige Stuhl und Hitler-Deutschland: Die Faszination des Totalitären* (München, 2004), 64ff., reaches the same conclusion on this point as Thomas Brechenmacher and Hubert Wolf.

[64] Volk, 321f., Doc. 148: Cardinal von Faulhaber on 7 December 1923 in his audience with Cardinal Secretary of State Gasparri.

The Catholic church congress held in Munich in 1922 proved to be a momentous event. In the presence of the nuncio, an open confrontation over the position of Catholics in the Weimar Republic that had been established through revolution flared up between the Center Party politician and president of the congress, Konrad Adenauer, and the host, Cardinal von Faulhaber[65].

As one of the parties supporting the first democratic German state, the Center Party[66] held governing responsibility almost continuously from 1919 to 1932. The so-called "Weimar coalition", however, could only achieve majorities if parties demonstrated a readiness to compromise in the pursuit of their goals and, in the case of the Center, through collaboration with ideological opponents in the liberal and socialist parties. In 1922 in Munich, Pacelli sided with Faulhaber and, on the issue of coalition government, showed a fundamental appreciation for the ever more pressing objections brought forth by the Vatican. Faulhaber argued that the Center party "did not present a unified image of principled clarity. [...] Without talking of politics, I wanted to issue a warning, so that the entranceway to the German people was not opened to bolshevism through eternal compromise and alliances with the Social Democrats. [...] I believe, however, that the Center Party will only achieve great things when it once again becomes the anvil and does not form a common bloc with the Church's old enemies"[67]. At the same time, however, Pacelli showed an appreciation for *realpolitik*, defending the Center Party (and the Bavarian People's Party, the BVP) as "the only party that we can count on when it comes to defending the interests of the Catholic religion in parliament"[68].

[65] Letter from Cardinal von Faulhaber to Reich Chancellor Wirth, 14 September 1922, in: Volk, 275f., Doc. 125.

[66] Cf. Winfried Becker, "Die Deutsche Zentrumspartei gegenüber dem Nationalsozialismus und dem Reichskonkordat 1930–1933: Motivationsstrukturen und Situationszwänge", in: *Historisch-Politische Mitteilungen* 7 (2000) 1–37; Robert Leiber, "Reichskonkordat und Ende der Zentrumspartei", in: *Stimmen der Zeit* 167 (1960/61) 213–223.

[67] EAM NL Faulhaber 1200.

[68] Wolf, 76–85; Hubert Wolf and Klaus Unterburger, eds., *Eugenio Pacelli: Die Lage der Kirche in Deutschland 1929* (Veröffentlichungen der Kommission für Zeitgeschichte, Reihe A: Quellen 50) (Paderborn et al., 2006), 167, 169. Cf. a letter with a similar line of argumentation, which Pacelli wrote from Rorschach to Undersecretary of State Pizzardo, 28 September 1932; published in Ludwig Volk, "Brüning contra Pacelli", in: *Rheinischer Merkur*, Nr. 48, 27 November 1970, 48. reproduction in: Ludwig Volk, *Katholische Kirche und Nationalsozialismus: Ausgewählte Aufsätze*, ed. Dieter Albrecht (Veröffentlichungen der Kommission für Zeitgeschichte, Reihe B: Forschungen 46) (Mainz, 1987), 315–320: "Brüning contra Pacelli". One document corrects the memoirs; in it, Pacelli comes to the conclusion: "For all its defects, the Center Party is still, as far as I can see, the only party that one can count on with any certainty in church matters, as the recent negotiations on the Concordat for Baden once again proved."

Incidentally, so far no evidence has been found in the Vatican files that Pacelli pressured Heinrich Brüning to form a coalition with the Nazi Party, as Hans Küng has portrayed the matter[69]. The Reich Concordat of 1933 was not an agreement to integrate Catholics into the Third Reich or to weaken their powers of resistance, but rather an attempt to establish a legal "interception line", as well as a legally defined protective space for a church that was separate from the state.

Other important endeavors for Pacelli included the efforts on behalf of a Catholic university, as well as lobbying for the idea of "Catholic Action". The latter he championed tirelessly, if not particularly successfully, with programmatic presentations at the annual competing events at Catholic church congresses. Cardinal Faulhaber considered this such a critical point that he included it in his short farewell speech for Nuncio Pacelli in 1929: "The German Catholics [...] do not want to remain behind the Catholics of other countries, even if they have their own peculiar principles and methods regarding work in social and public life and for the maintenance of associational life"[70].

When it came to the proper structure for theological studies, the training of priests, or the appointment of bishops, the nuncio possessed clear-cut views. The "Report on the Situation of the Church in Germany" from 18 November 1929, Pacelli's summarizing closing report of his nunciature, which was published in 2006, demonstrates that these criteria were actually applied[71]. Whoever did not meet these standards could not expect to receive a flattering characterization out of courtesy, not even Cardinal Bertram, the chairman of the Fulda Bishops' Conference.

Pacelli's relations to individual bishops varied. Speaking for the Bavarian bishops, Faulhaber reported in 1920: "His Excellency Pacelli is not only respected by the Bavarian bishops, he is admired – I have never heard a contrary voice – and he has also earned considerable renown within the offices of the state"[72].

---

[69] Küng (see n. 29).

[70] Cardinal Faulhaber in his talk during Nuncio Pacelli's stopover on 13 December 1929 at the Munich *Hauptbahnhof*; EAM NL Faulhaber 1320.

[71] Wolf and Unterburger (see n. 68).

[72] Letter from Baron Ritter zu Groenesteyn, 10 March 1920; EAM NL Faulhaber 1352. With all due trust, the chairman of the Freising Bishops' Conference nevertheless exercised caution in the matter of Pacelli's transfer to Berlin, which was discussed in early 1920: "I still will not venture to obtain a vote of the Bavarian bishops because, as I have heard more than once, the episcopate believes it must exercise the greatest restraint in matters of papal competence and especially in personal matters concerning the nunciature. The latter also because the episcopate, faced with the countless demands of the diocesan church towers, has not managed to construct a worthy nunciature building."

For the reverse view, an estimation made for the Freising Bishops' Conference that is comparable to the final report for the Fulda Bishops' Conference would be most welcome, but has not yet been found. Pacelli's contact with Cardinal Bertram of Breslau continued through the years to be characterized by a distanced propriety. The personal friendships he developed with Cardinal Faulhaber and Konrad von Preysing withstood even the strains of the Third Reich. For German Catholics during the years 1933–1945, this personal attachment constituted a form of support that can hardly be overestimated. Time and again, Pius XII's personal information channels to Berlin and Munich played an influential role in prior coordination of important decisions.

Eugenio Pacelli had a good memory in the positive as well as the negative sense. Accomplices as well as critics felt this in decidedly different ways. Examples that date back to the nunciature period include his relations to Konrad von Preysing, Clemens August von Galen, and Joseph Frings, the three German cardinals of 1945.

Another example, however, is the case of Konrad Adenauer. Adenauer and Pacelli were almost exactly the same age, born in 1876. Their mutual interests, which corresponded on central principles, made possible a mutual personal appreciation. Is it not astonishing, then, that the German chancellor received the Vatican's highest accolade for laymen, the Order of Christ, not from Pope Pius XII but only at his own farewell audience, from the hand of Pope Paul VI? Possibly, the interdiction originating in Munich in 1922, when Cardinal Faulhaber had written to tell Rome that it would be out of the question to bestow the usual honors on the president of the Catholic church congress following the incident there still applied to Adenauer[73]. For his part, Adenauer stuck to his position even after the death of Cardinal Faulhaber. In a letter thanking Monsignor Weissthanner for having written the brochure on the occasion of Cardinal Faulhaber's 80th birthday, Adenauer let it be known: "As much as I regret this controversy, I still believe I was justified in making those remarks"[74].

Pacelli considered achieving the concordat with Bavaria as his most important task. This agreement was reached only in 1925, after negotiations lasting years[75],

---

[73] Letter from Cardinal von Faulhaber to Monsignor Pizzardo, 19 December 1922, in: Volk, 278f., Doc. 127; EAM NL Faulhaber 1200. Cf. above the discussion of the Catholic church congress of 1922.

[74] Letter from Konrad Adenauer to Msgr. Joseph Weissthanner, 9 August 1962; copy in the archive of the Kommission für Zeitgeschichte, Bonn, NL Volk C III 3.

[75] Archbishop von Faulhaber wrote as early as 3 April 1922 to the Bavarian bishops: "The negotiations over the concordat have created a desperate situation in the last weeks." See Volk, 237ff., Doc. 110. Cf. the memorandum of the Apostolic Nunciature in Bavaria to Dr. Matt, Minister

as part of a package solution ratified by the Bavarian *Landtag*. In his Christmas letter to Pope Pius XI of 19 December 1924, Cardinal Faulhaber had to report that the concordat would not be concluded in that year because "all evil spirits between the portals of Hell and the gates of Munich were mobilized." It was to be hoped, however, that the "achievement of the century of our revered-by-all, intellectually grandiose Apostolic Nuncio Pacelli" would be concluded in the first weeks of the year 1925[76]. In these negotiations, Pacelli proved himself a legally trained, well prepared, and assertive representative of Vatican interests. That his promotion to cardinal and cardinal secretary of state in 1930 was justified by the quality of his work in Munich and Berlin was also a form of thanks for these diplomatic successes. Pacelli was not to blame for the lengthy negotiation period but it was all right with him that it delayed his move to Berlin. "I am doing all I can so that I don't have to move from Munich to Berlin. If need be, I would forego the cardinalship, would retreat into a private existence with a small pension or take over a small Italian diocese, anything but the hell of Berlin"[77].

"You know that it was with great preparedness for self-sacrifice that I consented to move to Berlin. As long as I was in Munich, although even there I wanted, for many reasons, to leave the nuncio existence behind me, the desire – I think understandable, for all-too-human reasons – to conclude the Bavarian concordat, for which I had already done so much work, held me back. Now in Berlin I have nothing but struggles and problems, and it is only for the love to God that I have taken this heavy cross upon myself. One can add that the climate in that city is not the best for my health"[78].

In 1925, Pacelli articulated his farewell mood publicly with the words: "By saying farewell to Munich, the city with the magnificent creations of its sense of art and living faith [...] I greet with a touched heart the noble Bavarian people, in whose midst during the past years I acquired a second hometown"[79].

---

for Education and Cultural Affairs, 27 September 1922; letter from Cardinal von Faulhaber to the Chairman of the Bayerische Volkspartei (Bavarian Peoples Party), 16 January 1923.

[76] Volk, 352f., Doc. 160.

[77] Letter from Nuncio Pacelli to Msgr. Pizzardo 1923, cited in: "Wie mutig war Pius XII.?", ‹http://www.welt.de/welt_print/article3035232/Wie-mutig-war-Pius-XII.html› (16 January 2009), 4; Pizzardo was familiar with the local conditions, from 1909 to 1912 he had himself served as secretary at the Munich nunciature.

[78] Pacelli to Msgr. Pizzardo, 8 December 1925; AA.EE.SS. Germania Pos. 511 P.O., fasc. 24, Bl. 95r; cited in: Besier, 68.

[79] *Bayerischer Kurier*, supplement "Aus Welt und Kirche", 16 July 1925. Pacelli's speech (Abschied aus Bayern; Farewell to Bavaria) is documented, with slight variations, in: Ludwig Kaas, ed., *Eugenio Pacelli: Gesammelte Reden* (Berlin, 1930), 47–50.

The *Bayerischer Kurier* commented on the speeches at the farewell ceremony held in the Odeonssaal using a writing style that, for today's ears, is at least as hard to get used to as the papal Christmas address of 1942 is for Rolf Hochhuth, yet it is still worth listening to: "One does not know whether one should marvel more at the perfected form of his German, the depth of thought, the love for Bavaria, his second home, or his deep sympathy for the Bavarian character and the Bavarian soul." In the same vein: the celebration in the Odeonssaal "was another one of those irresistible revelations of the millennia-old, unfading cultural power of the Roman Catholic Church, which triumphantly illuminated the smallness, powerlessness, and 'episode-like nature' of all anti-Roman opposition"[80]. "The myth of Rome's alienness to the German character, disproved a thousand times, has again been given the lie"[81]. "Dear Bavaria and Munich [...] you have showed again that you can be noble and loyal and sincerely grateful, to the pope as well as his illustrious envoy"[82].

By 1929, Eugenio Pacelli had come to terms with Berlin as well. On numerous occasions as pope, he mentioned again and again his time as nuncio in Germany. In his reminiscences, the years in Germany were "perhaps the best time of my life"[83].

When he departed, he was so popular that Berlin Catholics formed a 3 km-long torch-lit cordon for the doyen of the diplomatic corps, from the nunciature to the *Anhalter Bahnhof* railway station. His journey on a special train from Berlin to Rome was interrupted in Munich by a second farewell ceremony at the main railway terminus[84]. From that point, the Roman's mission in Germany was definitively a thing of the past but his German mission in Rome was nowhere near completed. As cardinal secretary of state and also as pope, Pacelli expressly reserved German affairs for himself.

Eugenio Pacelli never again visited his "second homeland". But he retained his popularity throughout the decades. The renaming of the Pfandhausgasse as Pacellistraße, on Otto Gritschneder's proposal[85]; the city of Munich's regular

---

[80] Ibid.

[81] Ibid.

[82] Ibid.

[83] Pope Pius XII on 11 March 1940 at the audience for Foreign Minister Ribbentrop, in: Pierre Blet, Robert A. Graham, Angelo Martini, and Burkhart Schneider, eds., *Actes et documents du Saint Siège relatifs à la Seconde guerre mondiale d'après les archives du Vatican*, 11 vols. (Vatican City, 1965–1981), here vol. 1, Nr. 258.

[84] Extensive reporting for example in *Münchner Neueste Nachrichten*, 14 December 1929. Cf. the nuncio's farewell letter to the German bishops and the response by Cardinal von Faulhaber, 13 December 1929; EAM NL Faulhaber 1320.

[85] Proposal by City Councilman Otto Gritschneder, 30 June 1950 (Antrag Nr. 580) to rename a street – "preferably in the inner city" – as "Pacellistraße" or "Pacelli-Platz"; Stadtarchiv München, Bürgermeister und Rat 1986.

greetings; the numbers of Bavarian pilgrims to Rome; and as the popular reaction to his death in 1958 are eloquent examples of lasting veneration. In spite of body language that insisted on distance and emanated authority, there was never another papal nuncio before or after him who was as close to German Catholics as Eugenio Pacelli. "He was talked about more than any German bishop or cardinal"[86]. In performing his core duties as nuncio in Germany, Pacelli managed a remarkable personal balancing act. He carried out Rome's detailed instructions for his office[87] more than satisfactorily and at the same time developed a bond of trust with German Catholics. Notwithstanding a recently expressed conjecture that a nuncio's basic set of tools includes limited prospects[88], Nuncio Pacelli was capable of learning and willing to learn. He understood the advice he received from the Royal Bavarian envoy at Christmas 1917, that Rome would do well to be somewhat more considerate of Germany's sensitivity to papal pronouncements – and despite all sympathy, he never forget on whose orders he served in Munich and Berlin. "Indeed, no one in the first half of the 20th century exercised a more lasting control over the ecclesiastical and political fate of German Catholicism than this true Roman, who in May 1917 took up the task, with unlimited self-confidence and cool passion, of representing Rome's interests in Germany"[89]. Cardinal Faulhaber had foreseen that there could be controversy extending even into our times. But that did not worry him when, on the occasion of Nuncio Pacelli's departure from Munich and with reference to Pope Pius XI, he said: "Public opinion can be falsified; history cannot be falsified. We have opened our archive and for these last years one need only read our files […] Nuncio Pacelli coordinated all his actions with these grand lines of a sovereign worldview and I say today: Keep calm, history cannot be falsified"[90].

Translated by Christof Morrissey

---

[86] Friedrich Muckermann, *Im Kampf zwischen zwei Epochen: Lebenserinnerungen* (Veröffentlichungen der Kommission für Zeitgeschichte, Reihe A: Quellen 15) (Mainz, 1973), 381.
[87] Wolf, 27–42.
[88] Ibid., 88.
[89] Scholder, *Die Kirchen und das Dritte Reich*, 99.
[90] Cardinal Faulhaber's farewell address in the name of the Bavarian bishops, 14 July 1925, in the Odeon. Munich; EAM NL Faulhaber 1320.

Introduction to the Presentation
"Pius XII and Modernity"

Manfred Weitlauff

Ladies and Gentlemen!

Since the task of moderating this evening of presentations has fallen to me, I, too, offer you a heartfelt welcome and thank you for your participation and the interest that that participation expresses. With this evening's proceedings, the General Directorate of the Bavarian State Archives, the Munich City Archive, and the Archive of the Archdiocese of Munich and Freising are inaugurating a four-part lecture series intended to accompany the traveling exhibition "Opus Iustitiae Pax. Eugenio Pacelli – Pius XII (1876–1958)", which opened in the Munich Carmelite Church last week. In my view, the lecture series sponsored by these three institutions to provide scholarly accompaniment to the above-mentioned exhibition is not only an excellent idea, it is a necessity. The papers presented as part of this lecture series and the discussions that – I hope – will follow each of them will provide the participants insights (in various respects) into the personality and actions of Pope Pius XII, in ways that attending the exhibition alone probably cannot. Especially since it barely touches on the important questions being asked about this pontificate today, if it touches on them at all.

Just this afternoon, I visited the exhibition and I have to confess: the only document there that really "moved" me is the letter of April 1933 by the independent lecturer Dr. Editha Stein (as she signed her own name) to Pius XI, in which she informed the pope of the oppression of the Jews then coming into effect and beseeching him to raise his voice against it. The letter was not answered, except for (if I am correctly informed) an indirect "verification of receipt" sent to the Archabbott of Beuron. Compared with this early plea for help, the "section" located immediately opposite, "Listen to the Pope's silence here", is simply dismaying.

Since this lecture series is being hosted in cooperation with three different institutions – one of the state, another municipal, the third of the church – it guarantees an appropriate critical counterweight to this exhibition. Its Vatican authors (if one may use that term) – namely the Papal Committee for Historical Scholarship that has been entrusted with preparing the exhibition and its, in this respect, very enterprising president (who is also accompanying it) – hope to achieve very specific aims. A few years ago, when I went down once again into the grottoes of St. Peter's and could not find the grave of Pius XII, though I knew in which niche his sarcophagus stood, the on-duty custodian responded to my question as to where Pio XII now lay with a short, precise "è in restauro". That really said it all, at least for those "in the know".

But of course it is not my task here to speak to you about Pius XII. It is only my modest duty to introduce to you the first of four invited speakers this evening, who will speak to you about Pius XII. Under the heading "Pius XII and Modernity", he will attempt to provide initial insights into this pope, who is well-known for his close ties to Bavaria, and his pontificate: into his thought and deeds, as well as into those future prospects for the Church in the modern era that may have proceeded from his papacy and whose effects are still felt today. We are especially curious to see what can be presented in this latter regard. It must be kept in mind, first of all, that the beginning of Pius XII's pontificate coincided with the start of World War II. In its early years, this papacy stood in the shadow of the heaviest political and military confrontations, with all their catastrophic consequences. After 1945, Pius XII's papacy was shaped by the emergence of rival blocs in East and West, which at the time could have escalated at any moment. Furthermore, the archival holdings on his papacy have not yet been opened to scholars, so that we still have to wait a long time for final judgments – to the extent that they are possible at all.

Allow me, then, to introduce our first speaker, Professor Franz Xaver Bischof. Born 1955 in St. Gallen, a Swiss citizen, Professor Bischof studied theology at what was then the Theological Faculty and is today the University of Lucerne, and at the Institut Catholique in Paris. In Lucerne, he was my first doctoral student and my first graduate assistant. In 1988, he earned his Dr. theol. *summa cum laude* with a brilliant dissertation on "The End of the Diocese of Constance, 1802–1803 to 1821–1827". In 1995, as a grantee of the Swiss "Nationalfonds zur Förderung der wissenschaftlichen Forschung" (National Fund for Promotion of Scholarly Research), he completed his habilitation, on the second half of the life of the Munich church historian Ignaz von Döllinger, while at the Catholic-Theological Faculty of the University of Munich, to which I was recalled in 1986, in the field of Medieval and Modern Church History. His habilitation was awarded the university's 1996 *Habilitationspreis*.

Since 1994, Professor Bischof has been scholarly coordinator of the *Historisches Lexikon der Schweiz* (Historical Encyclopedia of Switzerland) for the Canton St. Gallen. Following my retirement in the 2001–2002 winter semester, he held the Munich chair for Medieval and Modern Church history – the same chair once held by Döllinger – in an interim capacity; the process of a permanent appointment dragged on for years, not least because of general state austerity measures at the time. In 2004, Franz Xaver Bischof was appointed professor at the Seminar for Medieval and Modern Church History at the Wilhelms-Universität in Münster, Westfalia. In 2007, Professor Bischof was appointed, as my successor, to the "Döllinger" chair at the Catholic theology faculty in Munich, which he had previously held in a provisional capacity.

Professor Bischof is a board member of the "Vereinigung für Schweizerische Kirchengeschichte" (Union for Swiss Church History), co-editor of the renowned *Zeitschrift für Kirchengeschichte* and *Schweizerische Zeitschrift für Religions- und Kulturgeschichte*. He is also a member of the newly founded Commission for Theological History at the Bavarian Academy of Sciences and the Ecumenical Working Group of Protestant and Catholic Theologians in Germany, headed by Cardinal Karl Lehmann. Professor Bischof also currently serves as managing director of the board of the Martin Grabmann Research Institute at the Munich Theological Faculty.

Of his numerous publications – which focus on 19th and 20th century church, theological, and Catholic history but also include medieval and early modern topics – I would like to add to those already mentioned above the volume he co-edited with Stefan Leimgruber, *Vierzig Jahre II. Vatikanum. Zur Wirkungsgeschichte der Konzilstexte* (Forty Years of Vatican II: On the Historical Influence of the Council Texts), whose second edition appeared in 2005, and *Katholische Hochschulseelsorge an der LMU* (Catholic University Ministry at the Ludwig-Maximilians-Universität, Munich), which appeared in 2008.

Since appointment to his chair in Munich, Professor Bischof has once more pressed ahead with research on Ignaz von Döllinger. At the moment, he is working on a critical edition of Döllinger's French and English-language correspondents that is supported by the "Deutsche Forschungsgemeinschaft" (German Research Society).

Translated by Christof Morrissey

Pius XII and Modernity

Franz Xaver Bischof

"Pio XII: uno sconosciuto" – "Pius XII: An Unknown Quantity!"[1] That was the verdict pronounced in 2004 by Giuseppe Alberigo (1926–2007), the Italian historian of the papacy and Church councils, in view of the problems confronting biographers of Eugenio Pacelli, Pope Pius XII (1939–1958)[2], today. Alberigo was referring to the fact that Pacelli did not leave behind personal documents from any phase of his life or concerning any specific church matters; that beyond this the Roman sources on the papacies of Pius XI and Pius XII were not accessible and the literature on Pius XII, with few exceptions, is tainted by apologetic or polemical motivations. "We still know very little about this long and decisive pontificate", Alberigo reported, "too little about Pope Pacelli himself and too little about the decisions that he had to make in one manner or another"[3].

Since then, the Vatican archives on Pius XI's pontificate (1922–1939) up to his death on 10 February 1939 were opened to researchers in 2006[4]. It will take years before this massive amount of material can be evaluated, longer still for the archives on Pius XII to be opened and worked through in the same fashion. Nonetheless, a new chapter in scholarship on the Pacelli papacy has now been opened, particularly since Pius XII's pontificate can only be understood against the background of his own formative experiences. These include his time in the Rome of Leo XIII (1878–1903), Pius X (1903–1914), and Benedict XV (1914–1922), as well

---

[1]   Giuseppe Alberigo, "Pio XII: uno sconosciuto", in: *Cristianesimo nella Storia* 25 (2004) 987–996.

[2]   On Pius XII, encyclopedia entries in the following reference works: LThK² (Robert Leiber), LThK³ (Josef Gelmi), RGG⁴ (Günter Wassilowsky), TRE (Gottfried Maron) and *Catholicisme* (Roger Aubert); other selected works include: Andrea Riccardi, *Il Potere del Papa da Pio XII a Giovanni Paolo II* (Bari, 1993), 3–111; Georg Schwaiger, "Pius XII.", in: *Papsttum und Päpste im 20. Jahrhundert*, ed. Schwaiger (Munich, 1999), 271–309; Francesco Traniello, "Pio XII", in: *Enciclopedia dei Papi* (Rome, 2000), 632–645; Michael F. Feldkamp, *Pius XII. und Deutschland* (Göttingen, 2000); Philippe Chenaux, *Pie XII: Diplomate et pasteur* (Paris, 2003); Rudolf Lill, *Die Macht der Päpste* (Kevelaer, 2006), 153–174. An extensive but incomplete bibliography by Giovanni Castaldo and Alfredo Tuzi in *Opus iustitiae pax: Eugenio Pacelli – Pius XII (1876–1958)*, ed. Philippe Chenaux, Giovanni Morello, and Massimiliano Valente (Regensburg, 2009), 219–232.

[3]   Alberigo, 996.

[4]   On the Vatican Secret Archive and on the archive opening of 2006, see Hubert Wolf, *Papst & Teufel: Die Archive des Vatikan und das Dritte Reich* (Munich, 2008), 19–26.

as his service as nuncio in Germany from 1917 to 1929 and as Cardinal Secretary of State under Pius XI from 1930 to 1939.

It is to be hoped that, along with the range of archival sources, the focus of research will widen as well. That with it, the one-sided fixation on Pius XII's conduct in World War II and the debate about his "silence" on the Holocaust – a debate understandable in view of the magnitude of the Third Reich's crimes but often ungrounded in historical scholarship and, by now, thoroughly deadlocked – can be broken open, so that internal church perspectives and developments will attract increased attention[5]. These include the ecclesiastical-pastoral goals that, in my opinion, determined Pacelli's diplomacy and (church) policies, particularly in respect to his positioning toward the modern ideologies of communism and National Socialism, with their totalitarian structures, on the one hand, and the liberal-democratic order of the Western world, with its liberal freedoms, on the other; the reaction of the pope and the Roman Curia toward modernity; Pius XII's intellectual, theological, canonical, and spiritual profile; his magisterium, which he exercised extensively even during the war years; his conception of the Church, which undoubtedly presents the key to understanding his papacy; and, inseparably connected to this, the papal absolutism practiced by Pius XII, which Rudolf Lill correctly contends constitutes the "church-historical problematic"[6] of this long pontificate, which lasted from 1939 to 1958, culminating in the 1950 Marian Dogma of the Assumption.

My remarks here cannot even come close to mastering the themes sketched out above, and make no claim to do so. Instead, I intend to outline the main themes of Pius XII's pontificate in the context of modernity – which is shaped by the Enlightenment, liberalism, industrialization, technological and scientific progress, and social change – while employing a two-pronged approach. One the one hand, I examine external church policy, with a special view to the pope's stance toward National Socialism, Communism, and democracy; on the other hand, I consider internal church policy, primarily the magisterium and its significance in theological history. I would like to begin with a few comments on Pacelli's formative influences prior to his election as pope that are important for a wider understanding.

---

[5] For an evaluation of the debate about the pope's "silence", see José M. Sánchez, *Pius XII and the Holocaust: Understanding the Controversy* (Washington, 2002). On the same subject since then, see Thomas Brechenmacher, *Der Vatikan und die Juden: Geschichte einer unheiligen Beziehung* (Munich, 2005), 202–227; Wolf, 205–251; Dominik Burkard, "Pius XII. und die Juden", in: *Christ in der Gegenwart* 61 (2009) 25f., 33f., 41f.

[6] Lill, 154.

Election as Pope and Early Influences

That Cardinal Eugenio Pacelli was elected pope on 2 March 1939, his 63rd birthday – after a conclave that lasted only one day – hardly came as a surprise. He was considered the most talented personality in the College of Cardinals. His election can be seen first and foremost as the cardinals' reaction to the political crisis then coming to a head in Europe. In a difficult political period for the Church, Pacelli's election secured continuity with the outgoing pontificate, whose political orientation he had significantly helped determine since 1930[7]. The countries of the so-called Free World rightly saw in the new pope an ally against the totalitarian dictatorships in Germany, Italy, and Russia. At the same time, choosing the name Pius signaled idealistic agreement with his predecessor, even though the relationship between Pacelli and Ratti still elicits many unanswered questions. Yet Pius XI himself desired Pacelli as his successor. Whether intentionally or not, he had paved the way for him by sending his state secretary to Eucharistic congresses in South America, France, and Hungary, and for the first time ever, on a private mission to the United States, thereby making him known on a global scale[8].

The cardinals had elected a native Roman from a family of jurists that had maintained close ties to the papacy for generations, one of those families that, in a Rome divided by cultural politics, had not sided with the Italian nation state after unification in 1870 but rather with those popes who, on account of the lost papal states, considered themselves "prisoners in the Vatican", and that had stood loyally by the ultramontane piety and teachings of these popes[9]. Nevertheless, the highly talented Eugenio Pacelli attended a laicist state high school (Gymnasium), one that imparted a solid classical education. As a candidate for the priesthood, Pacelli attended the Jesuit Gregorian University and the Seminarium Romanum, the later Lateran University, as a non-resident student – a singular exception. He graduated in 1902 with doctorates in both church and civil law. While still a law student, he

---

[7]   On the 1939 conclave, cf. Alberto Melloni, *Das Konklave: Die Papstwahl in Geschichte und Gegenwart* (Freiburg, Basle, and Vienna, 2002), 91–94.

[8]   On the role and influence of Pacelli as Pius XI's Cardinal Secretary of State, see Chenaux, 165–223; Thomas Brechenmacher, "Teufelspakt, Selbsterhaltung, universale Mission? Leitlinien und Spielräume der Diplomatie des Heiligen Stuhls gegenüber dem nationalsozialistischen Deutschland (1933–1939) im Lichte neu zugänglicher vatikanischer Akten", in: *Historische Zeitschrift* 280 (2005) 591–645; Wolf, 253–306.

[9]   Cf. Andrea Riccardi, "Pius XII. und die Stadt Rom: Die 'Romanitas' Papst Pacellis", in: Chenaux, Morello and Valente, 21–35. Pius XII, writes Riccardi (ibid., 25), saw Rome not only as the city of his birth and the seat of the pope but as the center of the Catholic Church, which in Pius XII's eyes is "universal" because it is "Roman".

entered into service with the Roman Curia thanks to the network of family connections. There, he found his most important mentor in Cardinal Pietro Gasparri (1852–1934), the true architect of the 1917 codex reform. As Philippe Chenaux has convincingly demonstrated in his biography *Pie XII: Diplomate et pasteur*, that school of canon law that Gasparri also felt committed to appears to have been a decisive influence for Pacelli during this phase. This school reacted to the upheavals of the turn of the 20th century, and in particular the Roman question, with two new strategic positions. One was the doctrine of the Holy See as a subject of international law, whose existence did not necessarily depend on a territory of its own, which opened the way to the Lateran Treaties of 1929. Above all, however, the doctrine of *societas perfecta* emphasized the Church's jurisdictional independence, which it attempted to protect from any kind of state intervention in church matters, while at the same time claiming interpretative sovereignty in all cultural and social matters that affected the salvation of the faithful[10]. This legal interpretation of the Church as a perfect community prevailed in Vatican politics at just that time when Pacelli's steep ascent within the Curia was taking place, as Gasparri's closest collaborator in drafting the 1917 *Codex iuris canonici*, with its universalist, centralizing revision of canon law. It was this law that forged the resolutions of the First Vatican Council of 1870 into legal form and sought to recast the relationship between church and state to guarantee total church autonomy.

The view of the Church that Pacelli absorbed during his "apprenticeship" in the decidedly anti-modern Curia of Pius X – and with which, as pope, he would truly identify! – was that of the hierarchically organized universal church laid down in the *Codex* of 1917, one in which the will of the pope and the Roman headquarters extends to the remotest branches. To achieve this goal, both Pius XI and Pius XII depended on the proven politics of the concordat in their relations with the international community of states. "Concordats are instruments of the law"[11]; so Pius XII explained the importance of concordats to the president of the German Federal Republic, Theodor Heuss (1884–1963), as late as 1957. Independent of their respective political forms, concordats sought to "prepare the

---

[10] Chenaux, 49–53. On the young Pacelli's character, see also Riccardi, *Il Potere del Papa*, 29–34; Hubert Wolf and Klaus Unterburger, eds., *Eugenio Pacelli: Die Lage der Kirche in Deutschland 1929* (Veröffentlichungen der Kommission für Zeitgeschichte, Reihe A: Quellen 50) (Paderborn, Munich, Vienna, and Zürich, 2006), 26–32; Wolf, 42–46.

[11] Pius XII, "Rede an den Präsidenten der Bundesrepublik Deutschland", in: *Acta Apostolicae Sedis* 49 (1957) 1033–1036; German translation in: Arthur Fridolin Utz and Joseph Fulko Groner, eds., *Aufbau und Entfaltung des gesellschaftlichen Lebens: Soziale Summe Pius XII.*, 3 vols. (Fribourg, 1954–1961), III 3772f., here 3773.

space in which the Catholic Church or the Catholics of the country in question can develop and practice their worldview freely and peacefully"[12]. And in fact, concordat negotiations form a common thread through all phases of Pacelli's life's work, from the concordat with Serbia in 1914 to those with Franco's Spain in 1953 and Bolivia in 1957.

National Socialism, Communism, Democracy

Traditional concordat politics was the instrument, then, with which the Holy See reacted to the challenge of Nazism. In the Reich Concordat of 1933, the pope and Curia saw the opportunity to secure church life and pastoral care. It was intended to preserve "a legal basis of defense for Catholics [...] from which to defend themselves, as long as it was possible, against the constantly rising flood of religious persecution"[13]. With these words, Pius XII defended the concordat in his famous address to the College of Cardinals on 2 June 1945. "According to Roman logic, this in no way contradicted the keen awareness of the danger presented by Nazism, the '*völkisch* neo-paganism', and the threat to peace"[14]. Similarly, Pius XI had offered the Soviet dictator Josef Stalin (1879–1953) recognition by the Holy See, in accordance with international law, of the USSR's communist regime on three different occasions in the 1920s, in return for guaranteeing the Catholic Church's pastoral care – to no avail[15].

The sources confirm without doubt that Pacelli – an expert on, and friend of, Germany – fully realized the Nazi regime's inhuman and anti-church nature from the very beginning. They also reveal, however, that different views about how to deal with that regime existed within the Curia, as Hubert Wolf has shown. There was competition between those who wanted an official condemnation through the magisterium of the Holy Office, which would likely have exposed German Catholics to a severe hardship test, and those, led by Pacelli, who advocated diplo-

---

[12] Ibid.

[13] Pius XII, Address to the College of Cardinals, 2 June 1945, in: *Acta Apostolicae Sedis* 37 (1945) 59–168; German translation in: Utz and Groner, II 1800–1812, here 1803.

[14] Jean-Marie Mayeur, "Die katholische Kirche", in: Jean-Marie Mayeur, ed., *Erster und Zweiter Weltkrieg: Demokratien und totalitäre Systeme* (Die Geschichte des Christentums. Religion – Politik – Kultur 12) (Freiburg, Basle, and Vienna, 1992), 374–435, here 399.

[15] Cf. Hansjakob Stehle, *Die Ostpolitik des Vatikans 1917–1975* (Munich and Zurich, 1975), 43–131; Chenaux, 155–164; Gerhard Besier and Francesca Piombo, *Der Heilige Stuhl und Hitler-Deutschland: Die Faszination des Totalitären* (Munich, 2004), 79–92.

macy[16]. His pragmatic, calculating approach won out against the backdrop of the trauma engendered by the Kulturkampf, establishing considerations for the pastoral care and salvation of the Catholic faithful as the top guiding norm[17]. This position led, after the outbreak of the Spanish Civil War in 1936, to the simultaneous publication of the two encyclicals against Nazism and Communism in 1937. These clearly stated the total incompatibility between Catholic teachings, on the one hand, and Nazi ideology, with its glorification of blood, soil, race and nation, as well as communist doctrine, on the other, without identifying the German and Soviet regimes by name[18].

Under Pius XII, nothing changed concerning the principled rejection of National Socialist and communist ideologies, which were considered irreconcilable with Christianity. His inaugural encyclical *Summi pontificatus* of 20 October 1939 condemned, in the same style as the two 1937 encyclicals, the "false view of the state's unlimited authority" which "destroys the supranational community, undermines the foundations and significance of international law, leads to the violation of the rights of others, and makes all understanding and peaceful coexistence difficult"[19]. According to the New York Times, the encyclical was "a massive attack on all totalitarianism and the evils that, in the pope's view, it brought into the world"[20].

Corresponding with the pope's statement were frantic efforts to keep the peace. In the deceptive hope that he could profit from the moral standing that the papacy had gained in the international community during the interwar years, during the first months of his pontificate Pius XII attempted to prevent war through appeals for peace, calls to prayer, and a proposal for a five-power conference – true to his motto *Opus iustitiae pax*! After the outbreak of World War II, he concentrated on keeping Italy out of the conflict. When that failed too, he switched to a position of strict neutrality between the warring parties and thereafter to alleviating, within the

---

[16] Wolf, 253–306.
[17] Cf. ibid., 201f.
[18] Pius XI, Encyclical *Mit brennender Sorge*, 14 March 1937, in: *Acta Apostolicae Sedis* 29 (1937) 148–167; excerpt in: Anton Rohrbasser, *Heilslehre der Kirche: Dokumente von Pius IX. bis Pius XII.* (Fribourg, 1953), 559–582; Pius XI, Encyclical *Divini Redemptoris,* 19 March 1937, in: *Acta Apostolicae Sedis* 28 (1937) 87–96; excerpt in: Rohrbasser, 724–733.
[19] Pius XII, Encyclical *Summi pontificatus*, in: *Acta Apostolicae Sedis* 31 (1939) 413–453; German translation in: Utz and Groner, I 3–40, here 26.
[20] Cited in: Michael Burleigh, *Irdische Mächte, göttliches Heil: Die Geschichte des Kampfes zwischen Politik und Religion von der Französischen Revolution bis in die Gegenwart* (Munich, 2005), 839.

scope of limited possibilities, the sufferings of war and protecting Rome from military action[21].

Pius XII held fast to strict neutrality until the end of the war, despite continuous pressure from the democratic states, especially the U.S.A., to take sides against the totalitarian dictatorships. He was just as unwilling to legitimize the German war of aggression against the Soviet Union as a "crusade" against Bolshevism[22], as Nazis and Fascists wished and as some Italian and German bishops publicly did, including the Bishop of Münster, Clemens August von Galen (1933–1946)[23]. Neutrality was grounded above all in Pius XII's repeatedly expressed conviction that the pope, as head of a transnational church, must stand above the warring parties and must preserve the unity of the Catholic Church over and above all national differences, as well as in never-abandoned hopes that the pontiff could serve as a mediator in the event of peace efforts. This accorded with the policy the popes had pursued since Benedict XV but it constituted a clear overestimation on the part of Pius XII as to the possibilities of his office. The personal failure of Benedict XV as a mediator in 1917 probably also played a role[24]. The decision for neutrality was tied to the Pope's dilemma of having to choose between publicly aired protests,

---

[21] On Pius XII's conduct during World War II, see the relevant document collection: Pierre Blet, Robert A. Graham, Angelo Martini, and Burkhart Schneider, eds., *Actes et documents du Saint-Siège relatifs à la Seconde guerre mondiale d'après les archives du Vatican*, 11 vols. (Vatican City, 1965–1981). Selected literature includes: Owen Chadwick, *Britain and the Vatican during the Second World War* (Cambridge, 1986); Mayeur, 402–421; Pierre Blet, *Pie XII et la Seconde Guerre mondiale d'après les archives du Vatican* (Paris, 1997); in German, *Pius XII und der Zweite Weltkrieg: Die Akten des Vatikans* (Paderborn, 2000); Feldkamp, 124–155; Chenaux, 227–304; Victor Conzemius, "Weltkirche – Ortskirche Schweiz: Die Kirchenpolitik der Päpste Pius XI. und Pius XII.", in: Victor Conzemius, ed., *Schweizer Katholizismus 1933–1945: Eine Konfessionskultur zwischen Abkapselung und Solidarität* (Zürich, ²2003), 15–41; Harold H. Tittmann, *Inside the Vatican of Pius XII: The Memoir of an American Diplomat during World War II* (New York, London, Toronto, Sydney, and Auckland, 2004); Lill, 157–161.

[22] Pius XII, Address to the diplomatic corps, 25 February 1946, in: Utz and Groner, 2170–2175, here 2173: "Therefore We have, despite certain tendentious attempts to pressure Us, in particular been on guard against letting slip from Our lips or Our quill so much as one word, a single sign of endorsement or encouragement on behalf of the war effort against Russia in the year 1941." Cf. Pius XII, Christmas message of 24 Dezember 1951, in: *Acta Apostolicae Sedis* 44 (1952) 5–14; German translation in: Utz and Groner, 2156–2169, here 2158.

[23] Pastoral letter of Bishop von Galen, Münster, 14 September 1941, in: Peter Löffler, ed., *Bischof Clemens August Graf von Galen: Akten, Briefe und Predigten 1933–1946*, 2 parts (Veröffentlichungen der Kommission für Zeitgeschichte, Reihe A: Quellen 42) (Mainz, 1988), II 901–908, here 902: "The German people under arms have, since June of this year, stepped forth to thwart Moscow's militaristic attempt to export the heresy and violent rule of Bolshevism to Germany and Western Europe."

[24] See Wolf and Unterburger, 43–47; Wolf, 48–54, 90f.

which contained the risk of worsening the victims' fate, and maintaining "silence". The latter, to be precise, involved a form of speech that, while balancing legally protected interests in accordance with an ethics of social responsibility – in order to prevent even worse things from happening[25] – limited itself to speaking in the diplomatic style of the Curia, without directly naming the offenses in question, as in the case of the Christmas address of 1942[26]. On this question, the conclusion reached by Julius Cardinal Döpfner (1961–1976, cardinal in 1958), the Archbishop of Munich, still appears valid: "The retrospective judgment of history certainly justifies the view that Pius XII should have protested more energetically. In any case, however, one does not have the right to cast doubt on the absolute sincerity of his motives and the authenticity of his deepest reasons"[27].

Under the impression of World War II and the experiences with totalitarian forms of government, new thinking took hold in Rome. This change, about which there are still many open questions owing to the lack of sources, led to a positive affirmation of parliamentary and democratic forms of government. This "'Yes' to democracy as historical imperative for the hour at hand"[28] was pronounced by Pius XII in his radio address of Christmas 1944. In it, he stated his position on the elementary challenges of the political societal life of his times, took up the hopes

[25] Cf. for example Pius XII to the Italian ambassador in Berlin, Dino Alfieri, in: Blet, Graham, Martini, and Schneider, I 453: "The Italians surely know very well the terrible atrocities (orribile cose) that are now happening in Poland. We should employ fiery words against these atrocities and only the knowledge that We would worsen the fate of those unfortunates if We spoke more loudly keeps Us from doing so." Repeated statements by Pius XII using the same argumentation in: Burkhart Schneider, ed., *Die Briefe Pius' XII. an die deutschen Bischöfe 1939–1944* (Veröffentlichungen der Kommission für Zeitgeschichte, Reihe A: Quellen 4) (Mainz, 1966).

[26] Pius XII, Radio message, 24 December 1942, in: *Acta Apostolicae Sedis* 35 (1943) 9–24 (Latin translation; original in Italian); German translation in: Utz and Groner, 98–119. The decisive and controversial sentence regarding the annihilation of the Jews reads (ibid. 118): "Humanity owes this vow to those hundreds of thousands who, although personally innocent, are condemned to death or abandoned to a progressive impoverishment only on account of their nationality or their descent." On the reaction of the pope and the German bishops toward the destruction of the Jews, see also Mayeur, 406, 419–421, and Wolf, 205–251.

[27] Cited in: Roger Aubert, *Vom Kirchenstaat zur Weltkirche* (Geschichte der Kirche V/1) (Zurich, Einsiedeln, and Cologne, 1976), 198. Cf. the verdict of Gerhart Riegner, the later General Secretary of the World Jewish Congress, on the pope's address of 1942 in: Riegner, *Ne jamais désespérer: Soixante ans au service du peuple juif et des droits de l'homme* (Paris, 1998), 170; German translation in: Victor Conzemius, "Pius XII. – ein politischer Papst: Zum 50. Todestag von Eugenio Pacelli", in: *Stimmen der Zeit* 226 (2008) 669–678, here 676.

[28] Klaus Schatz, *Kirchengeschichte der Neuzeit II* (Düsseldorf, 2003), 144. On the process of rethinking in the Roman Curia, see also Peter Hebblethwaite, *Paul VI: The first modern pope* (New York and Mahwah, 1993), 193.

of the peoples for a democratic post-war order, and unveiled *his* understanding of, as he called it, "true democracy"[29].

This was new! For the first time, a Pope had declared democracy, and with it the modern order of free thought, as compatible with Catholicism[30]. Since the French Revolution of 1789, the popes had, in their permanent defense against modernity, repeatedly and explicitly condemned democracy and popular sovereignty. Since Leo XIII, they had settled on a posture of indifference toward all forms of government but Pius XII's position moved beyond this. It did not merely tolerate democracy but recognized it as a form of government suitable for the times. That was a step on the path to reconciliation between the Catholic Church and modern society, not, however, the recognition of the bourgeois-liberal constitutional state. The legitimation of democracy rooted in popular sovereignty and freedom of religion remained out of bounds. Instead, Pius XII, continuing Leonine teachings on the state, linked the recognition of democracy to the reservation that it was constructed "on the immutable principles of Natural Law and the revealed truths"[31] and – here, the consequence of this approach – must follow the word of the Church: "If the future is to belong to democracy, then an essential part of the fulfillment of its mission must fall to the Christian religion and the Church, which is the herald of the sermon of the savior and the resumer of his mission of salvation. It is indeed (the Church) that teaches and defends the truth, that imparts the supernatural powers of mercy for the realization of the existential order established by God and the purposes of this order, which is the foundation and guideline of every democracy"[32]. Such an interpretation of democracy was incompatible with modern, ideologically neutral constitutional government. Nevertheless, the impact of this speech about democracy on the blueprints for a political order in post-war Europe should not be underestimated. After 1945, "Christian Democracy" came to enjoy full approval by Catholics in countries such as Germany, France, and Italy, even if their relations with the Roman Curia, particularly in Italy, were by no means free of tension[33].

---

[29] Pius XII, Radio message to the world, 24 December 1944, in: *Acta Apostolicae Sedis* 37 (1945) 10–23; German translation in: Utz and Groner, I 1771–1788, here 1774.

[30] See Rudolf Uertz, *Vom Gottesrecht zum Menschenrecht: Das katholische Staatsdenken in Deutschland von der Französischen Revolution bis zum II. Vatikanischen Konzil (1789–1965)* (Politik- und kommunikationswissenschaftliche Veröffentlichungen der Görres-Gesellschaft 25) (Paderborn, Munich, Vienna, and Zurich, 2005), 363–405; Mayeur, 422f.

[31] Pius XII, Radio message to the world, 24 December 1944, in: Utz and Groner, I 1786f.

[32] Ibid.

[33] Cf. Maurilio Guasco, "Italien", in: Erwin Gatz, ed., *Italien und Spanien* (Kirche und Katholizismus seit 1945, vol. 3) (Paderborn et al., 2005), 15–106, here 19–35.

Pius XII linked recognition of democracy with a fundamental and irreconcilable anti-communism, which determined official Church and papal policies until his death in 1958. Since the 1930s, the Holy See had become ever more keenly aware of the international dimension of communism, which had established itself in the Soviet Union after the 1917 October Revolution and carried out severe persecution of the churches. In this, the Church was more far-sighted than the governments in many non-communist countries. As the Cold War set in after 1945, vast areas of Eastern and Central Europe were reshaped in the Soviet mold, a process everywhere accompanied by massive church persecutions. From 1949, China and other bordering Asian countries fell under communist rule[34]. Above all, however, the pope feared a communist takeover in Italy, where the Communists, who had been combated by the Fascists, constituted a major political force in 1945–1946. On the occasion of elections in Italy and France in 1946, Pius XII implored the duty of Catholics to vote, convinced that only Christian Democracy could defend the threatened values of religion and Christian civilization in Western Europe[35]. In the pope's imagination, the conflict assumed apocalyptic dimensions: "It became a struggle between Good and Evil"[36]. In 1949, the Holy Office issued the much debated decree that excommunicated and excluded from the sacraments not only those Catholics "who professed the materialist and anti-Christian doctrine of the communists"[37], but also those who published their writings or even just read them.

In his estimation of international communism, Pius XII unquestionably concurred with that of the United States and the Western capitalist countries. He therefore was widely considered a "Western" pope. That did not in the least deter him, however, from fundamentally and consistently rejecting the liberalism and individualism of the "Free World", as well as the values associated with them, in line with his predecessors. In his view, these contradicted "true freedom" and the "Christian order"[38]. Yet as part of his efforts on behalf of a "Christian Europe", Pius XII supported the nascent process of European unification as it was pushed

[34] On the consequences for the Church in these countries, see Gatz, ed., *Ostmittel-, Ost- und Südosteuropa* (Kirche und Katholizismus seit 1945, vol. 2) (Paderborn et al., 1999); idem, *Die Länder Asiens* (Kirche und Katholizismus seit 1945, vol. 5) (Paderborn et al., 2003).

[35] Pius XII, Address to the College of Cardinals, 1 June 1946, in: *Acta Apostolicae Sedis* 38 (1946) 253–260; German translation in: Utz and Groner, 2121–2131, here 2126f. (Decision for Christianity at the ballot box).

[36] Mayeur, 421–431, here 422. Cf. Guasco, 19–23.

[37] Decree of 1 July 1949, in: *Herder-Korrespondenz* 3 (1948/49) 487. On the consequences of the papal decree in Italy, see Guasco, 23–25.

[38] Pius XII, Christmas message, 24 December 1951, in: *Acta Apostolicae Sedis* 44 (1952) 5–15; German translation in: Utz and Groner, II 2156–2169, here 2166f.

forward largely by Christian Democratic politicians. In 1953, "with a view to the serious situation in which Europe finds itself", he described establishment of the European Economic Community as "a risk", but a "necessary" and "rational risk"[39]. As an organizational model, he proposed the example of Switzerland: "Switzerland is, in microcosm, that which not a few in Europe desire as a saving way out"[40]. Pius XII consistently refused, however, to identify the Catholic Church unilaterally with Western civilization and culture[41].

Magisterium under the Sign of Papal Authority

Despite Pius XII's great political significance, his pontificate should not be reduced to that aspect. During his nearly 20-year reign, Pius XII developed a magisterial productivity of extraordinary density, with forty encyclicals, an infallible pronouncement on doctrine, and hundreds of speeches, addresses, and writings on a wide range of issues and for the most diverse audiences. There is hardly a religious or social issue of his times on which Pius XII did not take a position[42].

Steps toward Reform

Among the encyclicals, those that Pius XII used to position himself vis-à-vis the inter-ecclesiastical new theological departures since the 1920s deserve special attention. These include the encyclical *Mystici corporis* of 1943[43], which intervened "in the scholarly debate about the ecclesiological use of the biblical image of Christ's body, with whose help Catholic theologians of the interwar years

---

[39]   Pius XII, "Il popolo, che abitava nelle tenebre". Christmas radio broadcast of 24 December 1941, in: *Acta Apostolicae Sedis* 46 (1954) 5–16; German translation in: Utz and Groner, I 301–316, here 313; Christmas radio broadcast of 24 December 1953, in: *Acta Apostolicae Sedis* 46 (1954), 5–16; German translation in: Utz and Groner, I 301–316, here 313.

[40]   Pius XII, Address to Swiss journalists, 14 April 1946, in: Utz and Groner, II 1768–1770, here 1769. Cf. Chenaux, 341–378.

[41]   Cf. Mayeur, 421–431, esp. 426.

[42]   Pius XII's statements on political, ethical-moral (especially marriage, family, and sexuality) and societal-social questions have been compiled by Arthur Fridolin Utz und Joseph-Fulko Groner into a "social summary" (Soziale Summe) (cit. in n. 11), which in its epic breadth extends to such topics as "The duties of a modern hotel porter" and "Fashion as a moral problem", material that requires considerable stamina on the part of today's reader.

[43]   Pius XII, Encyclical *Mystici Corporis* on the Mystical Body of Christ, in: *Acta Apostolicae Sedis* 35 (1943) 193–248; German translation in: Rohrbasser, 466–526.

attempted to broaden once again the post-Tridentine, institutionally narrow picture of the Church"[44]. With its fundamentally positive evaluation of that view, this encyclical remained, as Peter Hünermann notes critically, "trapped in the narrow conceptions of the Counter-Reformation"[45]. At the same time, this encyclical legitimized the existing hierarchy of offices[46]. The Church, according to the doctrine of First Vatican Council, is characterized as a "monarchically structured ruling organization"[47], lead by Christ's "Deputy on Earth". Indeed, "Christ and His Deputy" are – and here, Pius XII's claim to papal absolutism is all too clear – described as "only a single authority"[48] on Earth. The powers of bishops are derived exclusively from those of the pope[49]. In this latter question, only the Second Vatican Council brought overdue correction[50]. Nevertheless, with the biblical image of the body of Christ, *Mystici corporis* provided lasting inspiration to reflections on the Church until the start of Vatican II.

By identifying the body of Christ with the Roman Catholic Church as an – as he described it – "in its nature perfect community"[51], the pope undertook a demarcation from Orthodox and Protestant Christians. Of them it is said that, through baptism, they are aligned with the true church of Christ but do not belong to it. This conception of the church informed Pius XII's stance toward the ecumenical movement that emerged in the Protestant sphere during the 20th century. To be sure, the pope recognized the necessity for all Christians to work together in the struggle against the totalitarian ideologies[52]. But like his predecessors, he could envision a reunification only in the form of a return to the Roman Catholic Church[53].

---

[44] Günther Wassilowsky, "Pius XII.", *RGG*[4] 6 (2003) 1374–1377, here 1375. Cf. idem, *Universales Heilssakrament Kirche: Karl Rahners Beitrag zur Ekklesiologie des II. Vatikanums* (Innsbrucker theologische Studien 59) (Innsbruck and Vienna, 2001), 111–119.

[45] Peter Hünermann, *Theologischer Kommentar zur dogmatischen Konstitution über die Kirche 'Lumen gentium'* (Herders Theologischer Kommentar zum Zweiten Vatikanischen Konzil 2) (Freiburg, Basle, and Vienna, 2004) 263–582, here 279. Cf. ibid., 281.

[46] Pius XII, *Mystici Corporis,* 480, 486–488.

[47] Ibid., 480.

[48] Ibid., 487.

[49] Ibid.

[50] "Dogmatische Konstitution über die Kirche *Lumen gentium* (Apostolic Constitution on the Church *Lumen gentium*)", in: Peter Hünermann, ed., *Die Dokumente des Zweiten Vatikanischen Konzils: Konstitutionen, Dekrete, Erklärungen* (Herders Theologischer Kommentar zum Zweiten Vatikanischen Konzil 1) (Freiburg, Basle, and Vienna, 2004) 108–110 (Art. 21).

[51] Pius XII, *Mystici Corporis,* 499.

[52] Cf. Pius XII, *Summi pontificatus.*

[53] The *Instructio Ecclesia Catholica* of 20 December 1949 should be understood in this same sense: cautiously welcoming ecumenical initiatives, its sole purpose, in Pius XII's view, was to give non-Catholics the opportunity to get to know Catholic teachings; *Acta Apostolicae Sedis* 42 (1950) 142–147, here 144f.

In the same year, 1943, Pius XII's encyclical on the Bible, *Divino afflante spiritu*[54], appeared. Read with hindsight, it appears, in the assessment of the New Testament scholar Hans-Josef Klauck, "largely bland, almost over-cautious, in any case anything other than revolutionary, but measured against that which existed at the time it surely represents progress"[55]. After a half-century of "anti-modernistic and very restrictive defense against the historical-critical method in exegesis"[56], the encyclical was in fact received as liberating by contemporary Bible scholars and theologians. In his anti-modernist encyclical of 1907, *Pascendi dominici gregis*, Pius X had condemned the "wrong", historically minded form of exegesis; with the anti-modernist oath of 1910, he had forced Catholic theologians to commit to that position[57]. In the decade before World War I, however, the Papal Biblical Commission had repeatedly required Catholic exegetes to come up with answers, which, like the derivation of the Apostle Paul's letter to the Hebrews, were no longer tenable even then. From then on, Catholic exegetes navigated a difficult terrain, yet even in this field, thanks to its openness for historical inquiry, progress could not be impeded. When the scholarly exegesis was once again fundamentally questioned in Italy around 1940, it was the Papal Biblical Commission under the direction of the later cardinal Augustin Bea SJ (1881–1968), Pius XII's confessor, which repudiated such impertinence. In 1943, Pius XII himself intervened. In *Divino afflante spiritu*, he honored the work of Catholic exegetes very positively, emphasized that scholarly study of the Bible was theologically legitimate, called for the findings of modern archaeological and philological scholarship to be taken into account, and approved, for the first time, the literary genres in which the word of God is expressed in the Bible – albeit bound by the interpretations of magisterium and tradition. Despite lingering reservations and the renewed restrictions of 1950, this encyclical essentially opened the gates for modern Catholic exegesis. It was undoubtedly an important step on the way to the Dogmatic Constitution on Divine Revelation *Dei Verbum* of the Second Vatican Council. In addition, it facilitated the

---

[54]   Pius XII, Encyclical *Divino afflante spiritu*, 30 September 1943, in: *Acta Apostolicae Sedis* 35 (1943) 297–325; German translation in: Rohrbasser, 210–240.

[55]   Hans-Josef Klauck, "Die katholische neutestamentliche Exegese zwischen Vatikanum I und Vatikanum II", in: Hubert Wolf, ed., *Die katholisch-theologischen Disziplinen in Deutschland 1870–1962* (Programm und Wirkungsgeschichte des II. Vatikanums 3) (Paderborn, Munich, Vienna, and Zurich, 1999), 39–70, here 50.

[56]   Klaus Schatz, *Allgemeine Konzilien – Brennpunkte der Kirchengeschichte* (Paderborn, Munich, Vienna, and Zurich, 1997), 268.

[57]   *DH*, 3650–3654. On modernism and anti-modernism under Pius X, see most recently Claus Arnold, *Kleine Geschichte des Modernismus* (Freiburg, 2007).

progress of the Bible movement, whose roots extended farther back, as new Catholic translations of the Bible and, in France, theological works focused on the Bible began to appear from 1945 on[58].

Even the 1947 encyclical on the liturgy, *Mediator Dei*[59], was a response to an intra-ecclesiastical development that had already been in progress for some time. The modern liturgical movement of Benedictine origin was born in Belgium shortly before the First World War. In German and French-speaking lands, the movement enjoyed a respectable development, whereas in the Southern and English-speaking countries it experienced only patchy success[60]. Its concerns were taken up by scholars in the field of liturgical research, for example at the convent of Maria Laach under Abbot Ildefons Herwegen (1874–1946), by Catholic academic circles, and, in Germany, particularly by the Catholic youth movement, encouraged by Romano Guardini (1885–1968). From 1930 on – and especially after 1936, when the Nazi regime drove youth work back into the Church's inner realm – the modern liturgical movement was sustained by the efforts of young people in many Catholic parishes. Yet it was German bishops in particular who, along with some of the clergy, viewed this "new piety" with skepticism, occasionally even with open rejection[61]. Pacelli himself had issued an ambiguous verdict on the liturgical movement in his 1929 report *On the State of the Catholic Church in Germany*. He had welcomed without reservation the popular liturgical movement, which sought to familiarize "the faithful with church services, especially Holy Mass", but rejected the intellectual liturgical tendencies of Maria Laach, since these exaggerated "the value of the liturgy", neglected the "personal ascetic life", and opposed "popular prayer services and pious exercises not found in the liturgy, such as the Rosary"[62]. *Mediator Dei* attempted to end these conflicts while at the same bringing the liturgical movement under the control of the mag-

---

[58] Cf. Klauck, 50f.; Marcel Albert, *Die katholische Kirche in Frankreich in der Vierten und Fünften Republik* (Römische Quartalschrift, Supplementheft 52) (Rome, Freiburg, and Vienna, 1999), 51f.

[59] Pius XII, Encyclical *Mediator Dei*, 20 November 1947, in: *Acta Apostolicae Sedis* 39 (1947) 521–595; German translation in: Rohrbasser, 133–209.

[60] On the liturgical movement in the 20th century, see Reiner Kaczynski, "Theologischer Kommentar zur Konstitution über die heilige Liturgie Sacrosanctum Concilium", in: Peter Hünermann and Bernd Jochen Hilberath, eds., *Herders Theologischer Kommentar zum Zweiten Vatikanischen Konzil*, Vol. 2 (Freiburg, Basle, and Vienna, 2004), 24–44 (Succint overview).

[61] Theodor Maas-Ewerd, *Die Krise der Liturgischen Bewegung in Deutschland und Österreich: Zu den Auseinandersetzungen um die "liturgische Frage" in den Jahren 1939 bis 1944* (Studien zur Pastoralliturgie 3) (Regensburg, 1981).

[62] Wolf and Unterburger, 109–117, here 113, 115.

isterium. This encyclical has received rave reviews from some liturgical histori-ans[63]. In it, Pius XII recognized the liturgical movement in so far as he approved of its decisive concerns. As late as 1956, he described it as "a passing-through of the Holy Spirit through His Church"[64]. Although the actual inclusion of lay people remained limited and their participation was kept separate from the conse-cration and sacrificial authority of ordained priests, the encyclical already con-tained a demand for an intensive participation of the faithful, the *actuosa partici-patio*, which the liturgical constitution of Vatican II later accorded central importance. But the pope also repeated the reservations he had already expressed in 1929, warning of undesirable developments, above all the neglect of extra-Eu-charistic forms of piety and individual liturgical arbitrariness.

Picking up where *Mediator Dei* left off, further partial reforms that aimed to renew the liturgy followed under Pius XII: in 1951 the liturgy of the paschal night; in 1955 a reordering of the Holy Week; in 1957 the reduction of Eucharistic fast-ing, which made it possible to receive Communion during the late masses; and, in the same year, a general authorization for evening masses[65]. Further steps forward undoubtedly included the internationalization of the College of Cardinals and – against the background of decolonization of the "Third World" – the still cautious but purposeful continuation of Benedict XV and Pius XI's missionary policy. Here, the transformation of missionary districts into local churches with their own dioceses and efforts to establish an indigenous episcopate assumed central importance[66].

With hindsight, Pius XII's above-named reforms represent important stations on the road to Vatican II for how the Church was viewed, Bible scholarship, and renewal of the liturgy. From a church historical perspective, however, it would be an exaggeration to see in Pius XII an important trailblazer (Wegbereiter) for that council. The theology that would be so influential at the council grew to maturity

---

[63] Cf. Andreas Heinz, "Liturgiereform vor dem Konzil: Die Bedeutung Pius' XII. (1939–1958) für die gottesdienstliche Erneuerung", in: *Liturgisches Jahrbuch* 49 (1999) 2–38; Theodor Maas-Ewerd, "Papst Pius XII. und die Reform der Liturgie im 20. Jahrhundert", in: Martin Klöck-ener and Benedikt Kranemann, eds., *Liturgiereformen: Historische Studien zu einem bleibenden Grundzug des christlichen Gottesdienstes*, vol. 2 (Münster, 2002), 606–627; Klemens Richter, "Die Konstitution über die heilige Liturgie Sacrosanctum Concilium", in: Franz Xaver Bischof and Stephan Leimgruber, eds., *Vierzig Jahre II. Vatikanum: Zur Wirkungsgeschichte der Konzilstexte* (Würzburg, 2005), 29–49, here 33f.

[64] Pius XII, "Vous Nous avez demandé". Address of 22 September 1956 to the participants in the International Liturgical Congress of Assisi, in: *Acta Apostolicae Sedis* 48 (1956) 712.

[65] Kaczynski, 38–42.

[66] On the consistories of 21 February 1946 and 15 January 1946, see *Acta Apostolicae Sedis* 38 (1946) 103, 131–133; ibid., 45 (1953) 69, 86f.

largely outside the mainstream of Roman Neoscholastic theology, in the vise grip of surveillance by the magisterium and the bishops. That the Council texts themselves contained numerous references to Pius XII's documents does not contradict this. To the contrary: given the novelty of many topics, and the new positioning this occasioned, the Council's progenitors must have considered it opportune to point out continuities with the Church's tradition wherever possible.

The Anti-Modern Reversal

The second half of Pius XII's pontificate after 1950 was shaped by restorative differentiation. This found particular expression in the encyclical *Humani generis* of 12 August 1950[67], which in many passages can be read as picking up the thread of Pius X's anti-modernism. Indeed, that was how contemporaries interpreted it. Its publication cemented once more the primacy of Roman Neoscholasticism, which in the second half of the nineteenth century had been pushed through by the magisterium as the "Catholic 'normal theology'"[68] and which Pius XII also embodied, however open-minded he may have been on individual issues. *Humani generis* was aimed primarily at new theological beginnings, as they were connected in the post-war period to the *théologie nouvelle* in France and its innovative powers on the theological, spiritual, and pastoral levels; against theologians such as Jean Daniélou SJ (1905–1974), Henri de Lubac SJ (1896–1991), Yves Congar OP (1904–1995), and Marie-Dominique Chenu OP (1895–1990). Despite their individual differences, these theologians all had in common endeavor on behalf of new theological approaches – drawing on the Church's biblical-patristic tradition. Associated with this was the relativization, or rather the creative reinterpretation of Neoscholasticism and a critical but fundamentally positive engagement with contemporary philosophy, as well as concern with the existential questions about modern man, connected with efforts to explore new directions in practice, as well[69]. One such new direction was the highly innovative project of the French "worker priests", which Pius XII suppressed in 1953–1954[70].

---

[67] Pius XII, "Humani generis", in: *Acta Apostolicae Sedis* 42 (1950) 561–578; German translation in: Rohrbasser, 255–275.

[68] Peter Walter, "Die deutschsprachige Dogmatik zwischen den beiden Vatikanischen Konzilien untersucht am Beispiel der Ekklesiologie", in: Wolf, *Disziplinen*, 129–230, here 131.

[69] Cf. Albert Raffelt, "Die Erneuerung der katholischen Theologie", in: Mayeur, 216–237, here 226–232; Raymond Winling, "Nouvelle Théologie", in: *TRE* 24 (1994) 668–675; Albert, 48–54; Schatz, 267f.

[70] Émile Poulat, *Les Prêtres-ouvriers: Naissance et fin* (Paris, 1999).

Humani generis warned of the intrusion of historical-evolutionary thought into theology, and accused the unnamed theologian of "renewal mania", feelings of inferiority vis-à-vis modern science, an "imprudent irenics" and "contempt of the Church's magisterium", which was "portrayed as a drag on progress and a brake on scholarship"[71]. In this way, a "dogmatic relativism"[72] was introduced into theology and the Church doctrine written down in *Mystici Corporis* undermined. In its place, traditional apologetics and scholastic conceptions were to be retained, with, for example, no return to "the mode of expression of the Holy Scripture and the fathers"[73]. Above all, however, strict obedience to the Magisterium's authority and (even) its (not infallible) decisions was demanded. With reference to Luke 10:16 ("He who hears you hears me"), Pius XII prohibited further debate about matters which the popes had decided in their encyclicals[74]. "If this encyclical paragraph had been observed", as Otto Hermann Pesch has noted critically, there "could have been no Second Vatican Council"[75]. Bans on theological thought – even when decreed by the pope – could no longer be enforced in the 19th century, much less in the 1950s, dominated as that decade was by faith in progress – to say nothing of the present!

If, in retrospect, Vatican II took shape – and was to a considerable extent prepared – in the spiritual work and theological drafts of the pre-council period, it still cannot be overlooked, when seen from a theological-historical perspective, that this was not *the* theology of that era. Most of the theological approaches considered at the council were suspected of lacking orthodoxy. At the start of proceedings in 1962, it was by no means foreseeable that they would gain acceptance at the council. Particularly the *théologie nouvelle* was tainted by accusations of modernism up to the start of the council. Under Pius XII, its leading proponents had been subjected to almost the whole range of the Church's disciplinary measures and constrained in their theological and practical effectiveness. Often, their books had just barely avoided being put on the index. The inner-Church climate in which these theological pioneers were forced to carry out their intellectual efforts is documented by testimony from the eventual council theologian and cardinal Yves Congar. "[F]rom the beginning of 1947 until the end of the year 1956", Congar wrote, he had to endure "an unbroken succession of denunciations, warnings,

---

[71] Pius XII, "Humani generis", 262.

[72] Ibid., 261.

[73] Ibid., 260.

[74] Ibid., 263.

[75] Otto Hermann Pesch, *Das Zweite Vatikanische Konzil: Vorgeschichte – Verlauf – Ergebnisse – Nachgeschichte* (Würzburg, 1994), 40. Cf. ibid., 45.

restrictive or discriminatory measures, suspicious interventions"[76]. That theologians such as Congar would be rehabilitated a few years later and their ideas adopted at the council was not foreseeable during the last decade of Pius XII's reign. Far from it: both *Humani generis* and the Dogma of the Assumption of Mary articulated in the same year are indicators of the spirit that would have informed any council held at that time if Pius XII's plans from the years 1948 to 1951, which were kept strictly hidden from the public, had been realized[77].

The "Holy Year" and Marian Dogma of 1950

Perhaps as a substitute for a council, Pius XII declared 1950 a "Holy Year", in the course of which hundreds of thousands traveled to Rome. Its climax proved to be the proclamation of the dogma of the bodily Assumption of Mary into Heaven[78] – an event that found widespread acceptance in the Catholic Church but that met with fierce opposition in the Protestant world. Pius XII hereby made use of the Papal Magisterium in a way that could not be surpassed – this constitutes the only infallible ex-cathedra decision made to date since the proclamation of papal infallibility in 1870! – "even though not all scholarly difficulties had been cleared up"[79]. The dogmatization should probably be interpreted against the backdrop of the pope's preceding Marian statements and his personal devotion to the Holy Mother, particularly the cult of Fatima, to which he

[76] Jean-Pierre Jossua, *Le père Congar: La théologie au service du Peuple de Dieu* (Paris, 1967), 34; cit. also in Raffelt, 216–237, here 230. Cf. Étienne Fouilloux, "Congar, témoin de l'église de son temps (1930–1960)", in: André Vauchez, ed., *Cardinal Yves Congar 1904–1995* (Paris, 1999), 71–91; Yves Congar, *Journal d'un théologien 1946–1956* (Paris, 2000).

[77] On Pius XII's council plans, see Schatz, 271f.; Giovanni Caprile, "Pius XII. und das Zweite Vatikanische Konzil", in: Herbert Schambeck, ed., *Pius XII. zum Gedächtnis* (Berlin, 1977), 649–691.

[78] Pius XII, Apostolic Constitution *Munificentissimus Deus* on the proclamation of the dogma that the Mother of God Mary was taken up into heavenly splendor in body and soul, in: *Acta Apostolicae Sedis* 42 (1950) 753–771; German translation in: Rohrbasser, 328–347.

[79] Hubert Jedin, "Pius XII", in: Hubert Jedin, ed., *Handbuch der Kirchengeschichte*, vol. VII (Freiburg, Basle, and Vienna, 1979), 30–36, here 34. On criticism and ecumenical problems concerning the Marian Dogma of 1950, see Berthold Altaner, "Zur Frage der Definibilität der Assumptio B.M.V.", in: *Theologische Revue* 44 (1948) 129–140; ibid., 45 (1949) 129–142; ibid., 46 (1950) 6–20; Günther J. Ziebertz, *Berthold Altaner (1885–1964): Leben und Werk eines schlesischen Kirchenhistorikers* (Forschungen und Quellen zur Kirchen- und Kulturgeschichte Ostdeutschlands 29) (Cologne, Weimar, and Vienna, 1997), 98–120; Groupe des Dombes, *Maria: In Gottes Heilsplan und in der Gemeinschaft der Heiligen* (Frankfurt am Main and Paderborn, 1999), 104–122.

felt a special responsibility[80]. Following the failure of his peace initiatives during World War II, Pius XII consecrated the Church and all of humanity to the Immaculate Heart of Mary in October 1942[81] and did the same for the peoples of Russia ten years later[82]. In 1944, he prescribed the Feast of the Immaculate Heart of the Most Holy Virgin for the entire Church[83]. In 1954, to conclude the "Marian Year", which commemorated the dogmatization of the *Immaculata Conceptio* through Pius IX in 1854, Pius XII introduced the Feast of the Queenship of Mary[84]. In the pope's view, Mary was to serve as a role model and symbol for humanity threatened by materialism and war in a secularized world. This historical context becomes clear when Pius XII, in his apostolic constitution that defined the dogma, expressed his expectation that, in a time "when the false teachings of materialism and the corruption of morals that result from it suffocate the light of virtue and, by unleashing conflict and war, threaten to annihilate so many human lives [...] the truth of Mary's assumption reveals to all in a clear light the noble aim for which we are predestined in body and soul"[85]. The 33 canonizations of his papacy can be seen in the same light, in particular the 1951 beatification and 1954 canonization of Pius X[86].

Pius XII – a Modern Pope?

Taking stock of Pius XII's pontificate is not easy, if for no other reason than the problems already mentioned at the beginning of this text. Pius XII indisputably led the Church in an autocratic and strongly centralized fashion. In this, he grounded his actions in the Church's 1917 *Codex* and in the ecclesiology that underlay it. Following the death of his secretary of state in 1944, he did not nominate

---

[80] Cf. Chenaux, 400–404. On the pope's alleged visions of Fatima and Christ in 1950 and 1954, see Jean d'Hospital, *Drei Päpste: Pius XII., Johannes XXIII. und Paul VI.* (Vienna and Hamburg, 1971), 94–103.

[81] Pius XII, Radio broadcast to Portugal, 31 Oktober 1942, in: *Acta Apostolicae Sedis* 34 (1942) 345f.

[82] Pius XII, *Sacro vergente anno*, 7 July 1952, in: *Acta Apostolicae Sedis* 44 (1952) 505–511.

[83] Decree of the Congregation of Sacred Rites, 4 May 1944, in: *Acta Apostolicae Sedis* 37 (1945) 44–51.

[84] Pius XII, Encyclical *Ad Caeli Reginam*, 11 October 1954, in: *Acta Apostolicae Sedis* 46 (1954) 625–640.

[85] Pius XII, *Munificentissimus Deus*, 346.

[86] Pius XII, *Una celeste letizia*, 3 June 1951, Latin translation in: *Acta Apostolicae Sedis* 43 (1951) 462–468; *Quest'ora di fulgente trionfo*, 30 May 1954, Latin translation in: *Acta Apostolicae Sedis* 46 (1954) 306.

a successor, relying instead on the two leading figures in the Secretariat of State, Domenico Tardini (1888–1961) and Giovanni Battista Montini (1897–1978, from 1963 Pope Paul VI). Montini demonstrated sympathies for the new theological beginnings in France and in Italy supported the political independence of *Democrazia Cristiana*, which Pius XII never accepted; presumably for this reason, Montini was removed from the Curia in 1954 and remained in Milan in the rank of archbishop, without promotion to cardinal[87]. There is evidence to support the verdict reached – albeit with differing interpretations – by Jean-Marie Mayeur, Rudolf Lill, or Gottfried Maron, that Pius XII sought to combine elements of his predecessors' ruling styles: "the diplomatic style of Leo XIII, the reform activities and watchfulness of Pius X, the peace efforts of Benedict XV, as well as the wise statesmanship and scholarly sense of Pius XI"[88]. Beyond this, Pius XII was, in the verdict of Robert Leiber SJ, one of his closest collaborators, a "master of representation"[89]. He was also no less a master of symbolic communication, who understood exceptionally well how, at the dawn of the age of mass media, to stage the Pope as Christ's Deputy through film and photography and intensively promote the cult around his personality, while at the same time presenting "papal Rome as the protector of European traditions against the upheavals of the present, particularly communism"[90]. For many Catholics, and perhaps even more for non-Catholics, Pius XII, in his day, epitomized that which they associated with the Catholic Church.

The question remains, however, whether Pius XII's answers to the specific questions of his time were heard within the political, social, cultural, and church constellations of the 1950s. Did the pope's pessimistic worldview, which increasingly deepened in his final years, accord with the many new departures, the social change – which was naturally accompanied by a change in values – and the attitude toward life of the post-war period? One has only to read the Easter communication of 1957, which paints the dark, gloomy picture of a world gone off the rails, in which "everything (has become) relative and temporary" and for him, the pope, humanity appeared as "an infected and wounded body"[91]. Were the pope's increasingly reactionary tendencies no less than his constant appeal to the obedience of bishops, clergy, and faithful to the guidelines of the papal magisterium

---

[87]   Cf. Hebblethwaite, 242–259; Guasco, 32.

[88]   Mayeur, 24. Cf. Lill, 170; Gottfried Maron, "Pius XII", in: *TRE* 26 (1996) 674–677, here 676.

[89]   Robert Leiber, "Pius XII", in: *Stimmen der Zeit* 163 (1958–1959) 81–100, here 94.

[90]   Lill, 165.

[91]   Pius XII, Easter message, 21 April 1957, in: *Acta Apostolicae Sedis* 49 (1957) 276–280; German translation in: Utz and Groner, 2696–2702, here 2700.

really an adequate response to the internal Church reform deadlock, which indisputably existed at the end of Pius XII's pontificate? Were not the mobilizations of the 1950s – *Humani generis*, the "Holy Year", Marian dogma, the "Marian Year", canonization of Pius X, and the program for which that canonization stood! – which undoubtedly accorded with the piety and church-theological character of Pius XII, backward-looking responses, confined to the ultramontane tracks of the 19th century? Certainly, the answers to these questions must be formulated differently for their general and country-specific contexts. One should also not fail to recognize that Pius XII occasionally initiated or pushed ahead reforms and developments that reached their full effect after his papacy. In some matters, such as the introduction of secular institutes, he broke truly new ground[92]. Nonetheless, Pius XII was a backward looking preserver, not a reformer! He himself once more found expression for his view of the world and the Church in his last Easter missive of 6 April 1958, writing: "The shadow of Man does not extinguish the light of God but only lets it shine brighter still. A light lit by God over the world are the reliable watch of the Church over the doctrines, its tenacity in disseminating and defending the truth, its cautious wisdom toward renewals and upheavals, its non-partisan stance in the conflict between classes and nations, its resolution in the preservation of human rights, and its fearlessness before the enemies of God and of society"[93].

Against the backdrop of Pius XII's last decade, we may better understand why the cardinals in the conclave of 1958 effected a change. In his relationship to modernity, Pius XII's pontificate was in many respects closer to those of his namesakes from the 19th and 20th centuries than to the papacy of his immediate successor, John XXIII. That has had an impact not least on the assessment of this pope after his death.

Translated by Christof Morrissey

---

[92] Pius XII, Constitution *Provida mater Ecclesia*, 2 Februar 1947, in: *Acta Apostolicae Sedis* 39 (1947) 119–124.

[93] Pius XII, Easter message, 6 April 1958, in: *Acta Apostolicae Sedis* 50 (1958) 261–264; German translation in: *Herder-Korrespondenz* 12 (1957/58) 370f., here 371.

Introduction to the Presentation
"Pius XII and the Jews"

Hans Günter Hockerts

When I was asked to moderate the paper by Thomas Brechenmacher on "Pius XII and the Jews", I gladly accepted. It is a welcomed development that several core points of the exhibition will be illuminated by more in-depth presentations, particularly since the audience will have the opportunity to ask questions and enter into a discursive conversation. This series of presentations thereby opens a forum for discussion that could evolve into a provocative debate. That applies especially to the topic that will be covered here. The question of Pope Pius XII's reaction to the persecution and mass murder of the European Jews is not only one of the most widely considered but also one of the most controversial of recent history. This debate has been ongoing since the spectacular success of Rolf Hochhuth's play in 1963. In the meantime, it has branched out into so many directions that only a few experts retain a reliable overview of the whole debate.

Thomas Brechenmacher is one of those experts. The high regard in which he is held in specialist circles is illustrated by the following anecdote: a few weeks ago, a seminar on the current state of scholarship on Pius XII and the Shoah took place at the Holocaust memorial Yad Vashem in Jerusalem. The press was admitted only to the opening talks, given by Avner Shalev, the chairman of Yad Vashem's governing board, and Archbishop Antonio Franco, the apostolic nuncio in Israel. Afterwards, the journalists had to leave the room. The organizers were not interested in a public exhibition bout over such a controversial matter; rather, they were attempting to clarify, as objectively and profoundly as possible, the current state of scholarship. For that reason, we do not know in detail how the closed-door discussion at Yad Vashem transpired. But we do know that Thomas Brechenmacher belonged to the small circle of experts whom the organizers invited, because his word carries weight. For the sake of brevity, only one of his important studies can be highlighted here, *Der Vatikan und die Juden* (2005), which looks at the history of that relationship from the 16th century to the present. In the weekly newspaper *Die Zeit*, Hansjakob Stehle praised this work as "probably the most objective and thorough book to date on this controversial topic".

Brechenmacher's academic career began here in Munich. As a fellow of the "Studienstiftung des Deutschen Volkes" (German National Academic Foundation), he studied at Ludwig Maximilian University, acquiring his *Magister* (Master's degree) in 1990. After earning his doctorate at Berlin's Free University in 1995, he returned to Munich, where he completed his *Habilitation* (postdoctoral thesis) in the field of Modern History at the University of the German Armed Forces in 2003. Subsequently, he was a guest lecturer at the German Historical Institute in Rome. While there, he became one of the first researchers to have a close look at the newly opened Vatican archival collections beginning in February 2003. These included files from the Vatican Secretariat of State, the nunciatures in Munich and Berlin, and the Archive of the Congregation of the Faithful, as far as they pertain to relations between the Holy See and Germany during the papacy of Pius XI; in other words, the years 1922 to 1939. Since 2008, Thomas Brechenmacher has taught as Professor of Modern History at the Historical Institute of the University of Potsdam, with a speciality in German-Jewish history. How will this renowned specialist lead us through the difficult topical terrain – in some respects, we can even speak of a minefield – of "Pius XII and the Jews"? We eagerly anticipate the answer to that question.

Translated by Christof Morrissey

PIUS XII AND THE JEWS

Thomas Brechenmacher

1. The Church's traditional theology of the Jews and the differentiation between anti-Judaism and anti-Semitism

No one who studies Western ecclesiastical history can help but detect church teachings and modes of behavior directed against Judaism and the Jews, which periodically motivated and provoked acts, including violent attacks, against Jews[1]. Yet hostility was by no means the Church's guiding principle in its dealings with the people of the Old Covenant. To the contrary: as early as the days of Pope Gregory the Great (590–604), Catholic theology developed a set of teachings that governed the Church's relationship to the Jews until the Second Vatican Council in the 1960s. At the core of these teachings lay the realization that Jews indispensably belong to Christianity as the "reverse side of the coin", even if only as "witnesses" of Jesus Christ. Moreover, since there were hope and the promise that Jews would someday discover the "true faith" after all, violence perpetrated by Christians against Jews could never be justified. In fact, the Church believed it should, through its own exemplary bearing, offer the Jews incentives to make the decision to convert to Christianity. In line with this teaching, the Church's hierarchs, in particular the Pope, assumed the role of protector of the Jews, responsible for shielding them against Christian violence[2].

---

[1] The present article is based on comprehensive studies, of which only a few can be cited here: Thomas Brechenmacher, *Der Vatikan und die Juden: Geschichte einer unheiligen Beziehung vom 16. Jahrhundert bis zur Gegenwart* (Munich, 2005); Brechenmacher, "Teufelspakt, Selbsterhaltung, universale Mission? Leitlinien und Spielräume der Politik des Heiligen Stuhls gegenüber dem nationalsozialistischen Deutschland (1933–1939) im Lichte neu zugänglicher vatikanischer Akten", in: *Historische Zeitschrift* 280 (2005) 591–645; Brechenmacher, "Die Enzyklika 'Mit brennender Sorge' als Höhe- und Wendepunkt der päpstlichen Politik gegenüber dem nationalsozialistischen Deutschland", in: *Die Herausforderung der Diktaturen. Katholizismus in Deutschland und Italien 1918–1943/45*, eds. Wolfram Pyta, Carsten Kretschmann, Giuseppe Ignesti, and Tiziana Di Maio (Tübingen, 2009), 271–300; Brechenmacher, "Die Kirche und die Juden", and "Der Papst und der Zweite Weltkrieg", in: *Die Katholiken und das Dritte Reich. Kontroversen und Debatten*, eds. Karl-Josef Hummel and Michael Kißener (Paderborn, Munich, Vienna, and Zurich, 2009), 125–143, 179–195.

[2] In its classical formulation, this principle is transmitted in Pope Innocent III's constitution "Licet perfidia Iudeorum" of 1199: "Although the Jews' infidelity is to be condemned in many

As a complementary principle, of course, the Church hierarchy juxtaposed the responsibility for protecting Christians from Jews. Association with Jews, it was feared, could shake Christians in their faith and in the worst case even imperil their souls. To avert this danger, social relations between Christians and Jews were to be strictly regulated and minimized. These, then, were the religious grounds for segregating Jews within their own, partially enclosed residential areas, for prohibiting them from holding public office, practicing certain professions, charging "usurious" interest rates, and employing Christian servants, as well as requiring them to make themselves immediately identifiable by wearing a visible symbol on their garments. The four relevant constitutions of the Fourth Lateran Council in 1215 established a tradition of restrictive legislation against Jews, which in the Papal States existed into the 18th and 19th centuries, at least on paper, while also inspiring many other Christian states. Yet even these laws authorized neither violence against nor expulsions of Jews. For the top leadership of the Catholic Church – which wielded decisive teaching authority – the mission of dual protector prevailed in both principle and practice into the 20th century[3].

Numerous examples can be cited, whereby Rome – especially during phases in which the Church found itself on the defensive – was by no means immune to the tendency to interpret its dual-protector role in a one-sided manner, to the disadvantage of the Jews. During the final third of the 19th century, for example, when the collapse of the Papal States seriously jeopardized the continued existence of the Roman papacy, fears directed against the various intellectual, social, and economic currents of modernity – including secularization and relativism, pluralism, liberalism, capitalism, and socialism – coalesced time and again in a pronounced anti-Judaism[4]. Undoubtedly, there are connections, and even a fluent crossover,

---

respects, the Jews may not be persecuted by the faithful, since it is in the first instance through them that our faith is truly affirmed [...] Even if they prefer to persist in their stubbornness [...] since they appeal to the aid of our protection, we hear their petition and, in mild Christian gentleness and following in blessed memory the steps of our predecessors, grant them the shield of our protection." Innocent III, *Constitutio pro Iudaeis*, 15 September 1199, in: *The Apostolic See and the Jews*, vol. 1, ed. Shlomo Simonsohn (Toronto, 1988), 74f, nr. 71, here 74.

3   See Brechenmacher, *Das Ende der doppelten Schutzherrschaft: Der Heilige Stuhl und die Juden am Übergang zur Moderne (1775–1870)* (Päpste und Papsttum 32) (Stuttgart, 2004), 1–17; a shortened version without scholarly apparatus in Brechenmacher, *Der Vatikan und die Juden*, 19–26.

4   "Jewry, with all its Talmud inspired sects, always confronts Christianity in a crafty way", the one-time Cardinal Secretary of State under Pius X., Raffaele Merry del Val, recorded in the Holy Officium in 1928. In addition, "today, after the [First World] War, it is rising up more than ever and attempting to build up once again the Kingdom of Israel against Christ and against His Church." Archivio della Congregazione per la dottrina della fede (ACDF), S.O. 125/28 [Rerum

between an older Christian tradition of religiously motivated antipathy toward Jews – in other words, anti-Judaism – and the newer anti-Semitism, with its economic and racial argumentation.

When viewed from a broader historical perspective, however, it seems advisable to keep the two concepts separate. They identify two distinct phenomena, which, while related in their effects (antipathy toward Jews), depend on significantly different motivations and carriers. Concerning the narrower theme of the Catholic Church's conduct in the face of the Nazi genocide of Jews, a clear distinction between the terms "anti-Judaism" and "anti-Semitism" affords the possibility of additional insight. In purely theological terms, the dogma of the dual protector, though it may have been anti-Judaic, could never have led to genocide of the Jews. Nor could it have inspired devout Christians to believe that the Jewish people must be exterminated through murder. The Catholic Church's dogma does not provide any grounds for "inveterate" anti-*Semitism*, let alone "eliminationist" anti-Semitism.

On the other hand, the older, religious anti-Judaism – which is inherent in the Church's dogma and in the role of the dual protector – helps explain the "ambivalence" with which many Catholics, from the lay grass roots to the top ranks of the hierarchy, occasionally confronted the Nazi persecution of the Jews. The Church clearly condemned racial anti-Semitism. But a number of its officials repeatedly fell back into a mode of thought marked by prejudices and resentments. On the one hand, these drew on the religiously motivated anti-Judaism that was part of their socialization; on the other hand, they borrowed too unreflectively from the trappings of socio-economic anti-Semitism.

Eugenio Pacelli, Pope Pius XII, who grew up and was schooled in this theological tradition, does not constitute an exception. Even as late as 1942, in his Christmas Eve address to the College of Cardinals, Pius availed himself of anti-*Judaic* theological interpretations. Regarding a de-Christianized world mired in a hopeless war, the Pope challenged the cardinals not to descend into faint-hearted plaintiveness but to defend "the truth and virtue" as true servants of the Church. Such a stance still left open the possibility of a particular kind of lamentation and mourning, the kind "that weighed on the heart of the Redeemer [...] upon seeing Jerusalem, which opposed His invitation and His mercy with unbending blind-

Variarum 1928, n.2], vol. 1, nr. 20; Voto del Card. Segr. S.O. nelle Congr. di Feria IV, 7 March 1928. On the context of this pronouncement, cf. Brechenmacher, *Der Vatikan und die Juden*, 157–159; cf. also Hubert Wolf, "'Pro perfidis Judaeis'. Die 'Amici Israel' und ihr Antrag auf eine Reform der Karfreitagsfürbitte für die Juden (1928). Oder: Bemerkungen zum Thema katholische Kirche und Antisemitismus", in: *Historische Zeitschrift* 279 (2004) 611–658.

ness and dogged denial, which led it onto the path of guilt, and ultimately to deicide."[5] Here, Pius took up a core judgment of religious anti-Semitism, that of the deicide. Against the background of events taking place in 1942, the choice of this particular representation was undoubtedly ill-considered. We should keep in mind, however, that Pacelli was not talking about the situation of the Jews in a Europe dominated by Nazi Germany; rather, using a time-honored image, he was issuing an appeal to theologically trained cardinals – and only to them. The Pope's theological pronouncement was intended to be not political but metaphorical.

Was Pacelli an anti-Semite? It is well known that, as papal nuncio in Munich during the "soviet" revolution there, Pacelli sent a report to Rome in which he used adjectives to characterize the revolutionaries around Max Levien that suggest there were some Jews – if not all – whom he did not hold in particularly high esteem. Even if Pacelli did not write the report himself, he did forward it. On the other hand, we know from his time as nuncio in Munich and Berlin that he firmly rejected the plebeian anti-Semitism of the emerging Nazi movement. Furthermore, he expressly advocated concerns of the Jewish communities and even of Zionism.

The decisive point, of course, is not to tally individual findings and pit them against one another but rather to understand how the thought (and actions) of the papacy, Roman Catholicism's leading authority, toward Jewry and Jews began to change only slowly under Popes Pius XI and Pius XII, theologically as well as politically. This change came about as a result of the new challenge posed by social-Darwinist, racist anti-Semitism, as well as from confronting the persecution of Jews in Nazi Germany from 1933 onward.

At the same time, the connections between religious anti-Judaism and the newer anti-Semitism were initially either barely perceived or simply ignored. On 25 March 1928, Pius XI had racial anti-Semitism explicitly condemned in a decree of the Holy Office. "The Apostolic See", the text proclaims, "condemns [...] with particular emphasis the hatred of God's formerly chosen people, a hatred that today is commonly known as 'anti-Semitism'"[6]. The passage referred to the anti-Jewish antipathy of racial anti-Semites, which was a defining element of National Socialist ideology. With this decree of 1928, the Catholic Church emphatically rejected such a racist image of humanity.

---

[5] Pius XII, "Allocuzione della vigilia di natale al sacro collegio", in: *Discorsi e radiomessaggi di Sua Santità Pio XII*, vol. IV: 2 March 1942–1 March 1943 (Vatican City, 1960), 318–323, here 321.

[6] Decree S.O., 25 March 1928, cited here from reproduction and translation in: Georges Passelecq and Bernard Suchecky, *Die unterschlagene Enzyklika: Der Vatikan und die Judenverfolgung* (Munich and Vienna, 1997), 124f.

The argumentation employed by Pius XI and the Holy Office remained well within the traditional framework of the dual protector. "The Catholic Church has always viewed the Jews as the people who, until the appearance of the Savior, were the keepers of God's promises. It [the Church] has always prayed for the Jewish people despite, and even because of, their later blindness, and protected them from unjust persecution." In line with tradition, protection of Jews is here described as a core responsibility of the Church. At the same time, however, the theological judgment of "blindness" steadfastly cited in this passage suggests that a self-critical theological and historical engagement with the Church's own anti-Judaic traditions had not advanced particularly far in 1928.

Whether Pacelli had progressed farther theologically in 1939, or even three years later, than Pius XI and the Holy Office had in 1928 is doubtful, in view of his pronouncements to the cardinals at Christmas 1942. It is relatively certain, however, that against the background of events in the 1930s he developed a clear awareness of problems, including in a theological sense. This conclusion is supported by the story of the "suppressed encyclicals".

In June 1938, Pius XI, already seriously ill, had commissioned an encyclical against racism – with the working title *Societatis unio* – which, following his death, was never completed by his successor Pius XII. The reasons for this are still shrouded in mystery; perhaps we will learn more only when the archival files on Pacelli's papacy are opened. Nonetheless, it can be assumed with some plausibility that Pacelli considered the draft texts prepared for the encyclical by the Jesuits John LaFarge, Gustave Desbuquois and Gustav Gundlach as theologically inadequate. These texts were based on an unchanged theology of the dual protector. They rejected racist positions but still justified subliminally the traditional religious anti-Judaic judgments[7]. A "Jewish question" did indeed exist, Gundlach's draft argued (the same or similar passages can be found in the other authors' drafts), although not as a question of race but of Christianity. The "societal peculiarity" of the Jews could be justified on Christian-religious grounds alone. Through their "rejection" of the Lord Jesus Christ, the Jews had drawn a "deep, by their choice immovable boundary." The Jews, this passage implied, had removed themselves from society and this "peculiarity" was irreversible. The Jews, according to Gundlach, had "gambled away for good their exalted historical calling in God's plan for redemption."[8]

---

[7] The texts in: Passeleq and Suchecky and Anton Rauscher, ed., *Wider den Rassismus: Entwurf einer nicht erschienenen Enzyklika (1938): Texte aus dem Nachlaß von Gustav Gundlach SJ* (Paderborn, Munich, Vienna, and Zurich, 2001); cf. Brechenmacher, *Der Vatikan und die Juden*, 186f.

[8] Rauscher, 161f.

In the event of publication, such statements would almost certainly have been taken out of their context by the Nazi propaganda machine and used to construe the pope's supposed confirmation of anti-Jewish persecution in a manner contrary to the encyclicals' actual purpose. Such misappropriation had to be prevented at all costs. But a *new*, unambiguous theology of the Jews that could serve as the basis for a papal doctrinal letter did not yet exist on the eve of the Second World War. Pius XII's position regarding the planned encyclical on racism and anti-Semitism can be better understood in light of this theological dilemma; he did not reject the idea of an encyclical on the subject, only the existing drafts. Apparently, he did not believe an adequate theological basis for new drafts yet existed. And given the numerous clear condemnations of racial anti-Semitism issued by the Catholic Church's highest authorities up to 1939, an additional encyclical did not seem particularly urgent – in distinct contrast to the matter of organizing material relief efforts, which assumed central importance with the outbreak of war in September 1939.

The road the Catholic Church needed to travel before it could develop a new theology of the Jews, the *Nostra Aetate* of the Second Vatican Council in 1964, was still a long one in 1939. But the need for such a reorientation, one tied to fundamental historical and moral reflections about the anti-Judaic currents running through the theology and history of Christianity, seemed already to be germinating within Pacelli when he decided against having the encyclical *Societatis unio* reworked in 1939. Yet even without a new theology, it must be acknowledged that the papacy articulated its position on the persecution and (later) murder of European Jews unequivocally and with unmistakable clarity. Pius XI repeatedly condemned anti-Semitism even after 1928: in April 1938, in the so-called "syllabus on race" drawn up by the Papal Congregation of Seminaries and Universities (and issued on 3 May, the day Hitler arrived on a state visit to Rome); and on 6 September 1938 – one day after the Italian state had barred all Jewish students, teachers, and instructors from the country's schools and universities through its first race law – on the occasion of an audience with Belgian pilgrims but in actuality addressed to Mussolini: "Anti-Semitism is untenable. In a spiritual sense we are Semites."

Even the famous encyclical *Mit brennender Sorge* of 14 March 1937, with which Pius XII publicly denounced the Nazis' fight against the Church in Germany and whose text was in essence written by Pacelli himself, does not shy from a further rejection of racist theories. The "myth of blood and race" – National Socialism's main ideological fermenting agent – could never be brought into harmony with the Church's image of humanity, grounded in natural law. "Only superficial intellects could succumb to the misguided teachings, could speak of a national religion, could undertake the mad attempt to imprison God, the Creator of the whole world [...] within the boundaries of a single people, within the narrowness, defined by blood, of a single race." "The Old Testament people of the Covenant" were among the special bearers of the true, divine revelation; "Whoever wishes to ban the Bible story and the wise learning of the Old Covenant from church and school blasphemes against God's word."[9]

This unambiguous position by the Vatican was manifestly recognized and acknowledged even by Jewish politicians. In May 1938, the Zionist politician Moshe Waldmann reported to Jerusalem a conversation he had had with the Chief Rabbi of Rome. The chief rabbi, who maintained good contacts with the State Secretariat, had emphasized the exceptionally positive attitude of both the Pope and Cardinal State Secretary Pacelli toward "Jewish demands." Characteristic, said Waldmann, was the "readiness of Pacelli, that is to say the curia [...] to defend the Jews." The present state was "psychologically" so "favorable" that "under the right circumstances even [...] a change in the Vatican's position on the idea of a Jewish state in Palestine" could possibly be effected. The deeper motivation for the Holy See's disposition could hardly be better summed up than in Waldmann's own words: "The Vatican's opposition toward National Socialism's neo-paganism is fundamental."[10]

2. The Pope's Dilemmas

Fundamental opposition to Nazi ideology and the duty to defend all innocent victims of persecution, including the Jews – which was derived from both the Christian-Catholic image of humanity in general, as well as through the theology of the dual protector in particular – did not obviate the need for intensive consid-

---

[9] Encyclical of Pope Pius XI on the situation of the Catholic Church in the German Reich; text in: Dieter Albrecht, ed., *Der Notenwechsel zwischen dem Heiligen Stuhl und der deutschen Reichsregierung*, vol. 1: *Von der Ratifizierung des Reichskonkordats bis zur Enzyklika "Mit brennender Sorge"* (Veröffentlichungen der Kommission für Zeitgeschichte, Reihe A: Quellen 1) (Mainz, 1965), 404–443, here 411f. and 414; cf. Brechenmacher, *Die Enzyklika "Mit brennender Sorge"*.

[10] Memorandum by Moshe Waldmann on a conversation with Chief Rabbi Dr. Prato (Rom), Haifa, 26 May 1938 (Zionist Central Archives, Jerusalem), published in: Thomas Brechenmacher, "Pius XII. und der Zweite Weltkrieg: Plädoyer für eine erweiterte Perspektive", in: Karl-Joseph Hummel, ed., *Zeitgeschichtliche Katholizismusforschung: Tatsachen, Deutungen, Fragen: Eine Zwischenbilanz* (Veröffentlichungen der Kommission für Zeitgeschichte, Reihe B: Forschungen 100) (Paderborn, Munich, Vienna, and Zurich, 2004), 83–99, here 97–99.

eration of how this duty could be most effectively performed under the existing circumstances. As cardinal secretary of state and of course during his pontificate, Pacelli constantly wrestled with the question of whether to speak out or act against the secular crimes of his age. We can grasp this thanks to the most varied sources, four of which shall serve as examples here. As early as 4 April 1933, Pacelli telegraphed Nuncio Cesare Orsenigo in Berlin, instructing him to sound out possibilities for intervening on behalf of the hard-pressed Jews in Germany. He had been directed to do so by Pope Pius XI, but the characteristic formulation in the telegram to the nuncio was Pacelli's: it belonged "to the good traditions of the Holy See to fulfill its universal mission of peace and love" toward all people, "whatever social strata or religion they may belong to."[11] In May 1940, Pius XII complained to the Italian ambassador Alfieri: "The Italians surely know, and know well, of the terrible things that are happening in Poland. We should hurl words of fire against such things and the only thing that keeps us from doing so is the knowledge that we would only worsen the lot of these unfortunates if we were to speak."[12] On 30 December 1942, only a few days after his famous Christmas radio address – which is generally considered the most pronounced and clearest example of Pius' public statements against the persecution of the Jews – the Pope received the American chargé d'affaires Harold Tittmann. Tittmann wanted to know whom exactly the Pope had meant when he spoke in his homily of the "many hundred thousand people [...] who, without the slightest individual guilt and owing only to their nationality or their origins, are condemned to death or a slow impoverishment." In Tittmann's recollection, Pius responded somewhat testily that everyone had understood he was referring to the Poles, Jews, and hostages. He also added that, had he more specifically identified the Nazis' atrocities, he would have been compelled to name those of the Bolsheviks as well and that would surely not have given the Allies any special pleasure[13]. The Christmas address was in fact very well understood. The Reich Security Main Office (RSHA) in Berlin analyzed it in a lengthy report in January 1943. According to one of its

<hr>

11 Cf. Brechenmacher, "'So kann der Tag kommen, an dem man wird sagen können, daß etwas getan worden ist.' Pius XI., Pacelli und der Judenboykott im April 1933. Interpretation einer Quelle aus den neu freigegebenen Beständen des vatikanischen Geheimarchivs", in: Gisela Fleckenstein, Michael Klöcker, and Norbert Schloßmacher, eds., *Kirchengeschichte: Alte und neue Wege. Festschrift für Christoph Weber* (Frankfurt/Main, 2008), 361–370.

12 Montini's notes on an audience for the Italian ambassador Alfieri, 13 May 1940, in: Pierre Blet, Robert A. Graham, Angelo Martini, and Burkhart Schneider, eds., *Actes et documents du Saint Siège relatifs à la Seconde guerre mondiale d'après les archives du Vatican*, 11 vols. (Vatican City, 1965–1981), here vol. I, 453–455, here 455.

13 Harold H. Tittmann Jr., *Il Vaticano di Pio XII: Uno sguardo dall'interno* (Milan, 2005), 121f.

conclusions, the Pope had declared "his fundamental antagonism and his enmity toward National Socialism" in his address, "[e]ven if he does not call it by name." He "as good as accused the German people of injustice toward Poles and Jews [...] The Pope has made himself advocate and champion of these truest of war criminals."[14] Reich Foreign Minister Joachim von Ribbentrop threatened retaliatory measures in the event the Holy See intended to give up its traditional neutrality.

Four months after the reception for Tittmann, on 30 April 1943, Pius responded to a plea from the Bishop Konrad von Preysing of Berlin concerning the new wave of deportations from the German capital, "[to] try once more to intervene on behalf of the many unfortunate and innocent" victims: "We leave it to the senior shepherd who is acting on the scene to calculate whether, and to what degree, the danger of retaliatory measures in the event of episcopal pronouncements [...] make it appear advisable, despite the given motivations, *ad maiora mala vitanda*, to exercise restraint. Here is one of the reasons why We Ourselves impose constraints on Our own pronouncements."[15]

These citations refer to three central dilemmas in which Pius XII saw himself caught: 1.) How could the mission to practice *caritá universale* for all of humanity be reconciled with the Church's traditional mission of protecting its own constituents in a narrower sense, namely Catholics and in particular Catholics in Germany? Would not an open and unequivocal protest against the persecution of the Jews have meant exposing the Catholic Church in Germany to an incalculable risk? 2.) Might not an open protest have had a counterproductive effect precisely for those whom it was supposed to help, namely Jews and other "non-Aryans?" 3.) Would not a clear partisan stance taken by the Holy See against Germany and the Axis powers, and for the Allies, have meant losing an overall capacity for action, as well as the moral authority with which Pius XII hoped to become a peace envoy recognized by all sides? Would it not also have jeopardized the territorial integrity of the Vatican, which was premised (and few are aware of it) among other things on maintaining strict neutrality in foreign affairs, as stipulated in the 1929 Lateran Treaty with Fascist Italy?

---

[14] RSHA report, 22 January 1943, from the Politisches Archiv des Auswärtigen Amts, published in: Anthony Rhodes, *Der Papst und die Diktatoren: Der Vatikan zwischen Revolution und Faschismus* (Vienna, Cologne, and Graz, 1980), 233–235, cit. 233 and 235.

[15] Pius XII to Preysing, 30 April 1943, in: Hubert Gruber, *Katholische Kirche und Nationalsozialismus 1930–1945. Ein Bericht in Quellen* (Paderborn, Munich, Vienna, and Zurich, 2006), 484–489, cit. 486f. Citation from Preysing to Pius XII, Berlin, 6 March 1943, in: Burkhart Schneider, ed., *Die Briefe Pius' XII. an die deutschen Bischöfe 1939–1944* (Veröffentlichungen der Kommission für Zeitgeschichte, Reihe A: Quellen 4) (Mainz, 1966), 239.

If the Pope did not speak out more clearly than in his 1942 Christmas address, it was not because of dithering, cowardice, or excessive sympathy for Germany, let alone anti-Semitism. Rather, in view of the dilemmas outlined above, he decided to give priority to concrete action – in other words, attempting to rescue as many of the persecuted as possible – over speaking out publicly, the consequences of which he considered incalculable, perhaps even counterproductive. All of these considerations, however they are ultimately judged from a distance, took shape on the fundament of Pacelli's unshakeable conviction during, and about, the Second World War: that the Holy See could fulfill its "universal mission of peace and love" only by preserving its non-partisan stance and maintaining a position independent of all individual warring powers.

3. The Main Features of Action

Against the backdrop of this basic disposition, a brief summary of relief efforts undertaken by the Holy See becomes possible. In what way could *all* victims of the war – including, of course, the Jews – be given material aid as efficiently as possible? The immediate establishment of an information office for prisoners of war within the state secretariat in September 1939 was an initial and important step in this direction. With this venture, collecting data on prisoners, deportees, and missing persons was linked with efforts to provide material assistance to those identified by the tracing agencies. Four million pages of data contained in the information office's archive, opened in 2004, bear witness to this most extensive of Vatican relief operations[16].

The period of persistent diplomatic protests to the German government, which the Vatican had undertaken since 1933, and not only on behalf of the so-called "Catholic non-Aryans", had long since come to an end by 1939. That the Catholic Church would initially assist a group of persons who, despite their conversion from Judaism to Catholicism, were oppressed by the Nazis as "racial Jews" was in no way an example of "milieu egoism". Which institution, if not the Church, should have concerned itself with these Christians? Jewish relief organizations, confronted with the threat to their own co-religionists, in any case did not consider themselves responsible for these "non-Aryans". In September 1933,

---

[16] *Inter Arma Caritas. L'Ufficio Informazioni Vaticano per i prigionieri di guerra istituito da Pio XII (1939–1947)*, 2 vols. and DVD edition of the data sheets (Vatican City, 2004); on relief activities for Jewish victims of the war, see especially vol. 2, 643–716.

Cardinal Secretary of State Pacelli attempted to raise the issue of the "Catholic non-Aryans" with the Nazi regime; the reaction typifies the strategy the German authorities employed in dealing with the Church. Simply put, the Nazis refused even to acknowledge the Church's jurisdiction in the matter. In their view, neither the "purge of civil servants" nor the "Jewish question" had anything to do with confessional themes[17].

Berlin declined even to let the Holy See articulate a position in a political field that lay just outside the intersection of church and state interests delineated in the Reich Concordat; it was not about to tolerate the Church's efforts on behalf of "non-Catholic non-Aryans". This experience would repeat itself in countless cases, for the Holy See as well as the German bishops, until the final years of the war. The Nazi regime's agencies prohibited the Vatican's information office for war victims from becoming active in Germany. Nuncio Orsenigo, instructed time and again by the state secretariat to intervene with the Berlin authorities on behalf of Jews – whether baptized or un-baptized – repeatedly communicated the hopelessness of his efforts. "The situation of the Jews is off-limits for every well-intentioned intervention", he wrote in July 1942[18]. When in November 1941 Michael Cardinal von Faulhaber of Munich-Freising attempted to induce Adolf Cardinal Bertram, the Chairman of the German Fulda Bishops' Conference, to appear at the RSHA to protest mass deportations of Jews from the cities, both came to the conclusion that the "race fanatics" there would reject the petition out of hand because the bishops lacked formal jurisdiction in the matter[19].

But why had the Church not protested much earlier, for example in 1935, when the Nazis introduced the Nuremberg Laws, the decisive step toward a complete legal exclusion of the Jews in Germany? Where was the voice of Church dignitaries in November 1938, when the supposed "people's rage" violently turned against the Jews throughout the entire German Reich? It is true that neither the Holy See nor the German bishops issued an official and immediate protest against the Nuremberg Race Laws or the *Reichskristallnacht*. That does not mean, however, that both events were not recognized as blatant injustices, assessed and commented on. The reports of the papal nuncio Orsenigo from Germany in 1935 and also 1938 demonstrate that the perfidy of Nazi Jewish

---

[17] Confidential promemoria of the Holy See, 9 September 1933, in: Albrecht, 397, note 3.

[18] Orsenigo to Maglione, 20 July 1942, in: Blet, Graham, Martini, and Schneider, vol. VIII, 603f., cit. 604.

[19] Faulhaber to Bertram, Munich, 13 November 1941, in: Gruber, 462f., and Bertram to Faulhaber, Breslau, 17 November 1941, ibid., 465f.

policies was correctly diagnosed by papal diplomacy[20]. Nevertheless, no massive Church protest in particular against the persecution of the Jews took place.

The dissonance between the Nazi regime and the Catholic Church – including over the "Jewish question" – had been clearly articulated since 1933; so clearly, in fact, that a Jewish businessman from Rotterdam wrote to Pope Pius XI in 1936: "His Holiness, as well as His Eminence Cardinal Faulhaber, and many other of the higher Catholic clergy [have] publicly denounced the utopias of attacks on race and religion in Germany as un-Christian and in contradiction to the foundations of all religions and the Ten Commandments."[21] On the other hand, the Church did encounter criticism, not so much from Jews as from within its own ranks. In view of an impending pastoral letter from the bishops, the Church historian Joseph Schmidlin asked the Pope in August 1935, "why one does not move from just talking to taking unequivocal action [...] How much damage must [...] this rotten peace policy cause us, by lulling our friends to sleep and encouraging our enemies! Instead, the Church's powers of resistance will prove themselves as soon as it comes to an open struggle."[22] Yet could "open struggle" really be considered the *ultima ratio*? When the Holy See wanted to conduct an international information campaign against National Socialism in 1937, Faulhaber advised against it. He considered such a campaign "inappropriate and dangerous" at that time, since it could easily "provoke an intensification of oppression in the essential religious field." Above all, the Munich archbishop feared a renewed flare-up of morality trials against members of monastic orders, which the regime had orchestrated for propaganda purposes, as well as consequences for those Catholic schools that still existed[23]. Fear of the possible consequences of "popular rage" undoubtedly dampened the courage of Church dignitaries to publicly protest against the anti-Jewish pogrom of the so-called *Reichskristallnacht* of 9 November 1938. There had been precedents[24]. Nazi propaganda had left no doubt that it had proclaimed war on "World Jewry and also its black and red allies": "Yester-

---

[20] Cf. Brechenmacher, *Der Vatikan und die Juden*, 194f. and 198f.

[21] Joseph Salomon to Pius XI, Rotterdam, 22 February 1936, Archivio Segreto Vaticano (ASV), Archivio della Congregazione per gli Affari Ecclesiastici Straordinari (AES), Germania, pos. 692, fasc. 261, fol. 120rv.

[22] Joseph Schmidlin to Pius XI, Colmar, 5 August 1935, ASV, AES, Germania, pos. 686, fasc. 254, fol. 64r–66r.

[23] Cf. in detail, incl. proof of citations, Brechenmacher, *Die Enzyklika "Mit brennender Sorge"*.

[24] Just one month previously, rioters had devastated the archbishop's palace in Vienna, by order of Nazi Party offices. Cardinal Faulhaber, too, failed to protest to government offices against either anti-Semitic vandalism or the attack by an agitated mob on his residence in Munich and against his person on the evening of 11 November, a direct after-effect of the riots against the Jews.

day against the Jews, today against the Catholics!"[25] Even Bishop Clemens Count von Galen of Münster – usually among those bishops who recommended public pronouncements over diplomatic notes – did not step up to the pulpit to condemn the barbarity of the pogrom night. Several years later, he evidently regretted "not having protested immediately and publicly against this sacrilegious crime."[26] At the same time, careful considerations seem to have held him back from making a public appearance in November 1938. The fear that a protest by the bishop could have incalculable consequences for both the Jews and the Catholics of Münster most likely lay at the heart of these considerations, although the sources are not clear on this point[27].

The Church's room for maneuver vis-à-vis the Nazi regime was limited and it became even more so during the war. Courageous public appearances, such as those by Faulhaber, Galen, or Preysing, sometimes provoked severe reactions, which as a rule hit the bishops' subordinates rather than the bishops themselves. Galen expected to be arrested on numerous occasions, especially after he had delivered sermons against the Nazis' euthanasia program in July 1941. Some Nazi functionaries even called for his execution. In the end, however, the principle of punishing not the shepherd but those entrusted to his supervision prevailed once more. As a reaction to Galen's sermons, the Gestapo arrested thirty priests from the Diocese of Münster, several of whom lost their lives in concentration camps. One of Pius XII's dilemmas became especially apparent at this level as well: raised his voice publicly always had to factor in the consequences, for Catholics as well as Jews. The case of the Dutch Jews in summer 1942 demonstrated how counterproductive public protest could be: after Protestant and Catholic bishops in the Netherlands had spoken out against the deportations, the Gestapo not only carried out the transports as planned but had those "non-Aryan" Christians whom they had previously promised to except deported as well[28].

---

[25] Report by Faulhaber, Munich, 12 November 1938, in: Ludwig Volk, ed., *Akten Kardinal Michael von Faulhabers*, vol. 2: 1935–1945 (Veröffentlichungen der Kommission für Zeitgeschichte, Reihe A: Quellen 26) (Mainz, 1978), 604–607, here 604.

[26] Max Bierbaum, *Nicht Lob und nicht Furcht: Das Leben des Kardinals von Galen* (Münster, 1974), 393–395.

[27] Summary of the current state of research in: Heinrich Mussinghoff, "Bischof Clemens August von Galen und die Juden: Zum Forschungsstand", in: Hubert Wolf, Thomas Flammer and Barbara Schüler, eds., *Clemens August von Galen: Ein Kirchenfürst im Nationalsozialismus* (Darmstadt, 2007), 199–220, here esp. 205–207.

[28] Internuncio Paolo Giobbe, The Hague, to Maglione, Rome, 9 October 1942, in: Blet, Graham, Martini and Schneider, vol. VIII, 677f.; Orsenigo to Montini, Berlin, 28 July 1942, in: ibid., 607f.

Well before then, both Rome and the Church in Germany had switched – following their appraisal of the efficacy of speech and action – to a policy of providing material relief within the maneuver space that remained available. The "Caritas Emergency Service" (Caritas-Notwerk), chaired by Heinrich Krone, a former Center Party Reichstag deputy and the last chairman of the "Association for the Defense against Anti-Semitism", supported politically and racially persecuted Catholics. The work of the Caritas Emergency Service prepared the way for the "Relief Organization in the Episcopal Ordinariate in Berlin" (Hilfswerk beim Bischöflichen Ordinariat Berlin), founded in summer 1938 under the leadership of Cathedral Provost Bernhard Lichtenberg. Following Lichtenberg's arrest in 1941, Bishop Preysing personally took charge and designated the agency's managing director Margarete Sommer as the central contact person for "non-Aryans" who sought help[29]. These were by no means isolated acts. In his letter to Preysing from 30 April 1943, Pius XII expressly thanked the bishop and Berlin's Catholics for all their efforts on behalf of "so-called non-Aryans" and in this context expressed "a special word of paternal recognition as well as heartfelt sympathy for the imprisoned Prelate Lichtenberg". Margarete Sommer also referred to the Pope's letter to Preysing when, in a 1963 response to Rolf Hochhuth's play *The Deputy*, she wrote: "From my daily collaboration both with Count Preysing and with [...] Prelate Lichtenberg [...] I can assure you that we all helped Jewish people in the certainty that we were following the directives of the Vatican and the Holy Father."[30]

The Saint Raphael Association's "Special Relief Agency" (Sonderhilfswerk des St. Raphaels-Vereins) endeavored from 1933 on to enable "converted Jews and non-Aryans" to emigrate, above all to the United States of America, South Africa, Brazil, and Argentina. But because of increasing German restrictions and reduced foreign support during the visa process these efforts to assist emigration became an almost hopeless race against time.

During the war, the Holy See's influence was weakest in exactly those areas where the greatest number of civilian victims lost their lives. In those regions that the Germans had virtually hermetically sealed off from the outside world, particularly Poland, the Holy See no longer had access to any regular information channels after September 1939. The Polish Church had been destroyed. News reached the Vatican only sporadically, by way of the underground or the Polish govern-

---

[29] Jana Leichsenring, *Die Katholische Kirche und 'ihre Juden': Das 'Hilfswerk beim Bischöflichen Ordinariat Berlin', 1938–1945* (Berlin, 2007).

[30] Margarete Sommer, letter to Erwin Piscator, 11 April 1963, in: Walter Adolph, *Verfälschte Geschichte: Antwort an Rolf Hochhuth* (Berlin, 1963), 103f.

ment in exile. Nevertheless, premonitions about the fate of the deportees soon began to intensify. In July 1942, Nuncio Orsenigo became one of the first to report that accounts "of catastrophic transports and even mass killings of Jews" had been cropping up[31]. A report to the Vatican State Secretary from the Polish embassy, which continued to operate as an exile organization, on 19 December 1942 spoke of over one million murdered Polish Jews and precisely described the German extermination system, the selection for immediate killing of those considered "unfit for work", as well as the destruction "through labor" of those who remained. All this was happening in "places that have been specially prepared for this purpose."[32] By 5 May 1943 at the latest, there was no longer any reasonable doubt in the state secretariat, only incredulity, about the existence of death camps, death transports, and the use of poison gas. Of a pre-war population of approximately four and a half million Polish Jews, perhaps only 100,00 remained. The others had disappeared, without any further news as to their fate[33].

One of the earliest intelligence reports about the plan to completely annihilate Europe's Jews and its implementation, which was already underway, had been

[31] Orsenigo to Montini, Berlin, 28 July 1942, in: Blet, Graham, Martini and Schneider, vol. VIII, 608.
[32] Polish Embassy to State Secretariat, 19 December 1942, ibid., 755.
[33] Notes by the State Secretariat, 5 May 1943, in: Blet, Graham, Martini and Schneider, vol. IX, 274. Along with the state of contemporary information about the destruction of the Jews, the question about the recipients' realization of this knowledge must always be considered. On this, the fundamental work is Walter Laqueur, *The Terrible Secret: An Investigation into the Suppression of Information about Hitler's 'Final Solution'* (London, 1980). Among other things, it is worth considering to what extent the pope and the Vatican state secretariat, confronted with news of the systematic destruction of the Jews, were subject to a "hiatus between factual knowledge and absent recognition." This phenomenon, explainable in psychological or anthropological terms, also "strangely paralyzed" other actors, ones with greater means of power at their disposal, in the face of a break with civilization that exceeded the conventional capacities for imagination and prevented them from "recognizing Auschwitz for what it was." Dan Diner, *Gegenläufige Gedächtnisse: Über Geltung und Wirkung des Holocaust* (Göttingen, 2007), 21f. How else if not through "not wanting (or, for psychological reasons, being unable) to consider it possible" can we explain the discrepancy between the documented information about the events of annihilation and the shocked reaction of Pius XII, which the Jewish politician Moshe Shertok recorded in April 1945, after he had been received by the pope in a private audience? "I [Shertok] told him that it was my primary duty to thank him, and through him the Catholic Church, in the name of Jewish public opinion for everything that they had done in various countries to rescue Jews, for the rescue of children and Jews in general. He said: to save them from the terrible persecutions. I said: Those were not only persecutions. We were already used to persecutions before the war. This was a slaughter. He said: I have heard of some terrible things that happened in Poland and Hungary. I said: Not only to the Jews from those countries but to all Jews who were brought there. I told him that we believed we had lost five million Jews in this war in Europe. He said: Five million, really? That means that this made an enormous impression on him." Cf. Brechenmacher, *Der Vatikan und die Juden*, 223–225.

received in the Vatican one year previously, in March 1942. Two employees of the World Jewish Congress, Richard Lichtheim and Gerhart Riegner, had put together a comprehensive report on the situation of the Jews in those parts of Europe dominated by the Germans[34]. The so-called "Riegner Memorandum", which pleaded in particular for intervention on behalf of the Jews in the German client state Slovakia, led directly to increased diplomatic efforts by the Holy See to stop deportations from that country. But little was actually achieved; this was all the more depressing because the Slovak president Jozef Tiso was himself a Catholic priest. Only after the Slovak Catholic bishops issued a pastoral letter on behalf of the Jews did Tiso postpone further deportations in July 1943. But oppression resumed anew in 1944. This time, the Pope personally sent his chargé d'affaires in Bratislava to Tiso, in order to remind the president of his priestly dignity and conscience. Tiso responded to the Pope with a letter that revealed no understanding whatsoever[35]. What means of influence were left to the Vatican then? Whether a canonical disciplinary measure such as excommunication could have moved Tiso to a lasting change of course is a matter of speculation. As the head of a government that existed at the discretion of Germany, Tiso's scope for action was limited and would not have been expanded by his excommunication. No amount of protest could prevent the deportations from Slovakia. But the Church's interventions, combined with the efforts of various relief organizations that were supported and in some cases even guided by the Vatican, helped spare from the deportations, and eventually save, about one third of Slovakian Jews[36].

The case of Slovakia reveals another basic pattern that underlay the Vatican's actions: alongside persistent diplomatic intervention through nuncios and embassies, there were efforts in all countries to provide as much relief as possible. In concrete terms, this usually meant preserving specific, clearly identified groups from deportation: "non-Aryan Catholics", the newly baptized – not uncommonly, large numbers of baptismal certificates were distributed, without any preconditions – mixed marriages between Catholic and Jewish partners, children, the sick. Even more urgently than in the pre-war years, paths to emigration needed to be uncovered, emigrants financially supported, visas secured. In Romania, the

---

[34] Gerhart M. Riegner, *Niemals verzweifeln: Sechzig Jahre für das jüdische Volk und die Menschenrechte* (Gerlingen, 2001), 158f.; cf. also Blet, Graham, Martini and Schneider, vol. VIII, 466.

[35] Tardini to Burzio, 29 October 1944, in: Blet, Graham, Martini and Schneider, vol. X, 462, and Tiso to Pius XII, 8 November 1944, in: ibid., 475–477.

[36] Walter Brandmüller, *Holocaust in der Slowakei und katholische Kirche* (Neustadt/Aisch, 2003), 106; also Emilia Hrabovec, "Die katholische Kirche in der Slowakei 1939–1945", in: Lieve Gevers and Jan Bank, eds., *Religion under Siege*, vol. 1: *The Roman Catholic Church in Occupied Europe, 1939–1950* (Leuven, Paris, and Dudley, Massachusetts, 2007), 139–172.

apostolic nuncio and the leaders of Jewish communities cooperated closely to evacuate Jews from the territories occupied by Germany: working with the "War Refugee Board" and the apostolic delegate in Turkey and Greece, Angelo Roncalli, they were able to effect the emigration of more than a thousand Jews by way of Istanbul toward Palestine. Throughout the war years, Roncalli, who later became Pope John XXIII, functioned not only as an intelligence focal point in Southeastern Europe but also helped in all efforts to save the Jews of Greece and Bulgaria from deportations.

The policy of diplomatic intervention achieved its greatest success in Hungary, where the regent, Admiral Horthy, had the deportations of Jews stopped in July 1944 following a telegram from Pius XII[37]. The situation in Hungary resembled that in Slovakia; like Tiso, Horthy was under strong pressure from Germany and had little scope for independent decisions. Although the Pope's appeal to Horthy's conscience and humanity fell on more receptive ears than his earlier appeal to Tiso, in the long run it proved just as fruitless as in Slovakia. In October 1944, Horthy was overthrown and replaced by the fanatical anti-Semite Szalási, who immediately resumed the persecution of Hungary's Jews. Pius joined an appeal by the Hungarian bishops on behalf of the oppressed[38] – once more to no effect. At least a few thousand Hungarian "Catholic non-Aryans" were saved from the deportations through writs of protection issued by the nunciature. The moral force of the Holy See was not enough to achieve significant results in the face of existing power relations. This was evident in Croatia as well. Little could be done for the 40,000 Jews there, most of whom had been baptized. Those who managed to escape the persecutions of the fascist Ustasha regime by fleeing to the Italian-occupied territories before late 1941 were the lucky ones. Thanks in part to Vatican efforts, they were not sent back to Croatia. The Archbishop of Zagreb, Aloizije Stepinac, who had shown an initial proclivity to support the "Catholic" dictator Ante Pavelić, changed course as a result of the massacres of Serbs and Jews and protested publicly. The Holy See also distanced itself[39].

Italy and the territories it controlled in Dalmatia, Albania, Greece, and southern France remained free from deportations until September 1943. In Italy, help

---

[37] Pius XII to Horthy, 25 June 1944, in: Blet, Graham, Martini and Schneider, vol. X, 328; Cicognani to Maglione, Washington, 9 August 1944, Gratitude of the American Jews for the contribution to the "decisive improvement" of the situation in Hungary, in: ibid., 378.

[38] Pius XII to Cardinal Serédi, 26 October 1944, in: Blet, Graham, Martini and Schneider, vol. X, 460.

[39] Cf. Rhodes, 280–292, here esp. 288f.; Pierre Blet, *Papst Pius XII und der Zweite Weltkrieg: Aus den Akten des Vatikans*, 2nd edition (Paderborn, Munich, Vienna, and Zurich, 2001), 182–185.

for Jews initially consisted mainly of eluding deportations and creating opportunities for emigration. The cooperation between the Holy See and its special liaison to the Italian government, Father Tacchi-Venturi, with the Italian-Jewish relief organization "Delasem" (Delegazione assistenza ebrei emigranti, the "Delegation for Assisting Jewish Emigration") and the Saint Raphael Association proved effective. A Capuchin priest based in Rome, Benedetto da Bourg d'Iré, headed a highly active relief operation, especially for Jewish refugees from southern France, and personally reported its activities to the Pope[40]. Another cell was headed by Anton Weber, a German Pallottine priest. Through these organizations, several thousand Jews received support and around 25 million lira worth of relief monies were spent, taken largely from Church funds[41]. After the Germans occupied northern and central Italy in early September 1943, the situation in the country changed abruptly and Church organizations had to adjust to relentless persecutions and deportations of those they had been charged to look after.

When Rolf Hochhuth, citing an out-of-context quotation by the German ambassador to the Vatican, Ernst von Weizsäcker, suggests at the start of Act 3 in his play *The Deputy* that Pius XII was "silent" when the Jews of Rome were deported from beneath his own windows[42] it is nothing less than historical misrepresentation. True, the roughly 1,000 Jews who were seized in Rome on 16 October 1943 could not be freed. All efforts that immediately followed the news of a roundup in the Roman ghetto, including those of the Holy See, turned out to be in vain. But after 17 October, no further large-scale roundups or mass deportations took place in Rome.

Until it opens more of its archives, there can be no final verdict on whether the Vatican played a decisive part in halting the Rome roundup. It is indisputable, however, that an intervention took place, on two levels: in the form of a clear démarche from the state secretariat to Ambassador von Weizsäcker, as well as

---

[40] Capuchin General Donato da Welle to Marchetti Selvaggiani, 5 December 1944, on the activities of Father Benedetto; Archivio della Congregazione per la Dottrina della Fede (ACDF) S.O. 125/1928 [R.V. 1928, n.2], nr. 62.

[41] Numbers based on the account by Father Benedetto, Rome, 20 July 1944 and the summary compiled by Renzo De Felice, in: Renzo De Felice, *Storia degli ebrei italiani sotto il fascismo: Nuova edizione ampliata* (Turin, 1988 [reprint 1993]), Appendix, docs. 40 and 41.

[42] Ernst von Weizsäcker wrote to Berlin on 17 October 1943: "The curia is especially dismayed, since the proceedings transpired under the Pope's own windows, so to speak." Cit. from Saul Friedländer, *Pius XII und das Dritte Reich: Eine Dokumentation* (Reinbek, 1965), 144. The American historian Susan Zuccotti even adopts this citation for the title of her book, which is written with an accusatory tendency; *Under His Very Windows: The Vatican and the Holocaust in Italy* (New Haven, 2000).

indirectly and cleverly orchestrated through the rector of the German college of priests at Santa Maria dell'Anima, Monsignor Alois Hudal. Hudal, who is generally known only for helping former Nazi war criminals escape post-war justice, used his ties to the Wehrmacht and SS leadership on 16 October 1943, employing not humanitarian arguments (which the Nazi fanatics would doubtless have ignored) but rather military-strategic ones to bring the deportation of Jews from Rome to an immediate halt. With his initiative – to which the Vatican, in the person of the Pope's nephew Carlo Pacelli, had urged him – Hudal contributed to rescuing numerous Roman Jews from death[43]. Additionally, even before the roundup of 16 October, approximately half of the 8,000 Jews living in Rome had been able to go underground, a large percentage of them in Church properties: monasteries, convents, parishes, rectories, charitable foundations, children's homes, and orphanages, as well in the Vatican itself and in its extraterritorial properties. At the instruction of the state secretariat, not a few convents opened their cloisters to take in victims of oppression. Some stayed only a few days, before being transferred to other hiding places; the much larger part persisted for months in church institutions, enduring arduous conditions, until the withdrawal of the Germans and liberation through the Allies[44].

The Holy See and the Catholic Church as a whole developed far-reaching and diverse relief measures during World War II. Given the circumstances, these efforts often yielded results that were frustratingly meager. The figure of 700,000 to 860,000 Jews "to whose rescue the Catholic Church contributed" that has been "calculated" by Pinchas Lapide appears greatly exaggerated[45]; an estimate of around 100,000 is probably closer to reality. But even if only a small fraction of endangered Jews could be rescued, the Holy See accorded its relief operations the highest priority at all times. Saving lives took precedence and every individual life

[43] Cf. Brechenmacher, *Der Vatikan und die Juden*, 218–223, as well as comprehensive studies by the Italian historians Andrea Tornielli, *Pio XII: Il Papa degli Ebrei* (Casale Monferrato, 2001), esp. 277–305; Matteo Luigi Napolitano, *Pio XII tra guerra e pace: Profezia e diplomazia di un papa, 1939–1945* (Rome, 2002); and Andrea Riccardi, *L'inverno più lungo. 1943–1944: Pio XII, gli ebrei e i nazisti a Roma* (Rome and Bari, 2008), here esp. 123–140.

[44] For a list of the places of refuge, with numbers, see De Felice, Appendix, Doc. 40; cf. also Alessia Falifigli, *Salvati dai Conventi: L'aiuto della Chiesa agli ebrei di Roma durante l'occupazione nazista* (Milan and Turin, 2005), as well as Grazia Maria Loparco, "Gli Ebrei negli istituti religiosi a Roma, 1943–1944: Dall'arrivo alla partenza", in: *Rivista di Storia della Chiesa in Italia* 58 (2004) 107–210. Extensive documentary material is available at http://www.storicireligiosi.it/ebrei (2 April 2009).

[45] Pinchas E. Lapide, *Rom und die Juden* (Freiburg im Breisgau, Basel, and Vienna, 1967), 359, note 189.

counted. False speech, the Church leadership firmly believed, would have impeded that mission, perhaps even acutely imperiled it.

4. Concluding Thoughts

To describe and evaluate the relationship between Catholics and Jews between 1933 and 1945 is one of the more complex tasks for church historians to master. Sweeping generalizations, whether of an accusatory or apologetic bent, cannot do justice to the reality of this relationship. Historical judgment must be based on a serious effort to comprehend the respective postures in their larger contexts. A look at the Catholic Church's traditional theology of the Jews (the dual protector role) can help in this regard; it reveals fateful connections between anti-Judaism and anti-Semitism, without, however, promoting hasty, superficial conclusions about an "anti-Semitic" church. In order to judge the Pope's or the Vatican's stance regarding the Nazi murder of European Jews it is ultimately essential to understand the Holocaust in the context of the Second World War. In a remarkable essay on "importance and impact of the Holocaust", the historian Dan Diner recently articulated the observation that, since the 1980s, the Holocaust and the World War have been increasingly separated in public memory. This has encouraged the tendency to focus on the genocide of the Jews while neglecting the "overarching context" of the war. "The complex circumstances", writes Diner, "of the location of the front, diplomatic maneuvers, constellations of alliances, of neutrality, collaboration, occupation policy, tactical maneuvers and logistical constraints increasingly recede into the background as the annihilation of the European Jews is described and interpreted. The Holocaust creates its own narrative, as though it occurred separate from the events of the war."[46]

The role of the Pope within these "complex circumstances" only becomes comprehensible when, together with the Holocaust, it is viewed in the larger context of the Second World War. Only then does it become apparent that a narrative in which the Pope is situated in relation to that ultimate crime against humanity, the Holocaust, completely divorced from any historical context may make ethical-moral judgments easier to come by but only at the expense of a firm anchoring in reality. A dramatist such as Rolf Hochhuth can expertly isolate and highlight such an ideal-typical constellation. A historian, however, must do just the opposite: reconstruct the multi-layered nature of what really happened, precisely those

---

[46] Diner, 8–10.

thousand-fold "complex circumstances" of the war's events, within which the Pope – as well as other actors, such as the Allies – had to operate.

The higher the rank in the Catholic hierarchy, the more heavily responsibility weighed. That the conduct of individual members of that hierarchy, with the Pope at its head, could, in the context of the dilemmas described above, be erroneous or culpable doubtless holds true. It remains "thoroughly debatable", as Konrad Repgen summarized, whether the Catholic Church's countermeasures were pursued "in a timely fashion and with the greatest possible force in every case."[47]

Such findings, however, in no way justify sweeping judgments, such as that about the Pope's "silence", let alone an alleged affinity between the Catholic Church and National Socialism. In substance, Catholic dogma and Nazi ideology were irreconcilable. The Catholic Church's leadership repeatedly and unequivocally condemned racism and racial anti-Semitism. When in doubt, and always after careful consideration, the Church deferred strident and possibly counterproductive pronouncements in favor of concrete relief measures. The judgment of those born after these events may legitimately turn out to be ambivalent. In fairness, however – and in consideration of source-based scholarship – they should not question the fundamental serious-mindedness and truthfulness of the Pope's engagement with the Nazis' persecution of the Jews within the larger context of World War II.

Translated by Christof Morrissey

---

[47] Konrad Repgen, "Hitlers 'Machtergreifung', die christlichen Kirchen, die Judenfrage und Edith Steins Eingabe an Pius XI. vom [9.] April 1933", in: *Edith Stein Jahrbuch* 2004, 31–68, here 68; cf. also Repgen. "Widerstand oder Abstand? Kirche und Katholiken in Deutschland 1933 bis 1945", in: Klaus Hildebrand, Udo Wengst and Andreas Wirsching, eds., *Geschichtswissenschaft und Zeiterkenntnis. Festschrift zum 65. Geburtstag von Horst Möller* (Munich, 2008), 555–558, here 558.

Introduction to the Presentation "Pius XII and Michael Cardinal von Faulhaber"

Hans-Joachim Hecker

The organizers of this series of lectures have endeavored to complement the exhibition *Opus Iustitiae Pax: Eugenio Pacelli – Pius XII (1876–1968)*. Because of its approach and perspective, as well as the limits of this particular medium of representation, the exhibition naturally addresses some aspects only cursorily. For example, some elements that, given the exhibition's particular perspective, appear mainly as background to the later pontificate of Pius XII possess an independent historical significance of their own, particularly here in Munich. Pacelli cultivated relations with Bavaria and Germany, which he had established during his years in Munich and Berlin, beyond his time as papal nuncio, following his appointment to Cardinal Secretary of State and, later, his election as pope. In the difficult political times of the day, these relations necessarily assumed great political relevance.

Of the personal relationships that Nuncio Pacelli established in Germany, that with the Munich archbishop Cardinal Michael von Faulhaber was among the most important. The exhibition catalogue describes this association with Faulhaber – and incidentally that with Bishop Konrad von Preysing as well – as a "personal amicable relationship that withstood even the turmoil of the Third Reich." "For German Catholics during the years 1933–1945, this personal attachment constituted a not insignificant support."

Yet what concrete shape did this support take? This evening's lecturer, Professor Heinz Hürten, will shed light on that question with his presentation "Pius XII and Michael Cardinal von Faulhaber".

Allow me, then, briefly to introduce Professor Heinz Hürten. Professor Hürten is a native of Düsseldorf who, following his state exam, received his doctorate from the University of Münster in 1955. He earned his habilitation at the University of Bonn in 1970, where he also received his teaching license for Medieval and Early Modern History. From 1972, he was Senior Academic Director at the *Militärgeschichtliches Forschungsamt* (Military History Research Office) in Freiburg im Breisgau. In 1977, he accepted the chair for Modern and Recent History at the Catholic University in Eichstätt.

Professor Hürten's research specialties include the history of German Catholicism in the 20th century, particularly the complex of Christian exile and Christian resistance during the time of National Socialism. Of his numerous publications, including ones on Pius XII and Cardinal Faulhaber, I would like to mention two in particular. In 2002, Professor Hürten published the third volume of Cardinal Faulhaber's files, which covers the years 1945 to 1952. In 2007, *Akten deutscher Bischöfe über die Lage der Kirche* (German bishops' files on the situation of the Church), which encompasses the period from 1918 to 1933, appeared in two volumes. Both these volumes and the Faulhaber edition are part of the renowned series *Veröffentlichungen der Kommission für Zeitgeschichte*. These edited collections produced by Professor Hürten attest to an exceptional acquaintance with precisely those sources relevant to the time period with which today's lecture is concerned.

Translated by Christof Morrissey

Pius XII and Michael Cardinal von Faulhaber

Heinz Hürten

Scholarly findings have the likelihood of eventual obsolescence built into them; they do not claim to present the ultimate possible discovery, only that which can be securely concluded today; conclusions that, tomorrow, may be challenged or even disproved. We cannot escape this general problematic when we inquire into the relations that existed between the Munich Archbishop Faulhaber and Munich Nuncio Pacelli, who, over the course of decades, rose to become head of the Catholic Church. In all likelihood, in only a few years' time we will have an online version of the numerous letters that the Munich nuncio addressed to his superior authority, the Roman Curia. Even if in 1925 Pacelli left the Munich nunciature in other hands and thereafter was responsible only for the non-Bavarian part of Germany, one can assume that his correspondence as nuncio contains remarks about the Munich Archbishop not only from the years 1917 to 1925 but from 1925 to 1929 as well. Thus, some of what is said today may in the near future be amended, modified, or even disproved. But the answers to the questions that we are asked cannot wait for some unspecified date in the future, when we may know better. Let us then set about our task, in the knowledge that ours will probably not be the last words spoken on this subject.

When Faulhaber celebrated his eightieth birthday, Pacelli as pope wrote to him of "a deep need, coming from a sympathetic and grateful soul" to be among the well-wishers in spirit. Similar pronouncements of the high mutual regard that bound the two men are easily found[1]; their full force only becomes clear when one considers the importance of rank and authority in the Church hierarchy. But while there is no doubt about the high personal regard in which each man held the other, the same cannot be said about the underlying reasons for this. For the new archbishop and the new nuncio – whose respective postings in Munich were officially announced almost simultaneously, just one day apart on 26 and 27 May 1917[2] – were rather different personalities, and not only in their dissimilar backgrounds.

---

[1] Heinz Hürten, ed., *Akten Kardinal Michael von Faulhabers*, vol. III: 1945–1952 (Veröffentlichungen der Kommission für Zeitgeschichte, Reihe A: Quellen 48) (Paderborn, Munich, Vienna, and Zurich, 2002), nr. 255, cf. also nr. 337.

[2] Ludwig Volk, ed., *Akten Kardinal Michael von Faulhabers*, vol. I: 1917–1934 (Veröffentlichungen der Kommission für Zeitgeschichte, Reihe A: Quellen 17) (Mainz, 1975), LVI.

Faulhaber came from a family of peasant artisans, in which higher schooling and university studies lay beyond the accustomed professional horizon. Some have referred to this milieu as "German Catholicism's educational reserve"; it brought forth several leading figures in the German Church and lay movements. Faulhaber had dutifully served as a soldier, of which he remained proud for the rest of his life. He had even considered the possibility of becoming an officer before affirming his calling to the priesthood. For Pacelli, on the other hand, we know of no such diversions on his path to the priesthood and the highest Church offices, which had been predicted for him from an early date[3]. Both his father and grandfather had risen to prominence and honor while serving the Vatican curia as jurists; the grandfather had even acquired a noble title. The family's close ties to the highest circles of papal Rome gave the young, excellently educated Eugenio Pacelli the opportunity for a not unremarkable career, whose culmination, it must be said, was ultimately achieved – as in Faulhaber's case – only through his outstanding life's work.

Nor did Faulhaber's career progression to the priesthood and episcopal office conform to the ideal of a bishop's proper theological education that Pacelli cherished at the time he became nuncio in Germany. As Hubert Wolf has concluded with sufficient certainty, based on the final report Pacelli delivered in Rome at the end of his German nunciature and the influence he exercised on episcopal appointments, Pacelli was as skeptical about the education of priests and future bishops at state universities, which was the norm in Germany, as he was of the state's participation in the appointment of bishops[4]. Faulhaber, however, had studied at a state theological faculty in Würzburg, had been a professor at a state university in Strasbourg, and it had been the royal Bavarian government that had nominated him to the Holy Father for the bishop's chair in Speyer and the archbishop's throne in Munich, as stipulated by the old concordat between Bavaria and the Vatican. What the new nuncio may not have known was the deep impression that Faulhaber, while a student at Würzburg, had gained of one of his theological teachers, Herman Schell, who as one of the leaders of so-called "Reform Catholicism" had had some of his works end up on the index of banned books. Decades later, in his

---

[3]   In 1917, the Bavarian envoy to the Holy See, Freiherr Ritter zu Groenesteyn, attributed to him the potential "to be elected pope" in later years; Karl-Joseph Hummel, presentation manuscript "Pius XII. Opus iustitiae pax: Das Werk der Gerechtigkeit ist der Frieden", no further source particulars.

[4]   Cf. Hubert Wolf and Klaus Unterburger, eds., Eugenio Pacelli. *Die Lage der Kirche in Deutschland 1929* (Veröffentlichungen der Kommission für Zeitgeschichte, Reihe A: Quellen 50) (Paderborn, Munich, Vienna, and Zurich, 2006), 62f., 219.

autobiography, Faulhaber said he owed him more thanks than he could express in words[5]. Of course, Faulhaber never became personally close with Schell and in the theological debates about modernism and anti-modernism, which caused such an intellectual storm at the time he was teaching theology, he did not take a public stand. Similarly, Pacelli had not shown any especially close affinity to the anti-modernism then dominant in Rome; he too maintained contacts to influential exponents of Reform Catholicism, such as Baron Friedrich von Hügel and Franz Xaver Kraus, even if he ultimately did not let them determine his course[6].

What brought Pacelli and Faulhaber together may have been their common mentality, which inclined them to caution rather than aggressiveness. "On the basis of his character, [he was] more shy than dashing", Ludwig Volk described Faulhaber in his *Lebensbild*. The nuncio Pacelli could have been so described as well. But no less than Faulhaber, he possessed the talent to throw himself without reserve into fulfilling his calling, to rise up through that calling to hieratic greatness and thereby become "who he actually was"[7]. The basically conservative outlook they shared likely played a role as well. It led both men, immediately upon assuming their new offices in 1917, into deep antagonism toward their surrounding political environment but at the same time to a more profound understanding of the other's qualities. "It was God's wish", Pius XII wrote when Faulhaber celebrated his fortieth anniversary as a bishop and thirtieth as a cardinal, "it was God's wish that We [as the Pope referred to himself in the pluralis maiestatis, the "royal we", then still customary] through the years have been eyewitness and earwitness of your work as bishop, since as Papal Nuncio in Bavaria during the war and post-war period We lived through a turning point of the ages, which will always remain unforgettable for us."[8] It was the concurrent early days of their respective tenures in Munich, then, that underlay their lifelong bond. An early sign of Pacelli's esteem for Faulhaber can be seen in the fact that the latter's 1920 Lenten pastoral letter was printed in the *Osservatore Romano*[9], which almost certainly occurred through the nuncio's intervention. When Pacelli took on his additional nunciature for the entire German Reich in 1920, Faulhaber, rather than obediently awaiting the appointment of a successor sent by Rome, telegraphed the cardinal secretary of state, asking him "to let Monsignore Pacelli stay in Munich,

---

5   Volk, XLV.

6   Cf. Hubert Schiel, ed., Franz Xaver Kraus, *Tagebücher* (Cologne, 1957), 645f., entry from 30 January 1896.

7   Volk, LXXIX.

8   Hürten, *Akten Kardinal Faulhabers*, 606.

9   Volk, LXXVIII, n. 4.

at least until the conclusion of the Bavarian concordat." A planning committee had already been formed to "prepare a festive farewell" for Pacelli in the event that he did leave for Berlin[10]. Since the Bavarian concordat was not concluded until 1925, there ended up being plenty of time. (Already during a visit to Rome in 1919, Faulhaber had pressured the pope and the cardinal secretary of state to retain the nunciature in Munich, arguing that the unity of the Reich was fragile, perhaps even impossible to maintain in the long term, and that the Vatican's envoy would enjoy a "wholly different standing amidst a Catholic people" than a Reich nuncio in Berlin[11].)

There are statements from Faulhaber as well, confirming that the two men's close relations reached back to the time of World War I and the immediate postwar turmoil. When Pacelli left Germany in 1929, Faulhaber wrote to him, thankful for their mutual time in Munich, "in which the last year of the war and the first postwar years thoroughly shook up all established systems, including the religious one."[12]

The same outlook and a shared evaluation of the situation do not, of course, necessarily lead to commonality of action; to the contrary, some problems manifested themselves differently for the nuncio than for the archbishop. While the former could openly express his rejection of all revolutions, and of those whom they brought to power, the nuncio was primarily concerned with upholding the Church's neutral position and the dignity of the Holy See. Following the upheaval of 1918, Faulhaber wanted the nuncio to refrain from all contact with the Eisner government, in order to avoid "the appearance, in the eyes of the Catholic populace, that the Apostolic Nuncio had recognized the Eisner government and thereby legitimated the revolution." Any eventual meeting between Pacelli and the minister president would "thoroughly confuse [...] the people's consciousness."[13] The desire to prevent such an encounter also motivated Faulhaber's expressed wish that Pacelli should either leave the country or at least retreat to the monastery at Zangberg in order to guarantee his safety. The nuncio, who was continuously directed by the Curia not to favor Bavarian separatism or weaken the unity of the Reich in any way[14], in reality established no contacts with Eisner's

---

[10] Ibid., 149.

[11] Ibid., nr. 59, nr. 69, the quotation on 124.

[12] Ibid., 485.

[13] Ibid., 190f.

[14] Emma Fattorini, *Germania e Santa Sede: Le nunziature di Pacelli fra la Grande Guerra e la Repubblica di Weimar* (Annali dell'Istituto storico italo-germanico. Monografia 18) (Bologna, 1992), 103; Fattorini emphasizes these aspects as central to the directives that Pacelli received from Rome, without, however, indicating when these instructions took effect.

government other than those necessary to ensure the continued functioning of the nunciature. Even these he did not pursue personally but through his subordinate *uditore*. The treatment accorded this official while undertaking that mission convinced Pacelli that he could never submit himself, a representative of the Holy See, to such an encounter. Along with the other members of the diplomatic corps who still remained in Munich, the envoys of the other German federal states and Austria, Pacelli agreed to refrain from any actions that could be interpreted as a recognition of the Eisner government[15].

Whether the nuncio agreed with Faulhaber that he should leave Munich to avoid giving Eisner any opportunity for an encounter or whether it really was his weakened health that impelled him to leave for Rorschach in Switzerland cannot be clearly determined. On the day of his arrival, 22 November 1918, the house log of his residence there, "Stella Maris", identified only "vacillating health, a result of overwork" as the reason for his coming[16] and most historians concur. That Pacelli's trip to Switzerland could also have had a political motive, however, is suggested by one of Faulhaber's memoranda[17]. According to this document, the nunciature's *uditore* had asked him on 18 January whether the time was right for the nuncio to return. The archbishop advised against it because he again expected Eisner to attempt contact, even though the revolutionary government had been defeated in the Landtag election of 12 January 1919. Yet Pacelli left Rorschach on 31 January and returned to Munich, spending the most dangerous days of the Soviet Republic and the violent occupation through government troops in the city, when the nunciature suffered attacks from both sides[18].

Pacelli's initial impression was that the revolution had created a situation in Bavaria in which, as he wrote to Gasparri, "God's mercy alone" could save the Church[19]. Unlike the royalist patriot Faulhaber, however, Pacelli did not share a fixation with Bavaria as a core Catholic land that could only suffer harm through

---

[15] Pacelli to Gasparri, 15 November 1918, in: Fattorini, 310–314.

[16] Otto Walter, *Pius XII.: Leben und Persönlichkeit* (Olten and Freiburg, 1941), 149f. Walter quotes the entry in the Stella Maris house log for 22 November 1918, as well as Pacelli's farewell dedication of 31 January 1919; he appears credible on this point, despite weaknesses elsewhere.

[17] Volk, nr. 94. There are certain doubts about the reliability of this note because it obfuscates the violation of the nunciature's diplomatic immunity by government troops and, as a reaction to this, Pacelli's departure from Munich.

[18] On soviet republican troops' demands for the nuncio's car, as well as the house search of the nunciature by government troops, see Heinz Hürten, "Legenden um Pacelli", in: Konrad Ackermann, Alois Schmid, and Wilhelm Volkert, eds., *Bayern: Vom Stamm zum Staat. Festschrift für Andreas Kraus zum achtzigsten Geburtstag* (Munich, 2002), vol. 2, 503–511. On the "attacco delle truppe del Governo" see Pacelli to Gasparri, 5 May 1919, in: Fattorini, 325–327.

[19] Volk, 485.

"Reich unitarism".[20] He is not likely to have overlooked the fact, which Faulhaber also was forced to concede to himself, that it had been the Reich constitution of the Weimar Republic that had granted the Church greater freedom even in Bavaria than it had previously possessed under Bavarian law. (Consequently, Faulhaber wanted to secure this position through a separate concordat for Bavaria, in the event that the Reich broke apart, a plan he presented to Pope Benedict XV on 30 December 1919[21].) Furthermore, the nuncio in Bavaria had been instructed by the Curia to bolster the Reich as a bulwark against Bolshevism, a position that the egoisms of the federal states could only weaken[22]. As far as we know today, Pacelli did not take exception to the "anti-Bavarian" speech given by the Catholic Reich Chancellor Joseph Wirth at the 1921 Catholic Congress in Frankfurt, which greatly upset the Bavarians in the audience. By contrast, Faulhaber had been so distressed by the speech that he barred Wirth from attending the Catholic Congress in Munich the following year[23].

The most urgent task facing the nuncio was to reorder the legal status of an established church, which was even more difficult in Bavaria than elsewhere in Germany. The Bavarian king, as a Catholic monarch, had possessed rights within the Church that could not simply be transferred to a republican head of state. Faulhaber and the Bavarian episcopate played only a minor role in solving this problem. The successful concordat that ultimately emerged was, as Faulhaber explained to the bishops from outside Bavaria, "from beginning to end the work of the Apostolic Nuncio."[24] In fact, in his work on the Bavarian concordat, Pacelli did not meet with any well-developed demands on the part of the local episcopate, as he had in Prussia. The bishops there had, without any assistance from the nuncio, insisted on their rights at the state constituent assembly, established a commission to study problems concerning church law, and reached a unified position on what should be governed by concordat and what by parliamentary legislation[25]. For the Bavarian concordat, Pacelli did not have an expert German advisor, as he had for Prussia in the person of Ludwig Kaas, who also functioned as the bishops' representative to the nuncio[26].

---

[20]   Ibid., 177.

[21]   Ibid., nr. 59.

[22]   Ibid., 149.

[23]   Ibid., nrs. 125, 135.

[24]   Ibid., nr. 165.

[25]   Heinz Hürten, ed., *Akten deutscher Bischöfe über die Lage der Kirche 1918 bis 1933* (Veröffentlichungen der Kommission für Zeitgeschichte, Reihe A: Quellen 51) (Paderborn, Munich, Vienna, and Zurich, 2007), nrs. 60, 83–85.

[26]   Ibid., nrs. 85, 190.

Like the rest of the bishops in Bavaria, Faulhaber brusquely rejected the efforts of the Bavarian cathedral chapters to acquire a certain share in the process of appointing bishops[27], as was the case in Prussia and which the Fulda Bishops' Conference wished to preserve[28]. In the Concordat (article 14 §1), the Curia did grant a (non-decisive) role to the cathedral chapters. By contrast, the wish of the Bavarian bishops, who regularly sent Rome lists of suitable candidates for episcopal office, to be heard before a bishop's final appointment went unfulfilled. Faulhaber was also perturbed that the treaty with the Holy See was presented to the Bavarian Landtag, as part of a draft skeleton law, together with the Protestant church agreements, which seemed to him to knock the concordat down in rank. As a result, the new regulation did not fill him with "unalloyed delight"[29]. That such disappointments brought about a cooling of his relations to the concordat's chief negotiator, Pacelli, does not, however, emerge from the sources. And after World War II, there was no longer any sign of disappointment. In a confrontation with American occupation authorities, Faulhaber declared that anyone giving a speech on Bavarian schools that failed to mention the concordat and the Church as one of the parties to that treaty was guilty of no less than "objectively insulting the Pope".[30]

With the conclusion of the concordat, Pacelli's reason for staying in Munich disappeared. A new nuncio, Vassallo di Torregrossa, arrived in the Bavarian capital. Faulhaber's official relations with Pacelli consequently decreased. On some important tissues, such as the organization of Actio Catholica and perhaps also the military chaplains corps, there seem to have been differences of opinion[31]. But Faulhaber composed a heartfelt letter of thanks in the name of the Bavarian bishops when Pacelli was recalled to Rome. In his reply, the newly appointed cardinal secretary of state responded to something Faulhaber had written, perhaps not entirely to his liking: "For the openness with which Your Eminence expressed themselves I am sincerely grateful. If there were no other title upon which Your Eminence could establish the right as well as the duty to this frankness, then the friendship that has existed between us for years, growing stronger through loyal

---

27   Volk, nr. 117.

28   Hürten, *Akten deutscher Bischöfe*, nr. 120 2 d.

29   Volk, nr. 165.

30   Hürten, *Akten Kardinal Faulhabers*, 573.

31   Thus, Faulhaber wanted to have Actio Catholica organized along parish and diocesan lines, with a non-political orientation, cf. Volk, nr. 193; for Pacelli's differing view, cf. ibid., nr. 192. Differing opinions concerning military pastoral care may be suggested in nr. 210.

and successful collaboration, would alone suffice to make an open word from Your Eminence appear dear and valuable to me in every matter"[32].

The pressures that weighed on the Church in Germany with increasing intensity and severity from the moment Hitler assumed power automatically produced an intensified correspondence between the bishops and the Curia, especially with Cardinal State Secretary Pacelli, who devoted himself to German affairs with special concern. Ludwig Volk included an impressive series of such reports in his edited collection of Faulhaber's papers. The Cardinal Secretary of State's replies, despite their businesslike brevity, are usually not without a certain warmth, which at least hints at the old familiarity between the two men. Faulhaber belonged to the select circle of German bishops who were called to Rome in January 1937 to discuss the Church's situation in Germany. It was then that Faulhaber was given a task that demonstrates in a unique way the esteem in which he was held by Pacelli: he was to produce a draft encyclical with which the pope wanted to address German Catholics. Faulhaber wrote his draft in the nocturnal hours so that no one would learn of it. This text was extensively reshaped by Pacelli; to spiritual admonition and warning about Nazi heresy, he added a severe condemnation of church policy in Germany[33], which gave *Mit brennender Sorge* (With deep anxiety) its particular character and brought it more attention than papal encyclicals usually attract. This reshaping of Faulhaber's text does not, however, indicate disapproval of its author. In Pacelli's opinion, Faulhaber's thoughts and formulations were evidently good enough to be said to German Catholics as the pope's own words. What the changes to the original text effected was a change in aims. It was no longer intended just to console and boost the courage of the hard-pressed faithful in Germany while avoiding an aggravation of the Church's political situation, as Faulhaber had intended. Instead, the encyclical would go beyond just comforting the faithful, to show the world that Hitler's regime was in breach of contract and hostile to the Church. The changes to Faulhaber's draft, then, do not indicate a change in the relationship between the cardinal state secretary and the Munich metropolitan.

In March 1939, the cardinal secretary of state became pope. One of his first official acts was to discuss with the German cardinals the possibilities for making peace with the regime in Germany. Faulhaber and Bertram had provided him

---

[32] Ibid., nr. 210.

[33] A synopsis of Faulhaber's draft and the final text of the encyclicals in Dieter Albrecht, ed., *Der Notenwechsel zwischen dem Heiligen Stuhl und der Deutschen Reichsregierung*, vol. I: *Von der Ratifizierung des Reichskonkordates bis zur Enzyklika "Mit brennender Sorge"* (Veröffentlichungen der Kommission für Zeitgeschichte, Reihe A: Quellen 1) (Mainz, 1965), 404–443.

memoranda for this purpose. Once again, Pacelli demonstrated his greater feistiness. Whereas Bertram and Faulhaber advised him to give up positions that were already lost, the pope was not prepared to surrender any church rights[34].

An especially instructive source on Faulhaber's relations to Pope Pius XII are the *lettere autografe*, which have been published in the second volume of the *Actes et Documents du Saint Siège relatifs à la seconde guerre mondiale* (Rome, 2nd edition 1967). *Lettere autografe*, as they are published here, constitute a special type of text in the Holy See's correspondence with the bishops. They are less formal than papal breves and can be composed in languages other than curial Latin. They therefore enable a freer mode of expression than the rigidly formal correspondence of the Curia. At the same time, they carry more weight than the routine correspondence between the bishops and the state secretariat because they express the pope's view directly and in regard to particular situations. Of the 124 such texts collected in this edition, eleven are addressed to Faulhaber. Only Bishop Count von Preysing, with 18, and Cardinal Bertram of Breslau, with 12 such letters, rank above Faulhaber on the list of recipients. The higher total of letters addressed to Preysing is attributed by the publishers to the two men's acquaintance of many years: Preysing had been attaché at the Bavarian legation in Rome even before his ordination to the priesthood, at a time when Pacelli was still serving in the state secretariat. Bertram's privileged status on the list of *lettere autografe* recipients is easily explained by his position as Chairman of the Fulda Bishops' Conference, in which the Bavarian bishops participated from 1933 on. Faulhaber's privileged position as the pope's correspondent can most probably be explained by their mutual attachment, whose foundations had been laid in early Munich days. These are referred to in various ways. Pius XII sent Faulhaber his Christmas greetings in 1939 "in living memory of some solemn and edifying Christmases that We [experienced] in your beloved fatherland, surrounded by the heartwarmingly sincere faith of the devout German people in front of crèche and Christmas tree"[35]. In 1941, he spoke of the "sincere personal ties [...] that have connected Us to you for so many years and that count among our most cherished life experiences"[36]. "The greater the obstacles to a rapid and personal connection with Our

---

34   Reports on these conferences in Burkhart Schneider, ed., *Die Briefe Pius' XII. an die deutschen Bischöfe* (Veröffentlichungen der Kommission für Zeitgeschichte, Reihe A: Quellen 4) (Mainz, 1966), 317–327, 330–340.

35   Pierre Blet, Angelo Martini, and Burkhart Schneider, eds., *Actes et documents du Saint Siège relatifs à la seconde guerre mondiale*, vol. 2: *Lettres de Pie XII aux évêques allemands 1939–1944* (Vatican City, 1966), 109.

36   Ibid., 189.

brothers in apostolic office and the faithful in Germany become", he wrote in 1942, "the more fervently spiritual ties bind us: the memories of the years we experienced together with their difficult and also joyful occurrences"[37]. In his greetings on the occasion of Faulhaber's seventy-fifth birthday, the pope wrote: "You know how glad We were to live among you and with what enjoyment We worked for the best not only for the Catholic Church but the entire German people"[38]. The exchange of pleasantries is of course only a by-product of a correspondence whose most important theme was the fate of the Church in the existing circumstances, in all its aspects. Letter no. 78, to Faulhaber[39], on 2 February 1942 touches on not only their years of mutual experience but also on two of the Munich Archbishop's sermons, as well as "the resonance that the bishop's enlightened and courageous words find among the people" and their importance for "the moral resistance struggle of the faithful". The letter also discusses facilitating Sunday Mass and Holy Communion for the faithful, the pastoral care of soldier priests and the shortage of priests, "reports from the area of the war in the east", which were causing the pope "serious concern", the Dachau concentration camp, anti-Church propaganda, organizing the bishop's cooperative efforts, the *Osservatore Romano*, the war situation, the hope for peace, and Faulhaber's health. What comes across as chaotic in this listing is in fact skillfully structured in the letter's text, not unlike the musical artistry of a fugue.

In these letters to Faulhaber, there is one, by now frequently cited passage that illuminates this pope's position during the Second World War: "The current war has brought about an unspeakably difficult situation for the Holy See, in which an enormous sum of political and religious-ecclesiastical questions intersect and block one another in escalating dimensions and in ways that are no longer comprehensible for the uninitiated. [...] We have outlined our position on the questions of war with the term 'impartiality', not with the word 'neutrality'. Neutrality could be understood in the sense of a passive indifference, which is not an option for the head of the Church when confronted by such events. Impartiality for Us means evaluating matters in a spirit of truth and justice; whereby We, where public pronouncements on Our part are concerned, shall give the utmost consideration to the situation of the Church in the individual countries, in order to spare the Catholics there any avoidable difficulties"[40]. This explication of the guiding principles of his administration to someone slightly older but in church rank

---

[37] Ibid., 235.
[38] Ibid., 358.
[39] Ibid., 235–241.
[40] Ibid., 293ff.

unalterably subordinate demonstrates that it was not sentimental memory of better times that determined their mutual relationship but rather unreserved trust.

The years that followed, a time of hardship and poverty previously unknown in Germany, once again demonstrated how firm the bonds of friendship were between Pius XII and Faulhaber. Besides church-political issues, such as validity of the concordats, confessional schools and training of religion teachers, and the return of church buildings and properties, their correspondence is largely preoccupied with the expellee situation, those who had lost their homes to the bombing, and those who were pursued because of their political past, in cases where Faulhaber considered prosecution unjust. Time and again, Faulhaber had reason to thank the pope for relief shipments, which Sister Pascalina Lehnert was involved in organizing. In this way, she became one of Faulhaber's correspondents. The pope's donations included not only clothing, shoes, food, and medication, of which Insulin was in especially high demand; even balm for the Maundy Thursday Chrism Mass and the paper for a new printing of the Catechism also came by way of Rome[41]. Faulhaber himself was not ignored. In his own words, he returned from the consistory in 1946 having "received gifts worthy of a prince"[42]. In 1948, he expressed thanks for the gift of a robe and cape that Pius had sent him[43], for Christmas he received liturgical vestments and rosaries, a "fine portfolio", linen, "many practical items for desk and travels that are of incalculable value in these times"[44]. "We ask you", Pius XII wrote in response to Faulhaber's words of thanks, "to believe Us that the awareness of being able to help, and being permitted to help, those in need – and does this not include the bishops and the members of the Holy College, considering the practical impossibility of acquiring the outward attributes commensurate with their position? – is such a great and sweet reward in itself that the gratitude of the beneficiaries, particularly when it takes on the warm accents in the mouth of a so beloved and valued co-worker in Christ's Kingdom, as it is with you, positively begins to shame Us"[45].

Accompanying Faulhaber's perpetual testimonies of gratitude for the relief supplies sent by the pope was a no less expressive gratitude for Pius XII's doctrinal instructions, and both were reciprocated by Pius with equal thanks. If any confirmation of the Pope's esteem for Faulhaber were still needed, then his

---

[41]   Hürten, *Akten Kardinal Faulhabers*, nrs. 94, 97, 131.

[42]   Ibid., nr. 94.

[43]   Ibid., nr. 226.

[44]   Ibid., nr. 246.

[45]   Ibid., 436.

letters on the occasions of Faulhaber's 80th birthday, mentioned above, and his bishop's and cardinal's jubilee in the year 1951[46] provide more than adequate documentation.

What was the ultimate basis for this mutual high regard? Was it nothing more than a "friendship between men?" Hardly. Even in the most personal sections of their correspondence there is always a recognizable distance, the kind that separates a father and son even in the closest relationships. If both men, each in his own way, came to embody their respective offices and missions so completely that each obtained his individual profile only through this, then there was little space for anything else in their relationship outside of service to the Church. The admiration that they felt for one another was therefore not really based on sympathy, which may well have existed, but on each one's recognition of the other's greatness, which in turn arose from their devotion to their respective offices and missions. If this is ultimately what lent contour to their respective profiles, then the same is true of the establishment of that "intimate bond" that they speak of so often and clearly in their correspondence.

Translated by Christof Morrissey

---

[46] Ibid., nrs. 255, 337.

Introduction to the Presentation
"Pius XII in the Judgment of Posterity"

Karl-Joseph Hummel

The academic advisory panel for the exhibition *Opus Iustitiae Pax. Eugenio Pacelli – Pius XII (1876–1958)*, conceived by the Pontifical Committee of Historical Sciences, initially recommended showing the exhibition, after its opening in Rome, only at those two stations that were decisive for Eugenio Pacelli's diplomatic career: Munich and Berlin. (As a member of the panel, I was responsible for the nunciature period of 1917 to 1929.) Pacelli represented the Apostolic See in Munich from 1917 to 1925 and, in personal union, from 1920 to 1929 in Berlin. Following unexpectedly strong interest from individual visitors and in the media, the possibility of an English version that would be shown as a traveling exhibition, particularly in the United States, is now being discussed. Peripheral to its showing in Berlin (from 22 January to 7 March, 2009), a proposal was made to present the exhibition in Israel as well.

The exhibition is biographically oriented and consequently extends from Eugenio Pacelli's birth date on 2 March 1876 to the death of Pope Pius XII on 9 October 1958. The history of Pius XII's impact, now more than 50 years old, has intentionally not been made a subject of the exhibition. The organizers in Munich have therefore decided to offer four additional lectures as part of a program that accompanies the exhibition, which deal both with research topics as well as with interpretive issues that could not have been discussed while Pius XII was still alive.

On the first evening of this series, we concerned ourselves with Pius XII's relationship to modernity, on the second with Pacelli's relationship to the Jews. The third evening was devoted to the special bond of trust between Michael Cardinal Faulhaber and Eugenio Pacelli, about which we are now well informed by a whole series of new sources that became accessible with the opening of the Vatican archives up to 1939.

Tonight's program features "Pope Pius XII in the Judgment of Posterity". With this presentation, we are undertaking the attempt to re-tell, analyze, and render understandable a controversial history that began, at the latest, in 1963, with the premiere of the "Christian tragedy" of Rolf Hochhuth's *The Deputy*. After all,

Pope Pius XII – whose canonization, although a matter of controversy, should by no means be ruled out – is characterized in the play as a "criminal" and has been insulted by Hochhuth as "the most contemptible of all popes" and a "satanic coward". Just recently, on the 70th anniversary of Pius XII's election to the papacy, Hans Küng painted a portrait of this pontificate in the *Süddeutsche Zeitung* online edition. In it, Küng brings together all the negative elements from the Pius controversies in a comprehensive portrayal that contrasts sharply with the worldwide and indisputable esteem and deep respect accorded this pope on his death.

The numerous obituaries – from Christians and non-Christians alike – were full of recognition and great admiration for an exceptional life's work. Today, when we look back upon the five decades that have passed since 1958 and remember Eugenio Pacelli, we recognize that this once positive appraisal has largely been pushed to the margins as a result of fierce differences of opinion. For no other pope do the judgments of posterity diverge so greatly, is the discrepancy between a black-and-white popular image, on the one hand, and the differentiated findings of historical scholarship, on the other, so large. This is partly the result of the politically motivated confrontations that have accompanied the process of canonization, preparations for which are already well advanced, though a specific date cannot yet be named. The anticipated dates that have been proclaimed from time to time have in each case proven to be pure speculation.

Who determines the historical view we have of Pius XII? The opening of the Vatican archives up to the year 1939 has introduced a new dynamism into the debate about Pius. New sources enable new historiographical questions to be asked and have already forced us to make various revisions. To the assessments by contemporaries that predominated in the beginning and the political contours that were pushed to the forefront over the last 45 years have now, following the opening of important archives, been added revisions made from the perspective of historical scholarship.

In order to do justice to this new constellation, then, we could have invited a contemporary of Pius XII, a combatant from the politically-tinged debates about Pacelli, and a historian or political scientist who does scholarly work on Pope Pius XII to a podium discussion tonight. In part to preserve the character of a lecture evening, however, the organizer has decided on an even better solution: he has invited Professor Hans Maier, who in the course of his life has played, and continues to play, all three of those roles.

Hans Maier, born in 1931, belongs to the generation that personally experienced the Third Reich and the pontificate of Pius XII (1939–1958). Over the decades, he has served in various capacities dealing with church policy. In numerous publications, he has articulated his positions on many questions that lead directly to our topic, always preserving a scholarly distance. To sum up, all I can say is: Thank goodness for Hans Maier!

Professor Maier, I hardly need to introduce you as a person or as scholar here in Munich, in front of this audience. But permit me to welcome you very cordially and to offer my thanks that you happily agreed to take on this presentation, "Pius XII in the Judgment of Posterity", even though you knew that you would not be able to meet the high standards you set for yourself without engaging in much time-consuming additional reading. I am extraordinarily interested to find out how you are going to present this major topic here this evening.

Translated by Christof Morrissey

Pius XII in the Judgment of Posterity

Hans Maier

I

On 9 October 1958, at the 3:52 in the early morning, Pius XII – Eugenio Pacelli by family name – died of a stroke in the papal summer residence at Castel Gandolfo, following a brief illness. He was in the midst of his 83rd year of life and the 20th of his pontificate. When his coffin was transported in a solemn procession from Castel Gandolfo to Rome – Pius XII was the first pope since 1799 that did not die in Rome – it was escorted by hundreds of thousands of people on the streets. The world mourned a man who, in the judgment of many contemporaries, had elevated the Holy See "to the pinnacle of its prestige in the modern period"[1]. The twelfth Pius – to this day, he is the last of that name in the history of the papacy – was considered one of the greatest of all popes at the time of his passing. For some, he was even "the most admired and revered person of this century", as Radio Vaticana stated in its report of his death[2].

In his last will and testament, which the *Osservatore Romano* published one day after his death, Pius XII requested to be buried in a holy place. Monuments to him were not to be erected, however. Instead, the pope asked for the prayers of the faithful[3]. Pius XII's death produced a worldwide resonance, by no means only in Catholic countries but nearly everywhere. Only in the communist states was the resonance weaker. Representatives of many states traveled to Rome. The final requiem in St. Peter's Cathedral, which brought to a close nine days of mourning, was attended by 41 cardinals and by delegations from 53 countries. The best-known names from the world of politics included John Foster Dulles, Couve de Murville, Heinrich von Brentano, and Joseph Bech. The American secretary of state Dulles proclaimed upon his arrival in Rome: "The strength, the courage, and

---

[1] So wrote the *Frankfurter Allgemeine Zeitung*'s long-serving Italian correspondent Josef Schmitz van Vorst in an article of 10 October 1958, reproduced in: Rudolf Lill and Peter Martin Schmitz, eds., *Josef Schmitz van Vorst: Berichte und Bilder aus Italien 1948–1958* (Constancez, 1997), 370–373 (citation from 370).

[2] Katholische Nachrichten-Agentur (KNA) report, 9 October 1958.

[3] The last will and testament dated from 15 May 1956. German translation in: *Bonner Rundschau*, 11 October 1958 (Friedrich Lampe).

the leadership of His Holiness, Pope Pius XII, upheld the belief in a just peace for almost 20 years. During all these years, his determined struggle for the ideals of Christianity and his will to improve the lot of humanity were a constant, encouraging inspiration. The passing of His Holiness has plunged the whole world into deepest mourning but the inheritance that he left us will never be forgotten"[4].

In Italy, the deceased pope was celebrated above all as the *Defensor civitatis*, as the savior of the city of Rome during the war. Pacelli was, after all, a native Roman, the first pope since Innocent XIII (1721–1724) who had been born in the Eternal City. That Rome had not been destroyed in the war, that it survived as an open city, was attributed first and foremost to the pope. Obituaries recalled that Pius XII had hurried to the San Lorenzo district after the Allied air attacks there on 19 July 1943 and helped care for the wounded (to this day, the only public monument to Pius XII in Rome is in this part of the city)[5]. The Italian government ordered a three-day period of mourning for the whole country; the parliament, the courts, but also theaters and cinemas remained closed[6].

The pope's death evoked an especially lively response among the Germans. That was understandable: outside his native Italy, there was no other country with which Pius XII had such close ties as with Germany, where he had spent more than twelve defining years of his life as nuncio, in Munich and later in Berlin. According to his own statements, these years were "perhaps the best time" of his life. From the country of the Reformation, Pacelli had taken a comprehensive knowledge of the German language and German culture, as well as certain habits, and ways of thinking and working, even if his – in the meantime accessible – reports to Rome, particularly the "Final Report" of 18 November 1929, also contain instances of distancing and criticism[7]. In Rome, Pius was known as "Papa Tedesco", not always to the delight of the Italians or other nations[8]: his housekeeper[9], his private

---

4   Cit. in: *Neue Zürcher Zeitung*, 20 October 1958.

5   Illustration in the exhibition catalogue: Pontifical Committee of Historical Sciences, ed., *Opus Iustitiae Pax: Eugenio Pacelli – Pius XII. (1876–1958)* (Regensburg, 2009), 187.

6   KNA report, 11 October 1958.

7   Hubert Wolf and Klaus Unterburger, eds., *Eugenio Pacelli: Die Lage der Kirche in Deutschland 1929* (Veröffentlichungen der Kommission für Zeitgeschichte, Reihe A: Quellen 50) (Paderborn, Munich, Vienna, and Zurich, 2006), 60ff., 95ff., 219ff.

8   A telling anecdote in Giulio Andreotti, *Meine sieben Päpste* (Freiburg, 1982), 34: "After the death of Pius XII, Konrad Adenauer supported the appointment of the famous Jesuit pater Bea to cardinal. During a friendly conversation in his house in Rhöndorf he said to me that, until now, the Germans hadn't needed a cardinal of their own in the Curia because they [...] had had the Pope".

9   On Pascalina Lehnert there is now Martha Schad, *Gottes mächtige Dienerin: Schwester Pascalina und Papst Pius XII.* (Munich, 2007). Andreotti writes positively about her, noting especially her

secretary, his confessor, and many of his advisors and assistants were Germans. He conversed in German with many of his associates. He even gave two of his canaries German names, Hans and Gretchen[10].

Most of all, however, Pius XII was presumably the first head of state who – as early as 1944 – had warned against theories of collective guilt and after the war vigorously defended the Germans against the international ostracism that threatened, which included promoting three German bishops to the rank of cardinal. On 2 June 1945 he even spoke of the "outstanding qualities" of the German people in an address; who else dared say such a thing at the time? The pope expressed the hope that Germany would soon raise itself once more "to new dignity and to new life", once it had "thrown off the Satanic ghost of National Socialism and once the guilty had atoned for the crimes they had committed"[11]. Time and again, he lamented the expulsion of the Germans from Eastern Europe and warned "not to repay violence with violence but instead to let the power of the law answer"[12]. His protests against the notion of the collective guilt of all Germans did not lack for clarity. "There are great fallacies going around which would pronounce a human being as guilty and culpable only because he is a member or part of some community, without making the effort to inquire and investigate whether a personal act or sin of omission has really been committed. That amounts to arrogating the rights of God, the Creator and Redeemer, who alone in the mysterious plans of his always benign providence is master over events and as such – if his unlimited wisdom favors it – links the fates of the guilty and the innocent, of those culpable and those not culpable"[13].

The reaction of many Protestant Christians to the pope's death was also positive. In addition to Chancellor Adenauer and Foreign Minister von Brentano[14], the President of the Federal Republic, Theodor Heuss, Bundestag President Gerstenmaier, the bishops Dibelius and Lilje, as well as church president Niemöller honored the deceased[15]. True, the Protestant pronouncements also contain critical passages. Particularly the Dogma of the Assumption of Mary, proclaimed by

---

   objectivity and precision, and comments: "She also helped the pope practice his language skills; for me – who does not know German – it was surprising to hear how the pope gave the religious sister instructions in the German language." Ibid., 50.

10 Karl-Joseph Hummel, "Von Adolf Hitler bis Rolf Hochhuth: Eugenio Pacelli/Papst Pius XII. und die Deutschen". Paper at the opening of the exhibition "Pius XII. Opus Iustitiae Pax" in Schloss Charlottenburg, Berlin, 22 January 2009 (MS), 6.

11 Cit. in: *Rheinischer Merkur* 1958, Nr. 34: "Pius XII. und die Deutschen".

12 Letter to the German bishops, 1 November 1945; ibid.

13 Address at the General Consistory, 20 February 1946; ibid.

14 *Bulletin des Presse- und Informationsamtes der Bundesregierung*, Nr. 188, 10 October 1958.

15 Overview in: *Herder-Korrespondenz* (1958/1959) 207–210.

Pius XII in 1950, was mentioned as not helping to reduce the divisions between the confessions, as was the pope's conception of religious reunification in terms of a "return" to the Catholic Church. Nevertheless, it was repeatedly mentioned that, as nuncio in Germany, Pacelli had become acquainted with Protestantism in its country of origin from a personal vantage point and later, as pope, had spoken of Catholics and Protestants as "separated brothers". In his statement, Martin Niemöller probably expressed the basic tenor within German Protestantism when he wrote: "[...] and still, we are – even as Protestant Germans – deeply grateful to Pope Pius beyond his death. He was a great friend of our German nation [...] and he never allowed himself to be seduced into the general damning verdict of others; instead, he was the first who called for relief for the needy people of our nation. He also knew of the collective spiritual resistance that was put up in our nation; vis-à-vis the National Socialist rulers, he unequivocally stood up for the Christians of all denominations who had been thrown into concentration camps on account of this resistance and fortified them through donations and salutations"[16]. As in Germany, the Protestants in other countries expressed appreciation for the pope's person and achievements – in a long series that extended from President Eisenhower and UN General Secretary Dag Hammerskjöld to the Anglican Archbishop Geoffrey Fisher and the president of the Lutheran World Council, Franklin Cl. Frey. The Queen of England, whose coronation oath requires her to support the Reformed faith, ordered that the flags on all public buildings be lowered to half mast on the day of the pope's funeral[17]. In his blunt soldier's idiom, Field Marshal Montgomery called the late pope "a great Christian gentleman"[18].

In light of later judgments of Pius XII, we naturally have a special interest in the comments of Jewish personages of the time. Such statements were consistently characterized by respect, even by veneration and affection. The Israeli foreign minister Golda Meir was the first to lament the death of the pope before the United Nations General Assembly, with famous, often quoted words: "When fearful martyrdom came to our people in the decade of Nazi terror, the voice of the pope was raised for its victims"[19]. Nahum Goldmann, president of the World

---

[16] *Herder-Korrespondenz* (1958/1959) 208f. In his eulogy, Niemöller told of the silver crucifix that the pope had sent him in Dachau.

[17] Otto B. Roegele, "Der Tote spricht", in: *Rheinischer Merkur*, 17 October 1958.

[18] *Herder-Korrespondenz* (1958/1959) 209.

[19] "Pius XII. † im Echo jüdischer Nachrufe", in: *Freiburger Rundbrief* 19 (1958) 66–69; (here also the citations that follow). The German text reads: "Als für unser Volk im Jahrzehnt des Nazi-terrors das furchtbare Martyrium anbrach, erhob der Papst seine Stimme zur Verurteilung der Verfolger und in Barmherzigkeit für die Opfer."

Jewish Congress, wrote to Monsignor Tardini in the Vatican secretariat of state: With special gratitude we remember all that he did for the persecuted Jews during one of the darkest periods in their history." The Central Council of the Jews and the rabbinate in the Federal Republic of Germany conveyed their heartfelt condolences to the papal nuncio and to Cardinal Frings of Cologne. The chief rabbi in Jerusalem telegraphed Rome: "[T]he Catholics do not stand alone in their grieving over this loss." The chief rabbi of Rome, Dr. E. Tor, asserted "that Jewry will for all time remember all that which the Catholic Church did on the Pope's orders during World War II." In the New York German-Jewish weekly newspaper *Aufbau* of 17 October 1958, Robert M. W. Kempner, prosecutor at the Nuremberg War Crimes Trial, wrote a long article on Pius XII as an opponent of Nazism and his relief efforts on behalf of Jews. I cite three characteristic parts of this article: "Besides the condemnation of National Socialism by Pius XII, there were his active aid efforts, in the form of employing German Jews for archival work in the Vatican; taking in Jewish refugees, including many children, in monasteries and Catholic hospitals; protest actions against the inhumanity of the concentration camps by the Curia to Nazi diplomatic missions abroad and to the Foreign Office in Berlin; and many other humanitarian and diplomatic measures." – "When, after the fall of Mussolini, Rome was under Nazi administration, Pius XII did everything humanly possible to save the Jews of Rome. Many of them have the Vatican to thank for their lives. At that time, the idea emerged in the Nazi Party secretariat of *Reichsleiter* Martin Bormann to spirit the pope out of Rome and secure him as a hostage somewhere in occupied territory. Pius XII heard about these plans, naturally remained in Rome and by staying in the Holy City saved it from destruction. For reasons not yet verified, Hitler recoiled from giving an order to destroy Rome as long as the pope was there." – "Because he loved Germany without Hitler as almost no other pope before him had, he did everything within his power to hasten the end of the Hitler regime."

It is striking that in the Jewish as well as the other eulogies to Pope Pius XII, there is no mention of Auschwitz anywhere. We know that the word "Auschwitz" – and the image of the annihilation of the Jews associated with it – entered the public awareness only gradually in the post-war period[20]. Nowhere in the obituaries and acclamations of 1958 can one find the notion that the Jews would have

---

[20] Thus, the German bishop's *Hirtenwort* of 23 August 1943 and the Protestant Church in Germany's confession of guilt (*Stuttgarter Schuldbekenntnis*) contain no mention of the destruction of the Jews.

been better helped by loud, unambiguous protests on the part of the pope than by the varied diplomatic and humanitarian measures, as they were in fact taken by the Vatican[21]. In any case, the success of these measures – even if from today's vantage point it was only a partial success in mitigating the horrors – was credited to the pope and provided the basis for the overwhelmingly positive perception of the head of the Catholic Church among Christians, Jews, and others throughout the world.

II

That changed dramatically in the 1960s. During that period, the "pope who helped" was transformed into the opposite, into the "pope who was silent", silent on the crimes against humanity of the Holocaust, the Shoah. Almost from one day to the next, the historical figure of Pius XII appeared in a new and problematic light. All of a sudden, the pope was no longer measured by what he had done but by what he had not done – but which, in the new view of things, he should inevitably have done as Christ's deputy on Earth. In view of the deportations and the Nazi murder of the Jews, his conduct in time of wartime regarding Hitler suddenly appeared as a singular failure, as a grave sin of omission, as a "Christian tragedy" (Rolf Hochhuth). As always in the case of abrupt reversals in history, we must distinguish between the longer-term determinants and the immediate cause. One reason why the view of Pius XII changed undoubtedly lay in the new view of the Holocaust, which began to spread in the 1960s and eventually caught on all over the world. From an event closely woven into the proceedings of the Second World War, the Holocaust (Shoah) evolved into a topic that had a magnitude of its

---

[21] The position of Kurt R. Grossmann, responsible for restitution issues at the Jewish Agency, New York, is revealing (*Rheinischer Merkur*, 31 October 1958): "The question has often been asked, by the Jewish side as well, whether the pope could have done more to rescue the Jews than was done. That the Catholic Church helped children, in particular, to escape is an incontrovertible historic fact. The actions of Pater Benoit and of Gertrud Luckner in Germany, or the activities of French Catholics, would not have been possible without the practical assistance of Catholic clergymen, who thereby placed their freedom and even their lives at stake [...] the Jews are thankful that, in the time of their greatest persecution, the awareness set in that the conflict between Christianity and Judaism had lost its meaning and that Jews and Christians have to fight together for the defense of civilization founded on the belief in God the creator. That Pope Pius XII had this realization and stood up for it was a ray of hope in those dark days, which the Jews will surely not forget".

own[22], of significance not only to historians but also to philosophers and theologians ("God after Auschwitz")[23].

Dovetailing with this were new theological accents: in the statements of the popes who followed Pius XII, especially John XXIII and Paul VI, and – particularly pronounced – in the resolutions of the Second Vatican Council that convened in 1962. These concerned primarily the relationship between Christians and Jews, which was defined in a new way in the proclamation *Nostra aetate*[24]. Also up for debate were relations with the non-Christian religions, as well as the position of the Catholic Church in the modern world as such.

Of central importance in the conciliar pronouncements was the notion of religious and inter-human solidarity. The programmatic opening sentence of the "Pastoral constitution on the Church in the world of today" expressed it with the words: "Joy and hope, grief and fear of the people of today, especially the poor and the hard-pressed, are also joy and hope, grief and fear of the disciples of Christ." Inter-human solidarity was also implored by the programmatic social encyclicals of John XXIII, Paul VI and, later, John Paul II. This met with lively resonance particularly within German Catholicism. The declaration "Our hope", formulated by Johann Baptist Metz and adopted at the Würzburg synod in 1975, linked Christian hope in view of the horror of Auschwitz with an impassioned plea for a "new position on the religious history of the Jewish people", in memory of the fact "that there were Jews and Christians who proclaimed and called upon this God even in such a hell and after the experience of such a hell." From this, Metz derived a responsibility of the German church, in

---

[22] On the current state of research, see Raul Hilberg, *Die Vernichtung der europäischen Juden: Die Gesamtgeschichte des Holocaust*, 3 vols. (Frankfurt/Main, 1990); Waclaw Dlugoborski and Franciszek Piper, eds., *Auschwitz 1940–1945: Studien zur Geschichte des Konzentrations- und Vernichtungslagers Auschwitz*, 5 vols. (Oswiecim, 1999); Götz Aly, et al., eds., *Die Verfolgung und Ermordung der europäischen Juden durch das nationalsozialistische Deutschland 1933–1945* (document edition); nine volumes are planned; previously published: Vol. 1, *Deutsches Reich 1933–1937* (Munich, 2008).

[23] Theodor W. Adorno, *Erziehung nach Auschwitz* (Frankfurt/Main, 1963); Hans Jonas, *Der Gottesbegriff nach Auschwitz: eine jüdische Stimme* (Frankfurt/Main, 1987); Dan Diner, ed., *Zivilisationsbruch: Denken nach Auschwitz* (Frankfurt/Main, 1988); Johann Baptist Metz, "Kirche nach Auschwitz: Israel und die Kirche heute", in: *Festschrift für Ernst Ludwig Ehrlich* (Frankfurt/Main, 1991), 110–122.

[24] Original text in: *Acta Apostolicae Sedis* 58 (1966) 740–744; German translation in: LThK², vol. 13 (1967) 405–495, with an annotated introduction by Johannes Österreicher and excurses on Hinduism (Cyril B. Papali), Buddhism (Heinrich Dumoulin) and Islam (Georges C. Anawati).

particular, "to work, within the wider church, toward a new relationship of Christians to the Jewish people"[25].

Here, a new series of themes and motives come into focus. It seemed the obvious thing to do to tie them into a dramatic knot and present them to the public. This happened at a surprisingly early date and to considerable effect. Of course, the place where it occurred was neither a historical or theological seminar, nor a council or synod, but rather the stage.

Rolf Hochhuth's tragedy *The Deputy*, which premiered on 20 February 1963 under Erwin Piscator at the "Theater am Kurfürstendamm" in West Berlin, became the immediate impetus for a new evaluation and assessment of the role of Pius XII in World War II. With an abundance of performances in many countries, the play made an immediate impact on the international stage. It not only changed the existing image of Pius XII in the media and literature, but also exerted intensive influence on future historiography; its effects can still be felt today[26].

Hochhuth's drama does not deny its origins in Schiller. Written in a form of blank verse, it brings recent history to the stage – not as it really happened but as it could or should have happened, in the author's opinion. Morality rules in this play, and as always in presentations with sharply outlined positions of "for" and "against", with passionately involved personalities driven by an idea, the viewer – regardless of the many sensational elements – is moved and gripped. The effect of the "Christian tragedy", especially on young people, was considerable. The play fit the times, it satisfied the desire to knock outsized figures – such as a pope

---

[25] "Unsere Hoffnung: Ein Bekenntnis zum Glauben in dieser Zeit", in: *Gemeinsame Synode der Bistümer in der Bundesrepublik Deutschland: Beschlüsse der Vollversammlung* (Freiburg/Br., 1976), 71–111; this citation, 109.

[26] On the vigorous and controversial debate that immediately ensued, and in which Hannah Arendt, Karl Jaspers and Golo Mann, among others, participated, cf. Reinhold Grimm, et al., eds., *Der Streit um Hochhuths Stellvertreter* (Stuttgart, 1963); Fritz J. Raddatz, ed., *Summa iniuria oder Durfte der Papst schweigen? Hochhuths "Stellvertreter" in der öffentlichen Kritik* (Reinbek, 1963); Reinhard Hoffmeister, ed., *Rolf Hochhuth: Dokumente zur politischen Wirkung* (Munich, 1980); Karl-Heinz Wiest, "'Der Stellvertreter' – ein Stück und seine Wirkung", in: *Rottenburger Jahrbuch für Kirchengeschichte* 2 (1983) 203–248; Doris Rosenstein, "Rolf Hochhuth: Der Stellvertreter", in: *Dramen des 20. Jahrhunderts*, vol. 2 (Stuttgart, 1996), 126–156; Michael F. Feldkamp, "Der 'Stellvertreter' von Rolf Hochhuth in der Innen- und Außenpolitik der Bundesrepublik Deutschland: Mit einem Anhang ausgewählter Aktenstücke aus den Vatikanakten des Auswärtigen Amtes", in: *Geschichte im Bistum Aachen*. Beiheft 2: *Von Pius XII. bis Johannes XXIII.* (Neustadt/Aisch, 2001), 127–177; Thomas Brechenmacher, "Der Dichter als Fallensteller: Hochhuths 'Stellvertreter' und die Ohnmacht des Faktischen – Versuch über die Mechanismen einer Geschichtsdebatte", in: Michael Wolffsohn and Thomas Brechenmacher, eds., *Geschichte als Falle: Deutschland und die jüdische Welt* (Neuried, 2001).

– from their pedestals, to confront them with contemporary challenges that they were evidently not prepared to face, before which they failed. This was an extremely effective but certainly not unproblematic method. Of course a dramatist should be allowed to play with historical figures; Hochhuth made full use of this in *The Deputy*. But should an author have the liberty to stage history in an entirely new and invented way according to his fancy?[27]

Hochhuth's historical arrangement is as follows: a young Jesuit father, Riccardo Fontana, serving as a minutante in the Curia's foreign service, wants to impel the pope, whom he knows personally and whom he admires, to the long overdue protest against the persecutions of the Jews. But his pleas fall on deaf ears in the Berlin nunciature. In a roundabout manner, he works his way to Rome, into the proximity of Pius XII. Together with his own father, a Roman aristocrat, he speaks with the pope. But the head of the Church turns out to be a hesitating, weak, fearful shepherd, in the best case a cautiously tactical diplomat. He wants to weaken Hitler without harming, let alone destroying, the German people. In the intensifying war, he hopes for a mediating role. He is keeping all his options open. All attempts to move him to decisive action fail. And the protest against the persecution of the Jews, which, on Riccardo's urging, he eventually dictates to his scribe, is kept in such general terms that it achieves nothing. Hochhuth's hero takes the consequences: to the pope's dismay, he announces that he will attach the yellow star of David to his own soutane as a sign of solidarity. Dramatically, he promises:

> "I will wear this star until
> Your Holiness curses,
> before all the world, *that* man who
> is slaughtering Europe's Jews like cattle."[28]

The last act of the play shows Riccardo in Auschwitz. He has voluntarily followed the deported Jews there. In league with him is Gerstein, a historic person

---

[27] See the restrained verdict in Nicholas Boyle, *Kleine deutsche Literaturgeschichte* (Munich, 2009), 213: "Hochhuth's determination to find high-ranking personalities and hold them responsible for great crimes – Churchill in *Soldaten* (1967), Hans Filbinger, the minister-president of Baden-Württemberg, in *Juristen* (1979) – was on occasion highly effective (Filbinger was forced to resign). It did not, however, contribute to a comprehensive understanding of the historical and cultural context that had made the crimes possible".

[28] Rolf Hochhuth, *Der Stellvertreter* (Reinbek, 2006), 289f. Original German text: "Ich werde diesen Stern so lange tragen / bis Euer Heiligkeit vor aller Welt / *den* Mann verfluchen, der Europas / Juden viehisch ermordet."

who appears in Hochhuth's play under his own name. Gerstein was a member of the Confessing Church, was imprisoned in a concentration camp and, after his release, joined the SS because he hoped to organize resistance to the Nazi system from within its center. Naturally, both protagonists of resistance go down helplessly, both meet their deaths, because – as in Schiller – the True and the Beautiful cannot triumph in this world. The gas chambers of Auschwitz continue to operate. Yet the protest, once expressed, does not completely die away, it reaches posterity. In this "Christian tragedy" it testifies to the voice of truth, the struggle for freedom and justice that must constantly be fought anew. Riccardo's conclusion points to the future, it is an imperative: "God should not corrupt the Church/ just because a pope withdraws from his reputation."[29] In contrast to this, in the play's central scene in the Vatican palace, the pope retreats from the historic task that is placed before him in Hochhuth's drama. He defends himself by referring to the Jewish refugees the Church had rescued in the Roman monasteries. *His* summary rings stubborn and resigned: "That which it was granted us to do, happened."[30]

III

I have said it already: Hochhuth's portrait of Pius XII has decisively shaped the image of this pope among the wider public, right up to today. The pope who remained silent (or at least did not speak out loudly): this has been a fixed theme of Pius biographies ever since. Defenders as well as opponents have to engage it. But of course the debate continued after the *Deputy*. What came after Hochhuth? How did the image of Pius XII develop in the judgment of posterity during the years that followed? The debate was lively and remained controversial. It orbited continuously around the same questions, attempted to clarify the pope's behavior in individual situations. It could have been the hour of scholarship. Yet it took a long time before scholarship found its way out of the dramatic tracks laid by Hochhuth.

Guenther Lewy's The Catholic Church and Nazi Germany, published in New York in 1964, remained stuck in these tracks[31]. I got to know the author, an American political scientist, while he was working on the German version of this book with Eric Voegelin. Lewy's book is partisan; it attempts to destroy the "myth" of a Catholic resistance against the Nazi dictatorship – whereby he received

---

[29]   Ibid., 293.
[30]   Ibid., 292.
[31]   Guenther Lewy, *The Catholic Church and Nazi Germany* (New York, 1964).

116

inadvertent help from a whole series of all too apologetic publications from the immediate postwar years. Of course, it is not Pius XII but the German bishops in the Third Reich who are at the center of this study[32].

Lewy inaugurated a series of English-language efforts to investigate the subject of the Church in the Third Reich. These are strongly shaped by fixed opinions about that which is Catholic, by a preconceived image of the Church and its character. Catholicism appears as a commanding hegemon, uniform, monolithic, in essence barely changeable: a closed, potentially totalitarian entity. Owing to this structural similarity, it can, on the one hand, become a counterpart to modern totalitarianisms; on the other hand, it can also offer itself as an accomplice, come to terms and make pacts with them. What is decisive is that Catholicism remains the same in all its incarnations and, in effect, has no real history. In Daniel Jonah Goldhagen's book, this leads to a perspective that projects modern racial anti-Semitism back to the beginnings of the Church's history and sees the Holocaust prefigured in St. Paul's Letter to the Romans[33]. Naturally, there is no distinction made between Christian anti-Judaism and modern anti-Semitism. Texts such as *Nostra aetate* or the Second Vatican Council's *Declaration on Religious Freedom* are either not taken into account or, if they have been read, accused of insincerity. In John Cornwell's book, finally, Pius XII becomes – contrary to all source-based facts – "Hitler's Pope"[34].

Of course, scholarship's view of the pope is this so one-sided only where it is writing – in the words of Ludwig Volk – "Hochhuth prose"[35]. Where opinion is not fixed, where an open debate predominates, there are opponents but also defenders of this pope. Thus, opponents such as Suzan Zuccotti[36] and Michael

---

[32] The most thorough critique is by Ludwig Volk, "Zwischen Geschichtsschreibung und Hochhuthprosa: Kritisches und Grundsätzliches zu einer Neuerscheinung über Kirche und Nationalsozialismus", in: Ludwig Volk, *Katholische Kirche und Nationalsozialismus: Ausgewählte Aufsätze* (Mainz, 1987), 335–347.

[33] Daniel Jonah Goldhagen, *A Moral Reckoning: The Role of the Catholic Church in the Holocaust and Its Unfulfilled Duty of Repair* (New York, 2002); German translation under the title *Die katholische Kirche und der Holocaust: Eine Untersuchung über Schuld und Sühne* (Berlin, 2002).

[34] John Cornwell, *Hitler's Pope* (London and New York, 1999); German translation under the title *Pius XII.: Der Papst, der geschwiegen hat* (Munich, 1999). On this, see Heinz Hürten, "Pius XII. – Hitlers Papst?", in: *Stimmen der Zeit* 218 (2000) 205–208; Karl-Joseph Hummel, "Überzogene Anklage: Anmerkungen zur neuen Diskussion über Pius XII.", in: *Herder-Korrespondenz* 54 (2000) 129–135.

[35] See n. 32.

[36] Susan Zucotti, *Under His Very Windows: The Vatican and the Holocaust in Italy* (New Haven, 2000).

Phayer[37] and defenders like Margherita Marchione[38], José M. Sanchez[39] and Michael Burleigh[40] confront one another. Alongside them, there are others – including Philippe Chenaux[41], Emma Fattorini[42], Pierre Blet[43], Hubert Wolf[44] and Thomas Brechenmacher[45] – who, on the basis of new thinking and new sources, seek a middle path. Of course, none of these scholars has yet succeeded in constructing, and establishing internationally, a new paradigm of research on Pius that can lead beyond the old, often clichéd positions.

On this subject, José M. Sanchez wrote the following in 2002: "Everything that can be said has already been said. All critics and all defenders of Pope Pius XII have laid out their views clearly. Only a few opinions have changed in the last forty years since Rolf Hochhuth's dramatic accusations in *The Deputy* […] In fact, by this point, both critics and advocates of Pope Pius XII are citing one another in their works in ever-shrinking circles. In the words of the great literary scholar and Shakespeare expert Douglas Bush, one could say that what the studies on Pius XII and the Holocaust all have in common is 'intrepid repetition'."[46]

How can we overcome this present state, which can be to nobody's satisfaction? For historians, the silver bullet remains the reading and analysis of new sources. The Vatican Secret Archive contains many kilometers of files. With the

[37] Michael Phayer, *The Catholic Church and the Holocaust: 1930–1965* (Bloomington, 2000).

[38] Margherita Marchione, *Pope Pius XII: Architect for Peace* (New York, 2000).

[39] José M. Sánchez, *Pius XII. and the Holocaust: Understanding the Controversy* (Washington D.C., 2002); German under the title *Pius XII. und der Holocaust: Anatomie einer Debatte* (Paderborn, 2003).

[40] Michael Burleigh, *Sacred Causes: Religion and Politics from The European Dictators to al Qaeda* (London, 2006); German under the title *Irdische Mächte, göttliches Heil: Die Geschichte des Kampfes zwischen Politik und Religion von der Französischen Revolution bis in die Gegenwart* (Munich, 2008); second part, 575–1149, 1190–1228.

[41] Philippe Chenaux, *Pie XII: Diplomate et pasteur* (Paris, 2003).

[42] Emma Fattorini, *Germania e Santa Sede: Le nunziature di Pacelli fra la Grande guerra e la Repubblica di Weimar* (Annali dell'Istituto storico italo-germanico, Monografia 18) (Bologna, 1992); Emma Fattorini, *Pio XI, Hitler e Mussolini: La solitudine di un papa* (Turin, 2007).

[43] Pierre Blet, *Pie XII et la Seconde Guerre mondiale d'après les archives du Vatican* (Paris, 1997); German under the title *Papst Pius XII. und der Zweite Weltkrieg: aus den Akten des Vatikans* (Paderborn, 2001).

[44] Hubert Wolf, *Papst & Teufel: Die Archive des Vatikan und das Dritte Reich* (Munich, 2008).

[45] Thomas Brechenmacher, *Der Vatikan und die Juden: Geschichte einer unheiligen Beziehung vom 16. Jahrhundert bis zur Gegenwart* (Munich, 2005); Thomas Brechenmacher, "Teufelspakt, Selbsterhaltung, universale Mission? Leitlinien und Spielräume der Politik des Heiligen Stuhls gegenüber dem nationalsozialistischen Deutschland (1933–1939) im Lichte neu zugänglicher vatikanischer Akten", in: *Historische Zeitschrift* 280 (2005) 591–645.

[46] José M. Sánchez, "Papst Pius XII. und der Holocaust: Überlegungen zu einer Kontroverse", in: *Historisches Jahrbuch* 122 (2002) 521–529 (this citation, 521).

last great opening up of these records in 2003 and 2006, the entire tenure of Pope Pius XI (1922–1939) became available to researchers. (The opening of Pius XII's files is planned for 2014.) The new sources on Pius XI are important for research on Pacelli as well, since they contain a multitude of reports that the nuncio sent from Munich or Berlin to Rome – often more than one a day[47]. So far, nearly 5,000 reports have been discovered. To these can be added the reports (nearly a thousand) that Pacelli's successor, Cesare Orsenigo, sent from Germany to Pacelli, by then cardinal secretary of state in Rome. And finally, the notes from the pope's private conversations with his cardinal secretary of state alongside other sources, such as audiences with ambassadors, minutes from meetings of the various congregations, reports of the nuncios from all over the world and Rome's directives to them. Of course these sources must first be individually exploited. More than one hundred thousand archival items await working through. As concerns Pacelli's reports as nuncio in Germany, Hubert Wolf is currently working on making them accessible and available on the Internet[48].

Following "test drilling" in Pius XII's files in the Vatican Archive, the Münster-based historian Hubert Wolf summarized previous findings and supplemented them with new ones, presenting them to readers in his 2008 book *Papst & Teufel. Die Archive des Vatikan und das Dritte Reich* (Pope and Devil: The Vatican's Archives and the Third Reich). As a result, the old controversy surrounding the Reich Concordat can finally be consigned to the files, as was adumbrated at a colloquium of the German Historical Institute in Rome in July 2004. Konrad Repgen was proved right in his dispute with Klaus Scholder[49]. The Roman Curia did not play a directing role in the background regarding either the German bishops' decisions after the Nazi "seizure of power", the Center Party's consent to the Enabling Law, or the proposal for the concordat, which was made by the German side. To the contrary, the diplomat Pacelli expressly regretted that the German bishops had retracted their condemnation of the regime without receiving anything in return. The Center Party's self-dissolution, which he learned about from the newspapers, surprised and irritated him. He could now no longer use political

---

[47] Wolf, 24.

[48] Ibid., 26

[49] Klaus Scholder, *Die Kirchen und das Dritte Reich*, vol. 1: *Vorgeschichte und Zeit der Illusionen 1918–1934* (Frankfurt/Main, 1977); Konrad Repgen, "Über die Entstehung der Reichskonkordats-Offerte im Frühjahr 1933 und die Bedeutung des Reichskonkordats: Kritische Bemerkungen zu einem neuen Buch", in: *Vierteljahrshefte für Zeitgeschichte* 26 (1978) 499–534; Konrad Repgen, "Nachwort zu einer Kontroverse", in: *Vierteljahrshefte für Zeitgeschichte* 27 (1979) 159–161.

Catholicism as a bargaining chip in his negotiations and was forced to reach a speedy conclusion. A pistol had been put to his head, he confided to Ivone Kirkpatrick, the British chargé d'affaires at the Holy See[50].

Wolf's summary: "The Reich Concordat was a pact with the Devil – this was evidently perfectly clear to everyone in Rome – but it guaranteed pastoral care and the existence of the Catholic Church in the 'Third Reich'. The Curia itself did not pay for this either with the Center Party's consent to the Enabling Law or by rescinding the warnings against National Socialism. These steps were the fault of the German Church"[51]. Incidentally, Rome was prepared, and not only in this matter, 'to negotiate even with the Devil himself' (according to Pius XI): During his tenure as nuncio in Berlin, Pacelli more than once offered the Soviet Union diplomatic recognition, in return for a minimum standard of religious freedom and guarantees for pastoral care and the training of priests – yet the Soviet leadership rejected this[52].

On the Vatican's relationship to the Jews, the new sources offer illuminating details. Particular preconditions of thought, which long determined Rome's position on the Jews basically until Vatican II, come into focus. On the one hand, the popes always unequivocally rejected modern racial anti-Semitism. On the other hand, in Rome one still saw the synagogue – as in accounts from the Middle Ages – with blindfolded eyes, blind, stricken with delusion, and therefore prayed for the conversion of the Jews. The possibility of a separate Jewish path to salvation founded on the promises of the Old Covenant was not considered. The Catholic position was therefore an ambivalent one: it remained resistant to the rising racist tendencies while retaining the patronizing view of the "wrong-headed Jewish people", which was burdened with a curse. This made not a few susceptible to a spiritual anti-Semitism that left its traces in liturgy and homily.

As a result, the reaction of the Roman Curia to the anti-Jewish persecution that began in 1933 – and whose archival traces up to 1939 are now assessable – was hesitant and uncertain. Edith Stein's imploring letter of April 1933 to Pius XI – which became known in 2003 – may have been submitted to the pope and received a response, addressed to Arch-Abbott Raphael Walzer of Beuron, who had forwarded it, which Wolf published in 2008. But this reply was inexpressive and did

---

[50] Wolf, 194ff.

[51] Ibid., 202.

[52] Konrad Repgen, "Die Außenpolitik der Päpste im Zeitalter der Weltkriege", in: Hubert Jedin and Konrad Repgen, eds., *Handbuch der Kirchengeschichte*, vol. VII: *Die Weltkirche im 20. Jahrhundert* (Freiburg/Br., 1985), 36–96 (63ff.).

not address the author's plea to break the silence of the pope and the Church[53]. True, Pius XI did look for ways to reach the public the more Nazi anti-Semitism encroached on Italy. He was prepared and willing to lift his voice in protest. Yet he was already a sick man. Ratti was not capable of presenting personally his last speech as pope, from which the sentence "Spiritually we are all Semites" – a reckoning with racism – originates. As his successor, Eugenio Pacelli did not come back to this statement[54].

Thus, Pius XI's perspective yields new views of Pacelli and of the time before his election as pope. Ratti and Pacelli, Pius XI and the later Pius XII, appear as personalities in the mirror of nunciature reports and later the reports on the cardinal secretary of state's audiences with the pope. Their similarities, their mutual admiration, their cooperation come into focus. But their differences are also highlighted. Of Pius XI, Vatican experts said at the time that it was difficult to keep him from a public utterance – of Pacelli that it was equally difficult to get him to make the same. "Fisherman senior" and "Fisherman junior", as the Jesuit Gustav Gundlach referred to them in biblical-archaic terms (and with a quietly malicious undertone)[55], were, despite their close cooperation through the decades, two very different personalities.

Concerning the subject of Pius XII and the Jews, we will probably be able to acquire new insights only when the files of Pacelli's pontificate (1939–1958) are opened in a few years. Only then will a definitive verdict be possible, particularly on the papal rescue and relief efforts, their scope and their success. Could that also be the case for the alleged silence over the Holocaust?[56] Admittedly, Pius XII was a diplomat, not a martyr. Not that he was silent on the persecution of the Jews; claims to that effect were already refuted by wartime statements that became

---

[53] Wolf, 214–216.

[54] Ibid., 236f.; cf. Konrad Repgen, "Hitlers 'Machtergreifung', die christlichen Kirchen, die Judenfrage und Edith Steins Eingabe an Pius XI. vom April 1933", in: *Edith Stein Jahrbuch* (2004) 31–68; Angela Ales Bello and Philippe Chenaux, *Edith Stein e il Nazismo* (Rom, 2005).

[55] Wolf, 238.

[56] On this, see Repgen, "Außenpolitik der Päpste", 94–96. He emphasizes that the Secretariat of State was informed about the nature of the murder of the Jews relatively early and that it trusted this news; that it considered a public appeal "inadvisable" for fear of reprisals; that the Pope did indeed "speak out", (in the Christmas address of 1942, "those hundreds of thousands" who "without any fault on their part, sometimes only because of their nationality or race [stirpe], have been consigned to death or to a slow decline" were explicitly remembered), but that speaking out was "not his primary or exclusive means in the struggle against Hitler's Jewish policy." "The destruction of the Jews could not be undone through a public appeal, while drastic retaliation against Jews, against Catholics and the Church lay within the logic of the National Socialist system of rule." (Ibid., 96).

accessible long ago. Yet even his most unequivocal pronouncements remained diplomatically restrained in their language. This seemed to him to be dictated by the Holy See's necessary impartiality in the midst of war between leading powers[57]. Could the pope, through a more reckless word, a protest, an outcry have prevented or at least delayed the Holocaust, as the critics from Hochhuth to Goldhagen claim (often overestimating Rome's actual possibilities in the process)? Proof – as with all hypothetical "counterfactual" reflections – cannot be produced[58]. The speculations both for and against remain pure conjecture.

In assessing the impact and prospects of an open protest, the case of the Dutch bishops certainly played an important role. In February 1942, these had prepared a pastoral letter in which they condemned the deportation of Jews to the camps in the east. They insisted on reading this letter from the pulpit, despite the threats of the occupying power. Revenge followed promptly: all Jews who had been baptized

[57] On this, see Hanno Helbling, *Politik der Päpste: Der Vatikan im Weltgeschehen 1958–1978* (Berlin et al., 1981), 25ff.; Blet, passim, and Wolf, 27ff., 48ff., who highlights the influence of his early diplomatic experiences during World War I on Pacelli.

[58] A detailed debate in Sanchez, chapter 13: "Die Wirkungen eines scharfen Protestes: Hypothetische Geschichte" (The Effects of a Sharp Protest: Hypothetical History), 104–108. His conclusion: "It is therefore impossible to say what effect a papal protest would have had. [...] The files appear to confirm that Pius had no self-serving motives for his alleged silence; in reality, he had the noble motive of protecting the lives of innocent people, by foregoing a sharp protest. A different pope might have acted differently, voiced a sharp protest, and the result would presumably have been catastrophic, as Paul VI said in a commentary on Hochhuth's play. That would have preserved and heightened the moral integrity of the papacy – yet no one can say at what cost. As Pius was wrestling with this terrible decision, he may have foreseen the result and decided that an energetic protest would cause more harm than good, even though he knew that his reputation could suffer for it" (ibid., 108). In his unpublished drama *Pius*, W. Kurzka undertakes a "historical thought experiment": Pius XII dies on 14 February 1940 in Rome. His successor is elected by a hurriedly convened conclave: Louis Wegscheider, a South American with Swiss roots and long experience in Rome, who is seen as a neutral. He ascends the papal throne as Pius XIII. In contrast to his predecessor, he embarks on a radical political change of course and strikes a new tone in the relationship with other churches. He even convenes a synod. His protests against Nazism reach their high point in early 1942, when he learns of the program to annihilate the Jews resolved at the Wannsee Conference. He excommunicates Hitler, Himmler, Goebbels, and Bormann from the community of the faithful and absolves all soldiers of the personal oath they swore to Hitler. Of course he is arrested, brought to the priests' block at Dachau, and shot dead during an escape attempt. His successor Leo XIV repeals all of Pius XIII's decisions and sends the Führer of the Greater German Reich a declaration of loyalty. (I thank Professor Gerhard Schindler of Randersacker for making me aware of this text.) Thomas Brechenmacher sees in the tension between the "carità universale" for all of humanity imposed on the Church and the specific duty to care for Catholics one key to understanding Pacelli's conduct during the war; he describes it as a "dilemma" (letter to me, 15 September 2009).

as Catholics were deported and annihilated in Auschwitz. The best-known victims were Edith Stein and her sister. According to the testimony of his housekeeper Pascalina Lehnert, Pius XII knew about these developments[59] and one can assume – although there is no documentary evidence – it was in part for this reason that when he spoke out about the murder of the Jews in the years that followed, it was only in basic and general terms.

It was a cruel dilemma: should one rescue Jewish lives while foregoing spectacular public pronouncements (rescue, not rhetoric, in the words of Robert Kempner)? Or was it better to deliver an unconditional testimony, even at the cost of possible endangerment and destruction of Jewish lives? The conflict was not solvable, at least not with the means of politics and diplomacy. Even martyrdom cannot simply be expected, not even in extreme situations; it cannot be the rule for everyone. By proxy, many individuals, clerics as well as laypeople, preempted a Church decision for such a testament before courts, in prisons and in camps, and suffered in advance of it. The collapse of the Nazi regime spared the Church as whole the potential crucible of a "final solution".

IV

In conclusion, another look at the person. For nearly 20 years, Pius XII encountered many people: at audiences, church services, devotionals, processions. Time and again, Visitors who got close to him were fascinated by his person. "[T]his expired and humble man"[60], "a man like a ray of light. Behind him, night was darkening [...]"[61]. Godfried Bomans writes in his book *Römische Impressionen* (Roman Impressions): "The pope has very fine, delicately formed hands and knows how to play a pantomime that must be enchanting even to an Italian. The face is very flexible and glides with uncanny ease from one expression to the next. The eyes are deep and full of life, the large mouth could belong to an actor, if it wasn't that of an ascetic. Rarely have I seen a face that makes such an impression of immateriality. In it, the soul lights up like a mild light behind thin parchment. His entire appearance comes across as transparent, to which the slender figure

---

[59]   She reports that the pope planned a protest in August 1942, after the reports of the deportation of Jews from Holland, then changed his mind for fear that a protest would cost yet more human lives: M. Pascalina Lehnert, *Ich durfte ihm dienen: Erinnerungen an Papst Pius XII.* (Würzburg, 1986), 117, cit. in: Schad, 97.

[60]   Gottfried Bomans, *Römische Impressionen* (Munich, 1958), 35.

[61]   Reinhold Schneider, *Verhüllter Tag* (Cologne and Olten, 1956), 173.

clad in white contributes."[62] Thomas Mann, whom Pius XII granted a private audience on 29 April 1953, wrote in his diary: "Without the slightest inner resistance, the scion of Luther – who incidentally doesn't much like Luther – bent his knee before the white figure, deeply moved, and cherishes this moment."[63]

As with every important figure, in such a life moments of light and of shadow are collected. Whereas after the war the light was almost overpowering – at the time Pius was considered *the* media pope – since the 1960s the shadowy tones have predominated. For a long time they darkened the figure of light, in fact almost extinguished it. Yet we can hope that light and darkness together will yield the "light-darkness of a 'just' future image". Its contours are already recognizable[64].

Translated by Christof Morrissey

---

[62] Bomans, 35f.

[63] Cit. in: Hermann Kurzke, *Thomas Mann: Ein Porträt für seine Leser* (Munich, 2009), 181f.

[64] Esquilinus, "Pius XII.", in: *Hochland* 51 (1958/59) 185–189, here 185.

Sources on Eugenio Pacelli / Pope Pius XII in the Archbishop's Archive, Munich, and in the Archive of the Archdiocese of Munich and Freising

Peter Pfister

The core archival collections on the life and work of Eugenio Pacelli / Pope Pius XII are naturally to be found in Rome, in the Pacelli family archive and especially in the various collections of the Vatican Secret Archives. In view of the important way station that Munich constituted for the future pope, however, and in light of the strong ties he developed to Archbishop Michael Cardinal von Faulhaber while posted there, files on Eugenio Pacelli / Pius XII can be found in various church archival collections in the Bavarian capital as well.

Organization and Competencies:
The Archdiocesan Archive and the Archbishop's Archive

The Archdiocese of Munich and Freising contains two legally independent archives with their own distinct responsibilities. The Archdiocesan Archive (*Archiv des Erzbistums München und Freising*) documents the work of the local Catholic Church in Munich and Freising, in the manner of a historical archive. Since 1 February 1995, the registry of the archdiocese's general vicariate has been placed under the direction of the archive director, in the manner of an administrative archive. This administrative archive keeps the newer and regularly generated records pertaining to the existence and operation of the archive's establishing agency, the Archdiocesan Ordinariate of Munich (*Erzbischöfliches Ordinariat München*).

In addition to this institution, the Archbishop's Archive (*Erzbischöfliches Archiv München*), which has preserved the official records of the archbishops since 1821, is a local peculiarity. The archival collections of archbishops Lothar Anselm Freiherr von Gebsattel (1821–1846), Karl August Graf von Reisach (1846–1855), Gregor von Scherr (1856–1877), Antonius von Steichele (1878–1889), Antonius von Thoma (1889–1897), Franz Josef von Stein (1898–1909), and Franziskus Cardinal von Bettinger (1909–1917) were newly organized and rudimentarily catalogued by Helmut Witetschek, on commission from Julius Cardinal

Döpfner, in 1967. Witetschek discovered that the existing organizing system had been drawn up soon after Archbishop Michael von Faulhaber's assumption of his office in Munich in 1917, "after a rigorous purge of the files". This system was destroyed by the effects of war and the post-war period, although the surviving reference-material could be utilized for the new organization. It was thereby possible to reconstruct the old organizing system, in a certain sense, and to supplement it at certain points. These files have since been transferred for safekeeping to the Archdiocesan Archive.

The archival holdings of cardinals Michael von Faulhaber (1917–1952), Joseph Wendel (1952–1960), Julius Döpfner (1961–1976), and Joseph Ratzinger (1977–1982), as well as the registry files of Friedrich Wetter (1982–2007), are located partly in the Archdiocesan Archive, partly in the Archbishop's palace, as the property of the Munich Archbishop's See. Effective 1 January 1998, the archbishop transferred special authorization for the care of these collections, in regard to their archival administration, to the diocesan archivist.

The Collection "NL Faulhaber"

On the 50th anniversary of the death of Archbishop Michael Cardinal Faulhaber on 12 June 2002, Archbishop Cardinal Wetter decreed that the archival holdings from Cardinal Faulhaber be made available to researchers ten years before the expiration of the obligatory 60-year retention period mandated by the "Ordinance on the Safekeeping and Use of Archives of the Catholic Church", § 8 Nr. 3. This decision, intended to put an end to the speculations about the collection's contents, authorized the opening of the archive as a foundation for comprehensive, primary source-oriented research.

The "NL Faulhaber" collection encompasses approximately 100 shelf meters and contains about 3,000 files, whereby a single file can include up to several hundred individual documents. Alongside these files, there is a separate photo archive, which has now been fully digitalized and indexed. The organization contains the following sub-sections:

    I. *Kurie* (Curia)
   II. *Weltkirche* (Worldwide Church)
 III. *Kirche in Deutschland* (Church in Germany)
 IV. *Kirche in Bayern* (Church in Bavaria)
  V. *Diözesanverwaltung* (Diocesan Administration)

Systematic Categorization:

VI. *Seelsorge* (Pastoral Work)
VII. *Staat, Gesellschaft, Parteien* (State, Society, Parties)
VIII. *Kirchenkampf, Krieg, Entnazifizierung* (Struggle between Church and State, War, Denazification)
IX. *Persönliches* (Personal)

This prescribed organization[1], which in the first part (I to V) follows ecclesiastical regulation and in the second part (VI to IX) is systematically structured, is not without its problems, in as far as the same topics can be, and indeed are, categorized into different sections.

The sub-section "IX Personal" contains archival materials from the cardinal's childhood and youth, as well as on his scholarly career, which accords more with the content of a private collection. At the same time, however, these papers include documents having to do with his publications, as well as voluminous correspondence on anniversaries and other occasions. In this collection, then, private and professional documents can in many cases not be separated. An archival reorganization, however, would have required that the system of call numbers already used in some publications be changed and delayed the opening of Cardinal Faulhaber's files for many more years.

The "NL Faulhaber" collection also includes, among other things, letters, homilies, newspaper articles, hand-written (even stenographic) notes by the cardinal, position papers, subscripts, certificates, posters, and photographs, as well as diaries from various journeys undertaken in his student days. Further diaries remain in private hands. Currently, efforts are underway to unite them with the collection in the Archbishop's Archive[2].

---

[1] Cf. Heinz Hürten, ed., *Akten Kardinal Michael von Faulhabers*, vol. 3: 1945–1952 (Veröffentlichungen der Kommission für Zeitgeschichte, Reihe A: Quellen 48) (Paderborn, Munich, Vienna, and Zurich, 2002), XXVII–XXXVI.

[2] The nine sub-sections differ greatly in their respective volumes. The sub-sections "I Curia" and "II Worldwide Church" each contain around 100 files, "III Church in Germany" and "IV Church in Bavaria" around 200 files each, the sub-sections "VII State and Society" and "VIII Struggle between Church and State, War, Denazification" around 300 files each. The sub-sections "V Diocesan Administration" and "VI Pastoral Care" are considerably larger, with around 500 files each. The most voluminous sub-section, by far, is "IX Personal," with around 700 files.

Access and Scholarly Evaluation

Promoting historical research and historical education in the area of recent history count among the most important and therefore intensively pursued assignments and working goals of the Archbishop's Archive. Cardinal Wetter's 1998 decision to undertake a new cataloguing of Cardinal Faulhaber's files stood in fortuitous relation to the opening of the Vatican Secret Archive's Germany archive for the years 1922 to 1939, ahead of schedule, in February 2003. In concrete terms, this affected the archives of the nunciatures in Munich and Berlin, as well as the relevant files of the papal Secretariat of State for the period 1922 to 1939. Since then, Faulhaber's files in Munich and the relevant collections of the Vatican Secret Archives in Rome can be used correspondingly. To facilitate research, an exchange of finding aids took place between the Archbishop's Archive in Munich and the Vatican Secret Archive in 2003.

"From now on, insight can take the place of the previous presumptions and polemics", Cardinal Wetter stated in his greeting at the opening of the archival exhibition "Cardinal Michael von Faulhaber, 1869–1952".

Sources on Eugenio Pacelli – Pius XII in the Collection "NL Faulhaber"

Because of Cardinal Faulhaber's intensive contacts to Rome and his close relations with Nuncio Eugenio Pacelli, who became cardinal secretary of state in 1930 and pope in 1939, "NL Faulhaber" contains numerous documents that can be classified under the relevant areas of activity for Pacelli. The following files contain writings that pertain to Pacelli:

1050: Das Leben verschiedener Päpste: Leo XIII., Pius X., Benedikt XV., Pius XI., Pius XII. (Album mit Bildern), 1903–1940
The Lives of various Popes: Leo XIII, Benedict XV, Pius XI, Pius XII (album with photos), 1903–1940

1053: Zum Tod Papst Pius XI. und zur Wahl Papst Pius XII., 1939
On the Death of Pope Pius XI and the Election of Pope Pius XII, 1939

1055: Papst Pius XII. (Berichte, Predigten), 1929–1949
Pope Pius XII (Reports, Homilies), 1929–1949

1056: Papst Pius XII. (Zeitungsartikel), 1939–1951
Pope Pius XII (Newspaper articles), 1939–1951

1105: Papst Pius XII. (Enzykliken), 1939–1951
Pope Pius XII (Encyclicals), 1939–1951

1109: Papst Pius XII. auf dem Eucharistischen Kongress in Argentinien (Zeitungsartikel über Ansprache), 1939–1940
Pope Pius XII at the Eucharistic Congress in Argentina (newspaper article on speech), 1939–1940

1110: Papst Pius XII. (Ansprachen), 1938–1948
Pope Pius XII (Speeches), 1938–1948

1111: Papst Pius XII. (Ansprachen, Verlautbarungen, Enzykliken), 1938–1948
Pope Pius XII (Speeches, Official Statements, Encyclicals), 1938–1948

1112: Papst Pius XII. (Ansprachen, Verlautbarungen, Enzykliken), 1940–1952
Pope Pius XII (Speeches, Official Statements, Encyclicals), 1940–1952

1113: Papst Pius XI. (Enzyklika); Papst Pius XII. (Enzyklika, Ansprache), 1937–1951
Pope Pius XI (Encyclical); Pope Pius XII (Encyclical, Speech), 1937–1951

1130: Papst Pius XII. an Konrad von Preysing und Michael Rackl, 1939–1945
Pope Pius XII to Konrad von Preysing and Michael Rackl, 1939–1945

1131: Papst Pius XI. und Papst Pius XII. an die deutschen Bischöfe, 1926–1952
Pope Pius XI and Pope Pius XII to the German Bishops, 1926–1952

1150: Eingaben an die Päpste Benedikt XV., Pius XI. und Pius XII., 1920–1943
Petitions to Popes Benedict XV, Pius XI, and Pius XII, 1920–1943

1152: Faulhaber – Päpste Pius XI. und Pius XII., 1933–1944
Faulhaber – Popes Pius XI and Pius XII, 1933–1944

1153: Faulhaber – Papst Pius XII., 1945–1947
Faulhaber – Pope Pius XII, 1945–1947

1154: Faulhaber – Papst Pius XII., 1947–1951
Faulhaber – Pope Pius XII, 1947–1951

1170: Wahlanzeige von Papst Pius XII. an Hitler (Abschrift) und Antwort, 1939
Election Announcement of Pope Pius XII to Hitler (Copy) and Reply, 1939

1200: Faulhaber – Kardinalstaatssekretariat, 1911–1932
Faulhaber – Cardinal Secretariat of State, 1911–1932

1201: Faulhaber – Kardinalstaatssekretariat, 1933–1944
Faulhaber – Cardinal Secretariat of State, 1933–1944

1202: Faulhaber – Kardinalstaatssekretariat, 1945–1952
Faulhaber – Cardinal Secretariat of State, 1945–1952

1203: Kardinalstaatssekretär Pacelli (Ansprachen), 1932–1938
Cardinal Secretary of State Pacelli (Speeches), 1932–1938

1259: Vatikanische Informationsstelle (Vermisstensuchstelle), 1942–1946
Vatican Information Office (Search Office for the Missing), 1942–1946

1300: Nuntiatur Berlin, 1926–1944
Nunciature Berlin, 1926–1944

1320: Nuntiatur München, 1912–1950
Nunciature Munich, 1912–1950

1395: Santa Maria dell'Anima in Rom, 1878–1951
Santa Maria dell'Anima in Rome, 1878–1951

1550: Papstspenden, 1918–1923
Papal Donations, 1918–1923

1552: Vatikanhilfe nach dem Zweiten Weltkrieg, 1946–1947
Vatican Aid after World War II, 1946–1947

1553: Papsthilfe (Schwester Pascalina), 1946–1949
Papal Aid (Sister Pascalina), 1946–1949

1554: Vatikanhilfe nach dem Zweiten Weltkrieg, 1948–1950
Vatican Aid after World War II, 1948–1950

3503: Reaktionen auf die Rede Faulhabers beim Katholikentag in München, 1922
Reactions to Faulhaber's Speech at the Catholic Congress in Munich, 1922

3602: Zentralstelle des Volksvereins für das katholische Deutschland (Faulhaber – Pacelli, Faulhaber – Bertram, Marx, Brauns), 1912–1933
Central Office of the Popular Association for Catholic Germany (Faulhaber – Pacelli, Pacelli – Bertram, Marx, Brauns), 1912–1933

3621: Katholische Jugend (Auseinandersetzungen mit der Hitlerjugend); Zentrale in Düsseldorf, 1933–1934
Catholic Youth (Conflicts with the Hitler Youth); Central Office in Düsseldorf, 1933–1934

3710: Una Sancta; Christlich-Jüdische Vereinigung (1950–1951); Rotary; Hochkirchliche Bewegung (1926–1928), 1918–1951
Una Sancta; Christian-Jewish Union (1950–1951); Rotary; High Church Movement (1926–1928), 1918–1951

4006: Beteiligung der bayerischen Bischöfe an den Kosten des Umbaues des Primizaltares von Papst Pius XII. (Faulhaber – bayerische Bischöfe, Faulhaber – Hudal)
The Bavarian Bishops' Share in the Costs of Rebuilding the Altar form Pope Pius XII's First Mass (Faulhaber – Bavarian Bishops, Faulhaber – Hudal)

4062: Freisinger Bischofskonferenz, 1930
Freising Bishops' Conference, 1930

4105: Kundgebung der bayerischen Bischöfe zur Volksabstimmung am 12. November 1933, 1933
Rally of the Bavarian Bishops on the Plebiscite of 12 November 1933, 1933

5007: Fall von Weihbischof Anton Scharnagl, nach 1945
Case of Auxiliary Bishop Anton Scharnagl, after 1945

5522: Zurückstellung der Kleriker an Ordenshochschulen vom Wehrdienst, 1936–1937
Deferment of Clerics at Religious Institutions of Higher Learning from Military Service, 1936–1937

5898: Berufung von Professor Hans Barion und Sebastian Schröcker nach München; Schließung der Münchener Theologischen Fakultät, 1934–1939
Vocation of Professor Hans Barion and Sebastian Schröcker to Munich; Closing of the Munich Theological Faculty, 1934–1939

6760: Militärseelsorge, 1917–1930
Military Pastoral Care, 1917–1930

6790: Verhandlungen über die Exemtion der Militärseelsorge; Katholische militärische kirchliche Dienstordnung, 1925–1931
Negotiations over the Exemption of Military Pastoral Care; Catholic Military Church Regulations, 1925–1931

6954: Schulreform (Episkopat, Kultusministerium, Militärregierung, Päpstlicher Beauftragter, Erzbischof Münch), 1948
School Reform (Episcopate, Culture Ministry, Military Government, Papal Representative, Archbishop Münch), 1948

7261: Zu Goebbels, Göring, Himmler, Hitler, Mussolini, 1933–1949
On Goebbels, Göring, Himmler, Hitler, Mussolini, 1933–1949

7480: Zu den Konkordatsverhandlungen zwischen dem Hl. Stuhl und der Bayerischen Staatsregierung, 1906–1924
On the Concordat Negotiations between the Holy See and the Bavarian State Government, 1906–1924

7482: Zum Bayerischen Konkordat 1924 und zu den Ausführungsbestimmungen, 1918–1940
On the Bavarian Concordat 1924 and on the Terms of Implementation, 1918–1940

7608: Reichstagswahlen, 1930–1936
Reichstag Elections, 1930–1936

8060: Pressestimmen gegen Kardinalstaatssekretär Pacelli, 1927–1937
Press Commentaries against Cardinal State Secretary Pacelli, 1927–1937

8062: Angriffe gegen Papst Pius XII., 1938–1940
Attacks against Pope Pius XII, 1938–1940

8102: Doppelmitgliedschaft katholischer Organisationen, 1934–1937
Double Memberships of Catholic Organizations, 1934–1937

8106: Katholische Verbände und Art. 31 des Reichskonkordats, 1933–1939
Catholic Associations and Article 31 of the Reich Concordat, 1933–1939

8150: Kampf um die Bekenntnisschule, 1922–1938
Struggle over the Confessional School, 1922–1938

8180: Abbau der klösterlichen Lehrkräfte und Klosterschulen, 1936
Drawdown of Monastic Teachers and Schools, 1936

8203: Denkschriften der deutschen Bischöfe an Hitler 1935–1936 (mit Entwürfen); Aufzeichnungen Faulhabers und Korrespondenz über seinen Besuch bei Hitler am 4. November 1936, 1933–1939
Position Papers of the German Bishops to Hitler 1935–1936 (with Drafts); Notes by Faulhaber and Correspondence about his Visit with Hitler on 4 November 1936, 1933–1939

8217: Reaktionen auf die Enzyklika "Mit brennender Sorge", 1937
Reactions to the Encyclical "Mit brennender Sorge" (With Deep Anxiety), 1937

8318: Predigtverbote (P. Rupert Mayer), 1937–1938
Prohibitions on Sermons (P. Rupert Mayer), 1937–1938

8353: Sittlichkeitsprozesse gegen Ordensmänner, 1936–1937
Morality Trials of Religious, 1936–1937

8381: Gesetz zur Verhütung erbkranken Nachwuchses (Sterilisierung), 1933–1940
Law on Contraception against Hereditarily Defective Offspring (Sterilization), 1933–1940

9263: Autobiographie (stenographische Aufzeichnungen und Stoffsammlung)
Autobiography (Stenographic Notes and Collection of Materials)

9299: Papst Pius XII. (Graphische Drucke von F. Spoltare)
Pope Pius XII (Graphic Prints by F. Spoltare)

On account of the partially problematic organizing system described above, the possibility that additional documents pertaining to Pacelli may be situated in other files cannot be ruled out.

Additional Collections of Sources on Eugenio Pacelli – Pius XII

Although the collection "NL Faulhaber" contains the bulk of the materials on Eugenio Pacelli – Pius XII in the Archbishop's Archive and the Archdiocesan Archive, aspiring researchers can also be directed toward several additional holdings that promise to yield potential returns. The files of Cardinal Wendel, whose time in office largely coincided with Pius XII's pontificate, contain documents that reflect the Munich archbishop's contact with the pope and his state secretariat. This collection is currently being organized and catalogued, on the directive of Archbishop Reinhard Cardinal Marx. Its opening to scholarly researchers is projected for 2014, concurrent with the files on the papacy of Pius XII. The papers of Anton Scharnagl, the canonist, *Landtag* deputy, and auxiliary bishop who died in 1955 and whose good connections to Pius XII dated back to Pacelli's tenure as nuncio in Munich and Berlin, contain correspondence with the cardinal secretary of state which, above all, concern problems of church-state relations.

In addition to these episcopal records, two fragmentary sections of personal papers located in the Archdiocesan Archive can also be mentioned. Records of the Bavarian minister of war, Philipp von Hellingrath (1862–1939), who served in that office from 1916 to 1918, contain three of Pacelli's letters from the year 1918. And eighteen of the nuncio's letters from the years 1917 and 1918 are included in the partial literary estate of German Reich Chancellor Georg Count von Hertling.

Literature

Peter Pfister, Susanne Kornacker, Volker Laube, and Thomas Forstner, eds., *Kardinal Michael von Faulhaber 1869–1952: Eine Ausstellung des Archivs des Erzbistums München und Freising, des Bayerischen Hauptstaatsarchivs und des Stadtarchivs München zum 50. Todestag* (Ausstellungskataloge der Staatlichen Archive Bayerns 44) (Munich, 2002).

Peter Pfister, ed., *Michael Kardinal von Faulhaber (1869–1952): Beiträge zum 50. Todestag und zur Öffnung des Kardinal-Faulhaber-Archivs* (Schriften des Archivs des Erzbistums München und Freising 5) (Regensburg, 2002).

Peter Pfister, "Das Erzbischöfliche Archiv München", in: Peter Pfister, ed., *Julius Kardinal Döpfner und das Zweite Vatikanische Konzil* (Schriften des Archivs des Erzbistums München und Freising 4) (Regensburg, 2002), 41–46.

Guido Treffler, "Das Konzilsarchiv von Julius Kardinal Döpfner im Erzbischöflichen Archiv München", in: Peter Pfister, ed., *Julius Kardinal Döpfner und das Zweite Vatikanische Konzil*, (Schriften des Archivs des Erzbistums München und Freising 4) (Regensburg, 2002), 47–55.

Translated by Christof Morrissey

Index

Illustrations

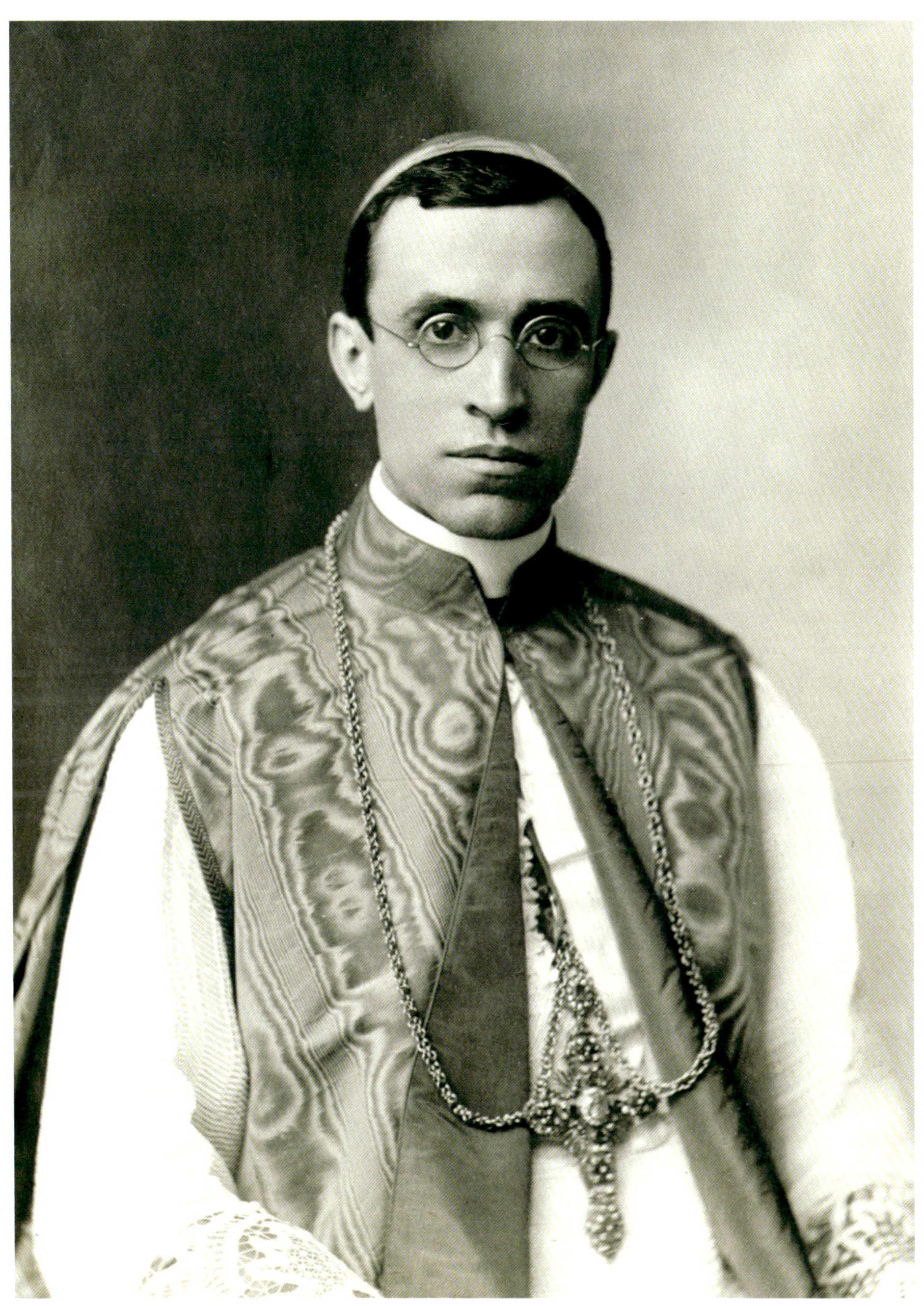

Eugenio Pacelli as a young archbishop
(AEM Dokumentation Personen, Pius XII.)

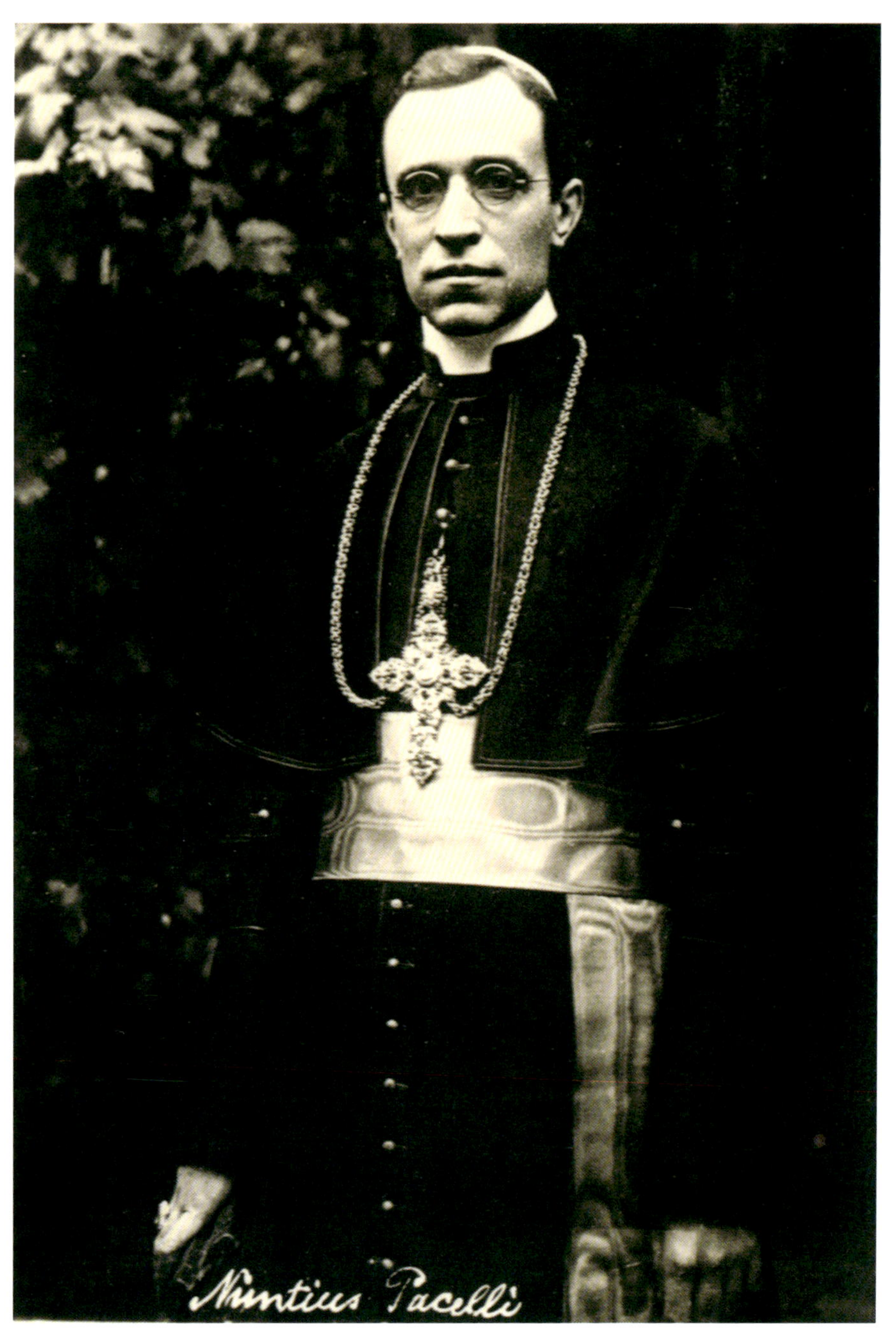

Nuncio Eugenio Pacelli at Bad Adelholzen, Bavaria, 1923
(Archiv der Barmherzigen Schwestern, Munich)

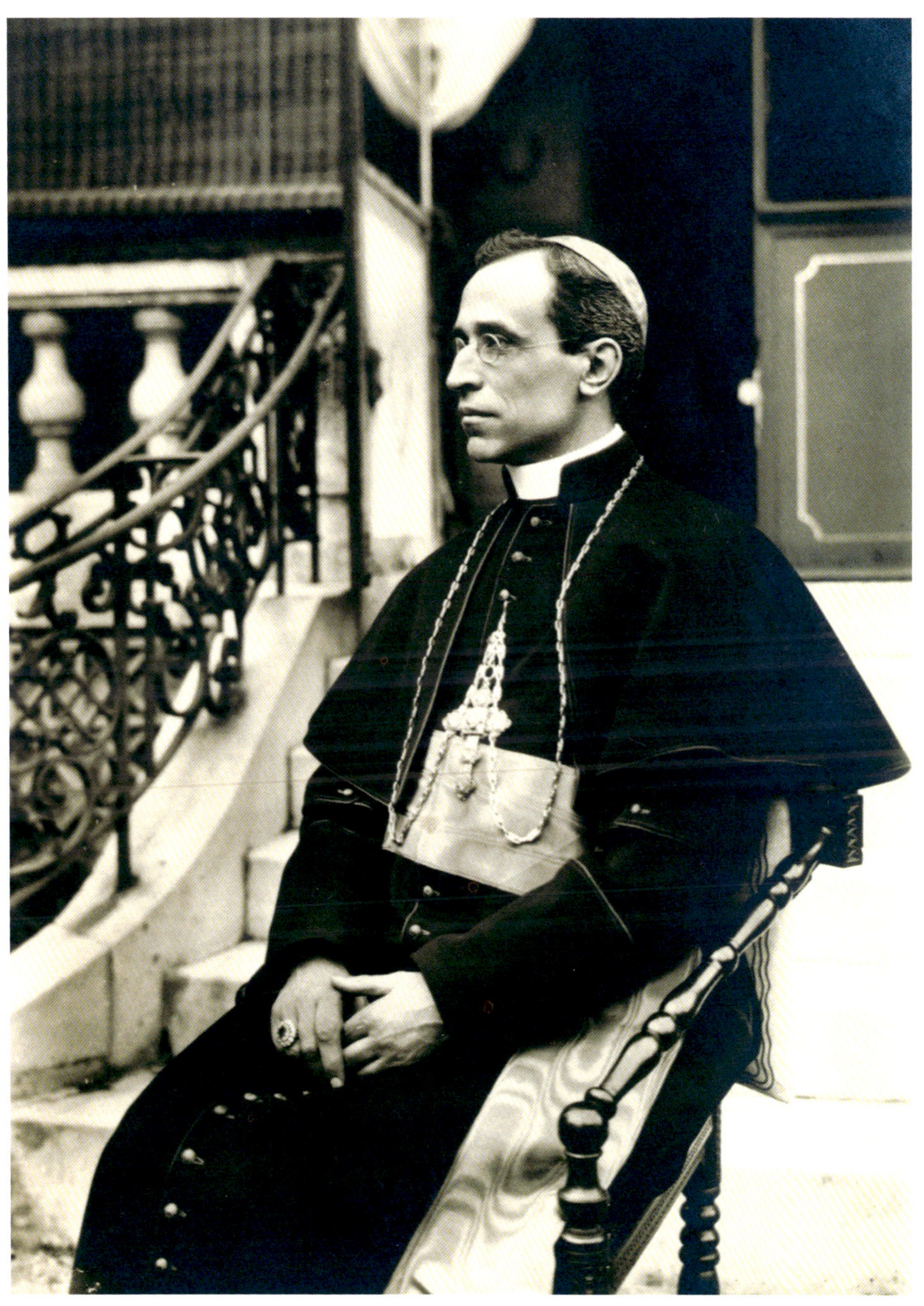

Nuncio Eugenio Pacelli at Bad Adelholzen, Bavaria, 1923
(Archiv der Barmherzigen Schwestern, Munich)

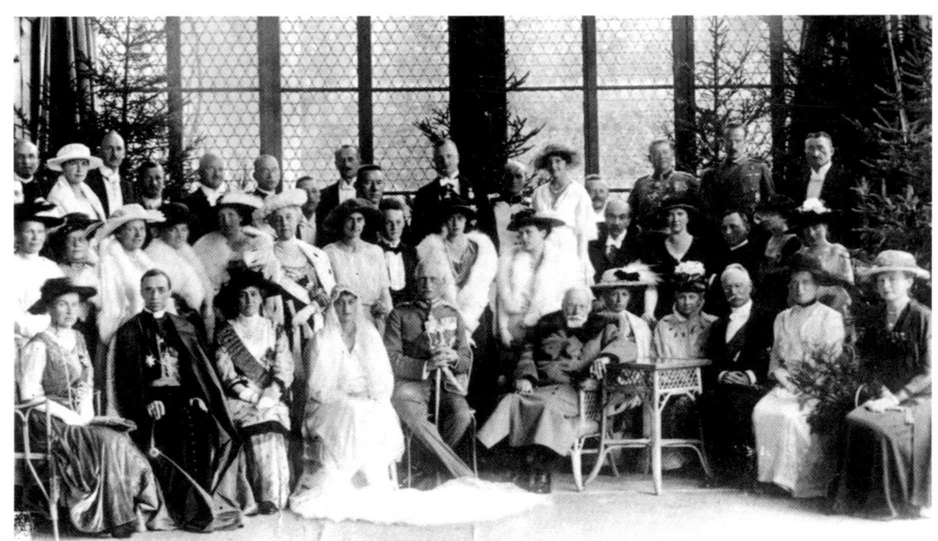

Wedding of Crown Prince Rupprecht of Bavaria with Antonia of Luxembourg at Lenggries, Bavaria, 7 April 1921
(AEM Dokumentation Personen, Pius XII.)

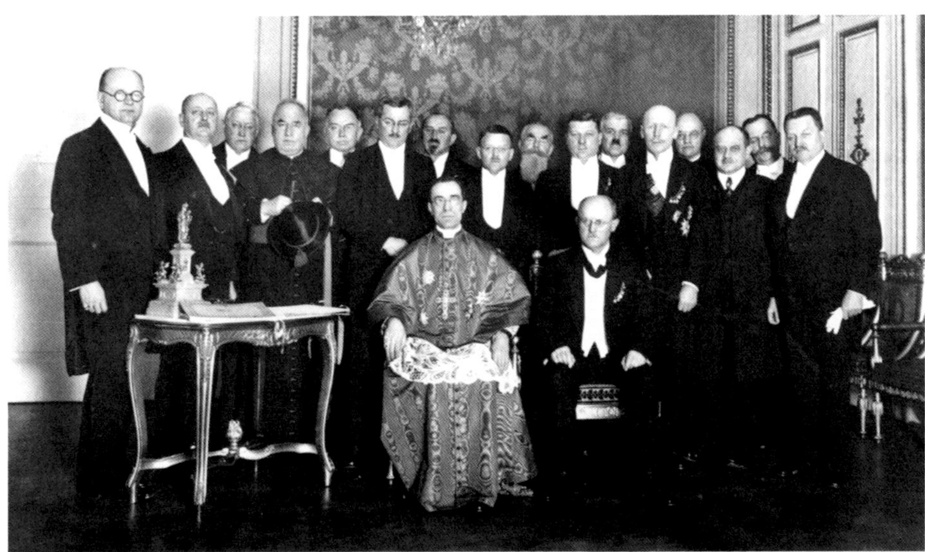

Nuncio Pacelli and the Bavarian government, having exchanged the ratification documents of the concordat between the Holy See and Bavaria, 24 January 1925
(Bayerisches Hauptstaatsarchiv, Munich)

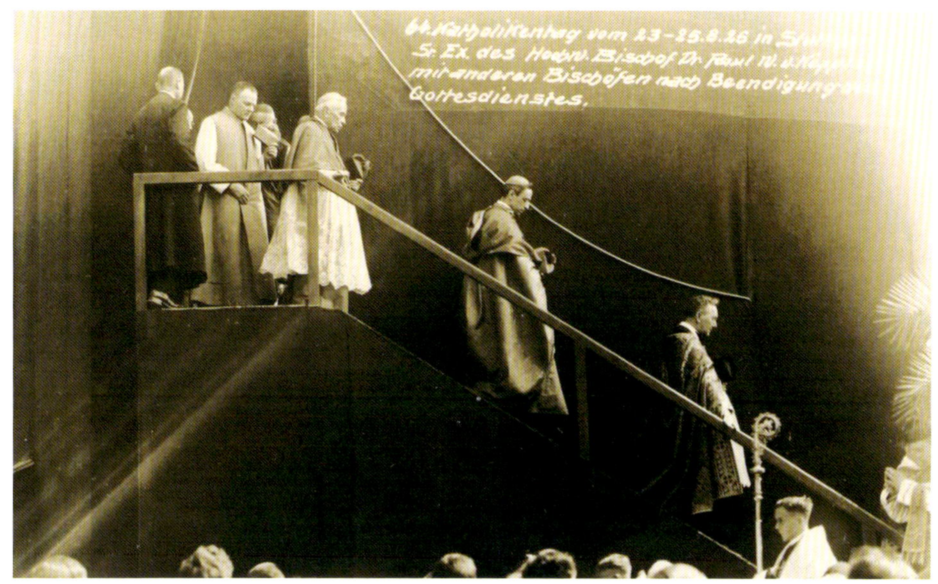

*Pacelli at the 64th congress of German Catholics (Katholikentag) at
Stuttgart (23–25 August 1925) (AEM Dokumentation Personen, Pius XII.)*

*Pacelli with Prelate Johann Pfaffen-
büchler (Superior of the Barmher-
zige Schwestern), Paul von Stengel
(in charge of Vatican Affairs at the
Bavarian foreign ministry), and
Franz Rubenbauer (director of
Munich's central railway station),
atop Mount Wendelstein, Bavaria,
11 October 1927
(AEM Dokumentation Personen,
Pius XII.)*

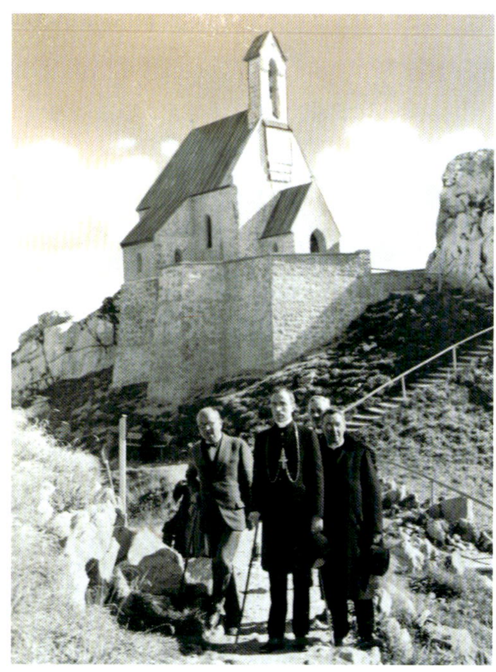

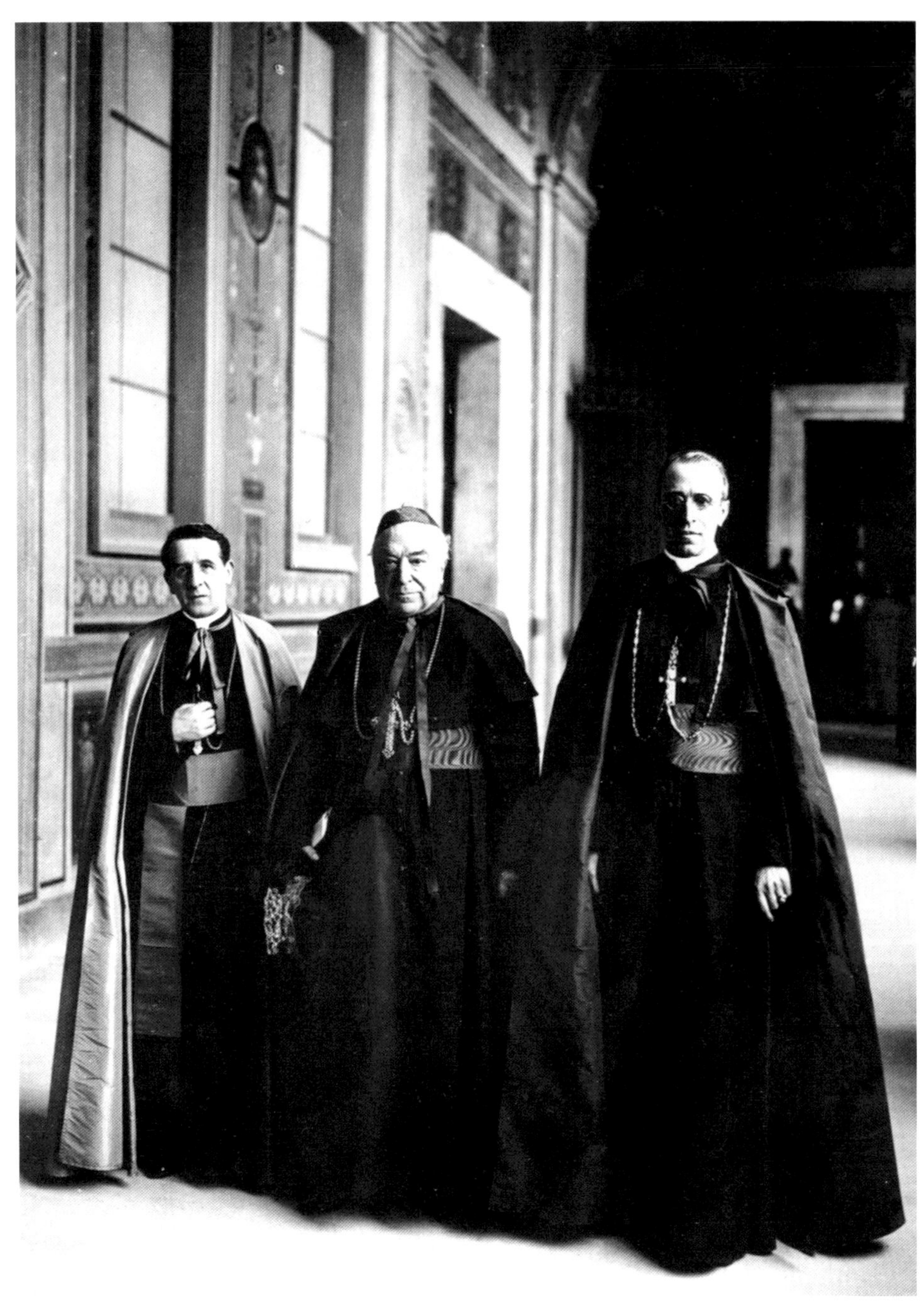

Pacelli with Pietro Cardinal Gasparri and Archbishop Giuseppe Pizzardo (left)
(AEM Dokumentation Personen, Pius XII.)

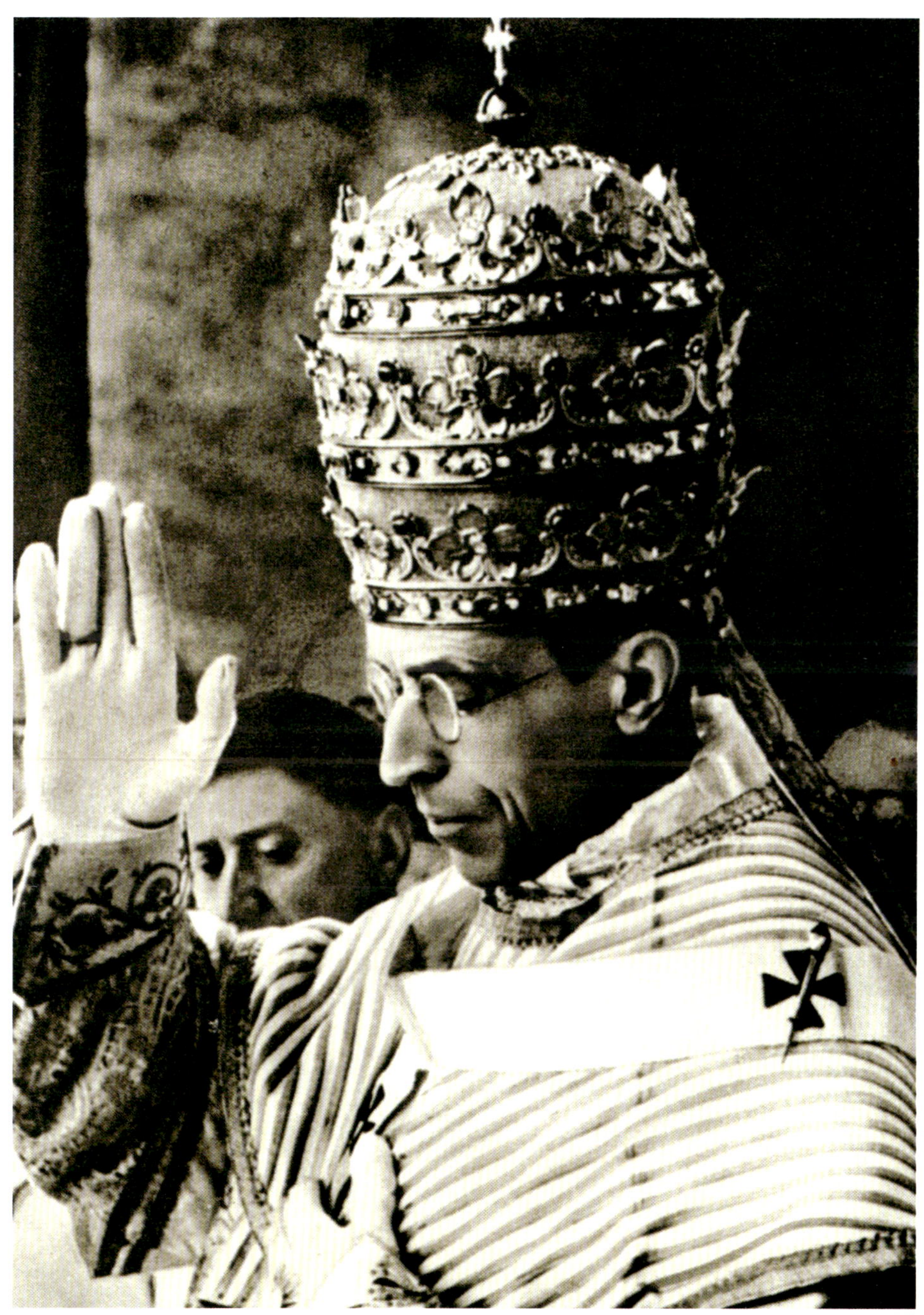

Pope Pius XII after his coronation, 12 March 1939
(AEM Dokumentation Personen, Pius XII.)

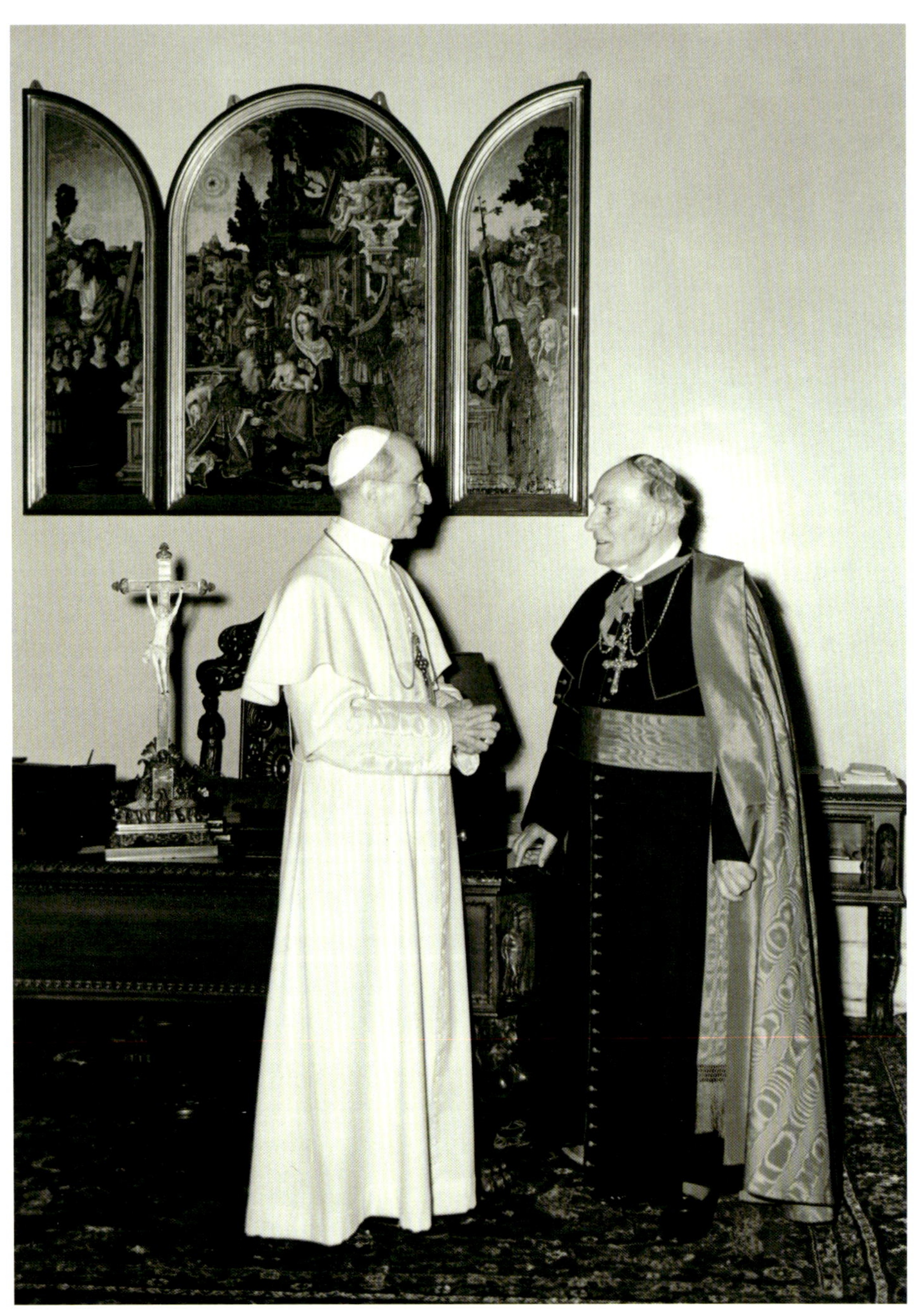

*Pius XII and Michael Cardinal von Faulhaber, February 1946
(EAM NL Faulhaber)*

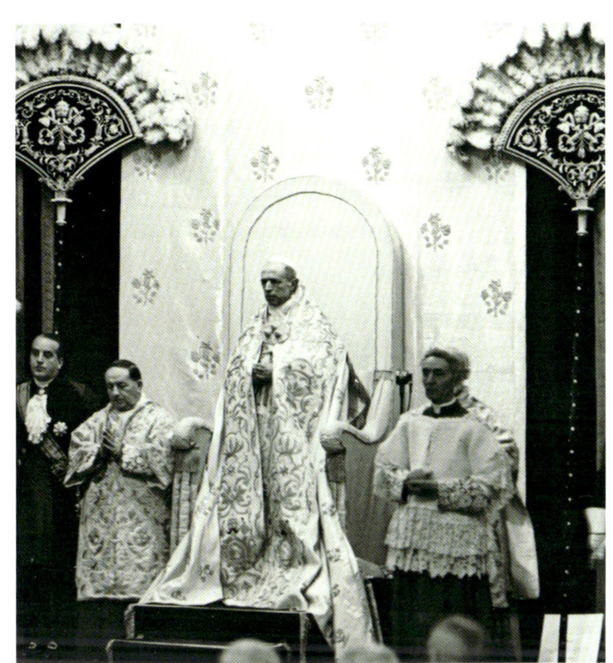

Pius XII during the canonization of Jeanne de Lestonnac, 15 May 1949 (EAM NL Faulhaber)

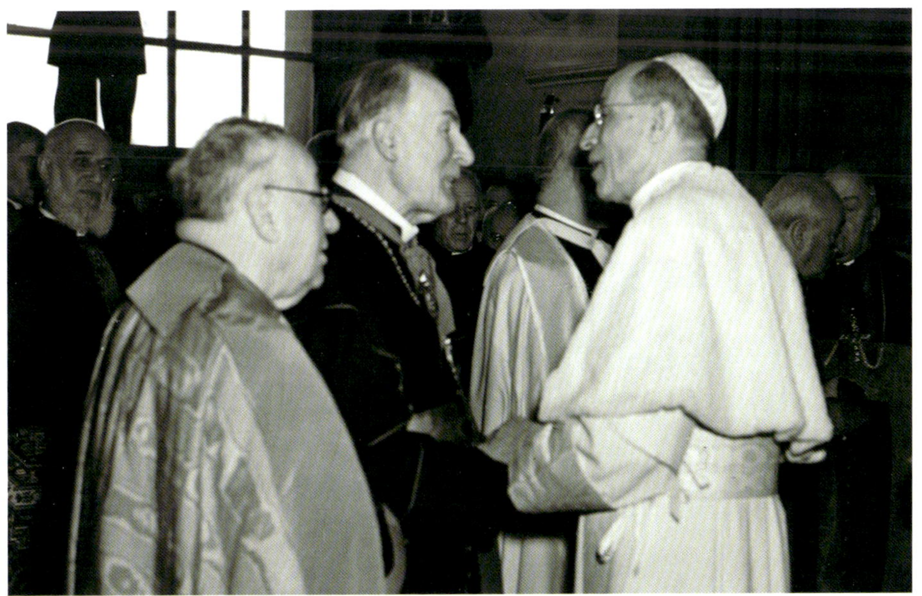

Pius XII and Michael Cardinal von Faulhaber during an audience, 1 November 1950 (EAM NL Faulhaber)

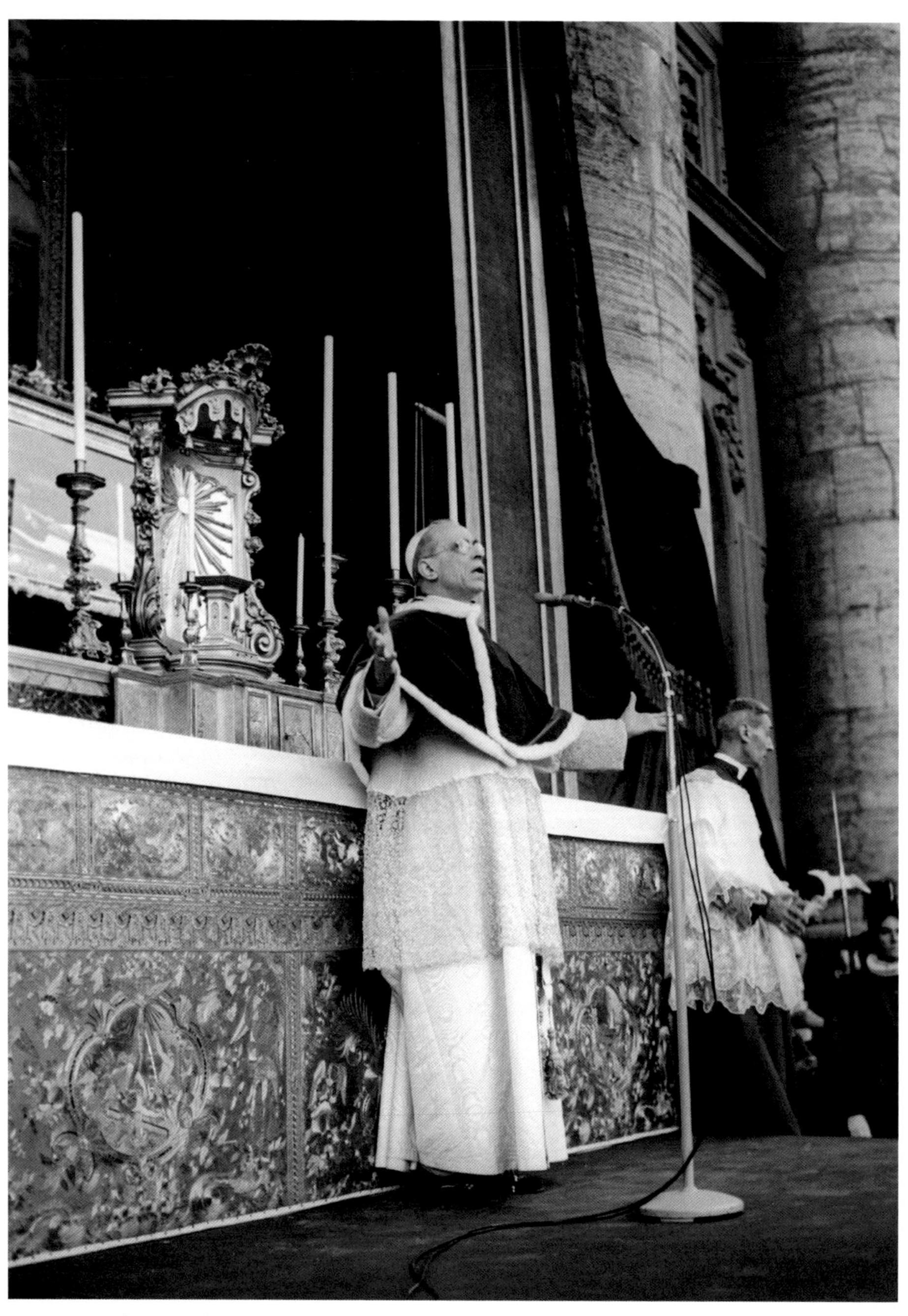

Pius XII during the beatification of Pope Pius X in St Peter's Square, 3 June 1951 (EAM NL Faulhaber)

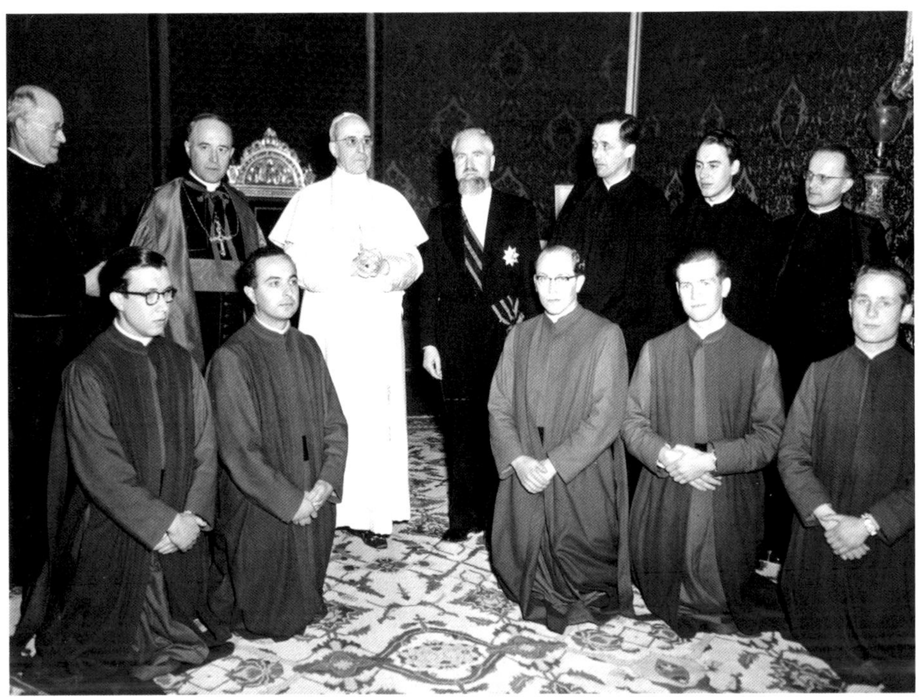

Audience with Pius XII and (standing left to right) Joseph Thalhamer (canon of Munich cathedral), Archbishop Joseph Cardinal Wendel (Archdiocese of Munich and Freising), Bavarian Minister of State Alois Hundhammer, Franz von Tattenbach SJ (Rector of the Roman Collegium Germanicum), unknown, and Matthias Defregger (Cardinal Wendel's secretary); (kneeling) candidates for the priesthood from the Roman Collegium Germanicum
(AEM Dokumentation Personen, Pius XII.)

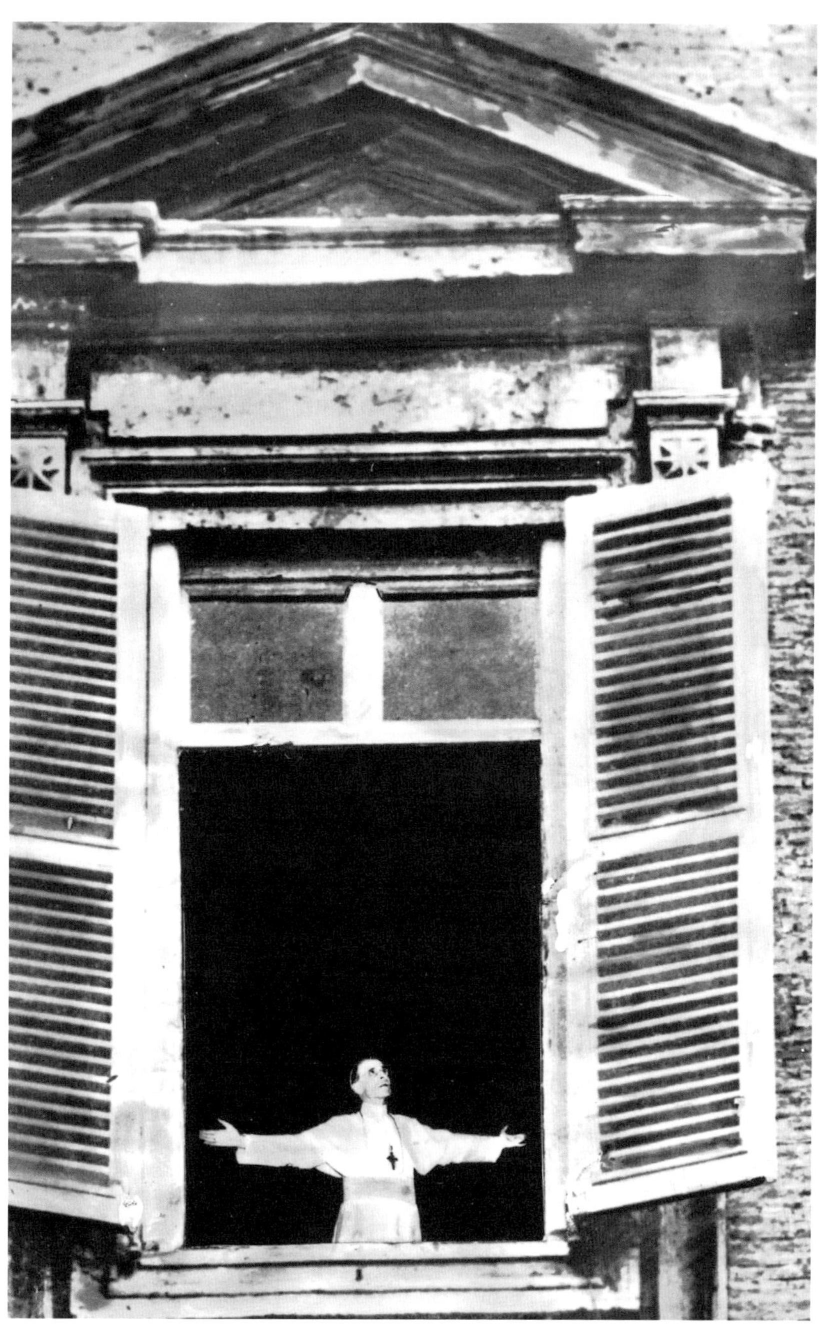

*Pius XII at the window of the Apostolic Palace
(AEM Dokumentation Personen, Pius XII.)*

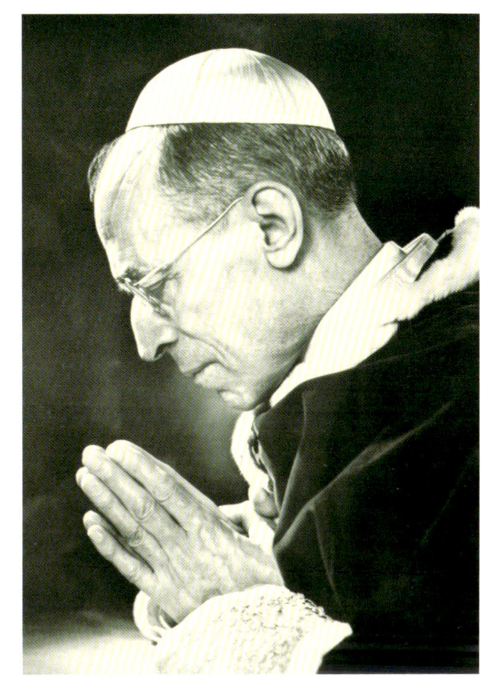

Pius XII
(AEM Dokumentation
Personen, Pius XII.)

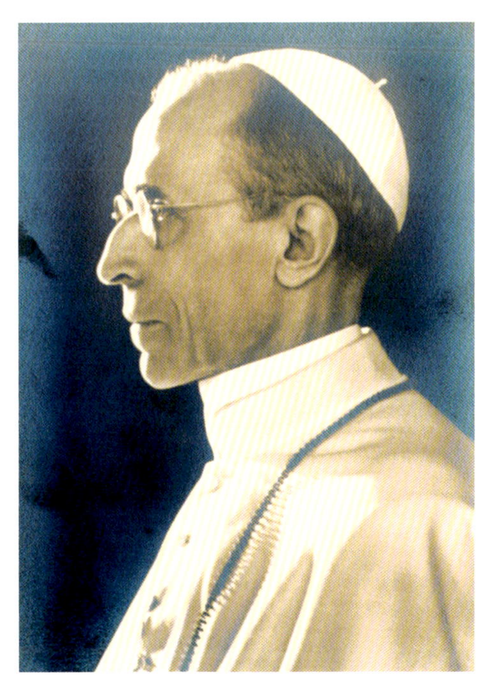

Pius XII
(AEM Dokumentation Personen,
Pius XII.)

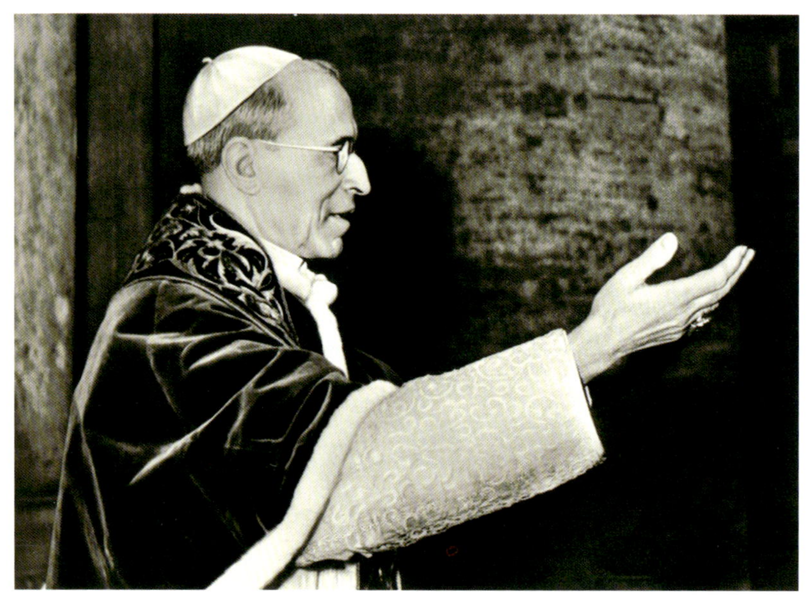

Pius XII
(AEM Dokumentation Personen, Pius XII.)

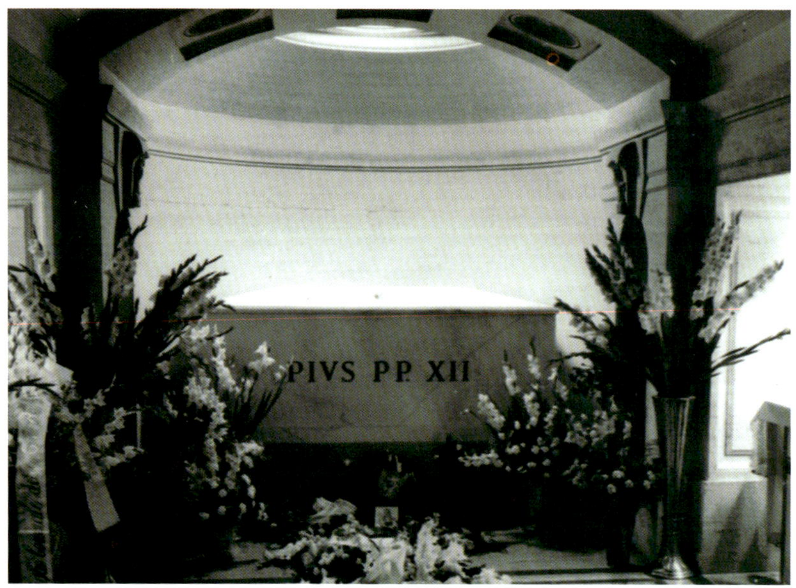

Tomb of Pius XII
(AEM Dokumentation Personen, Pius XII.)

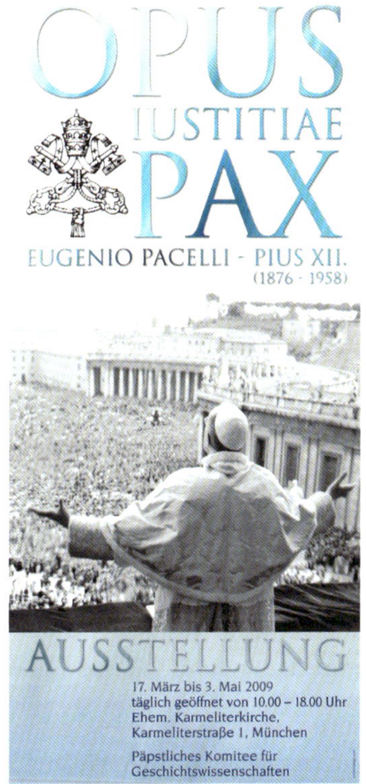

*Banner for the exhibition "Opus Iustitiae Pax"
at Munich, 17 March to 3 May 2009
(AEM Dokumentation)*

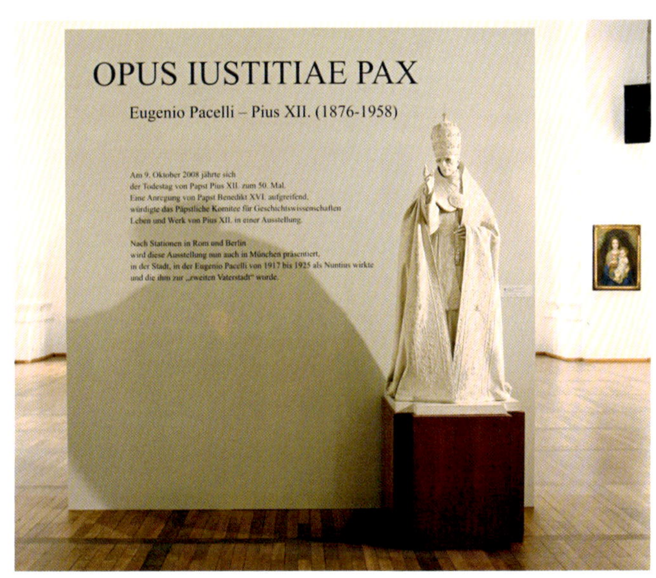

*Entrance area of the
exhibition "Opus
Iustitiae Pax" at
Munich, former church
of the Carmelites
(AEM Dokumen-
tation)*

155

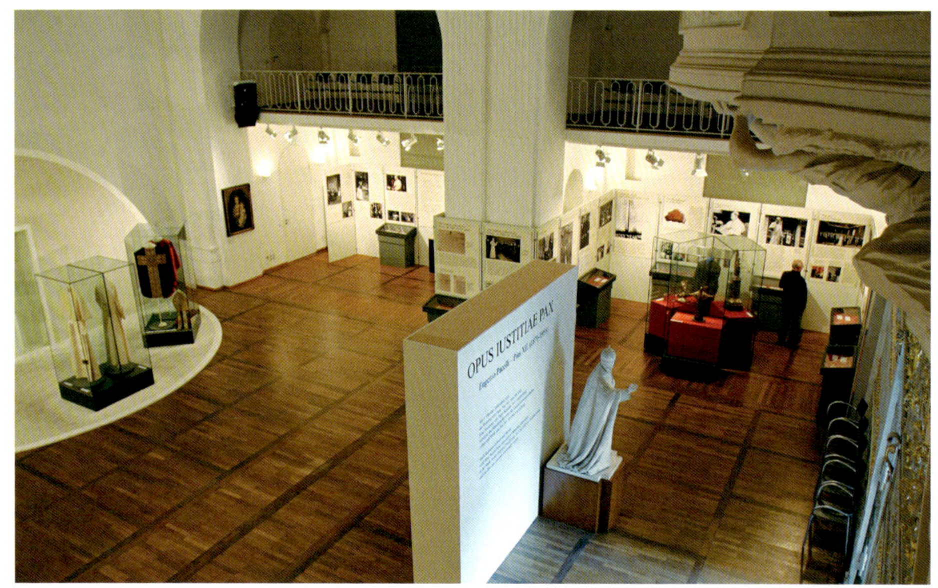

View of the exhibition room
(AEM Dokumentation)

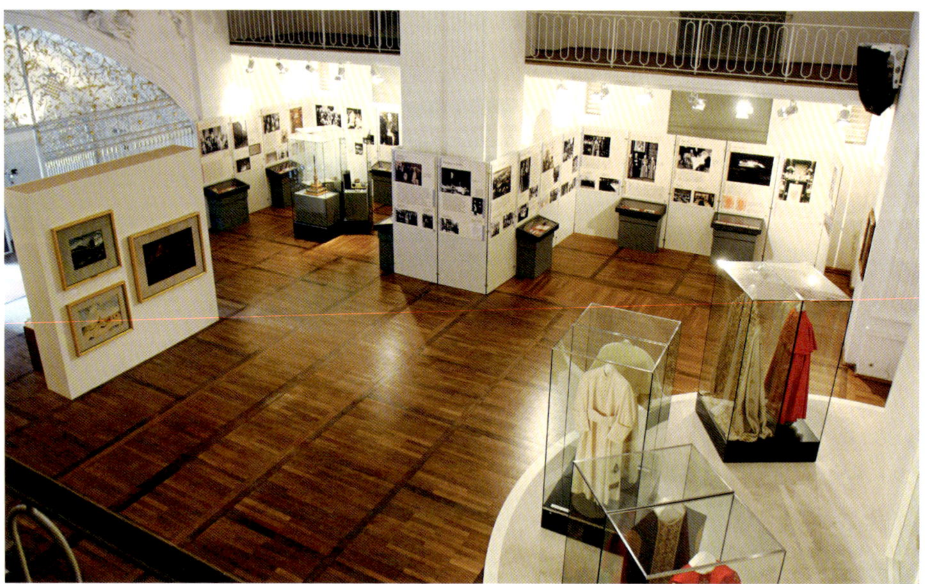

View of the exhibition room
(AEM Dokumentation)